CEDRIC ROBINSON

D1452455

Black Lives series

Elvira Basevich, *W. E. B. Du Bois*
Utz McKnight, *Frances E. W. Harper*
Joshua Myers, *Cedric Robinson*

Cedric Robinson

The Time of the Black Radical Tradition

Joshua Myers

polity

Copyright © Joshua Myers 2021

The right of Joshua Myers to be identified as Author of this Work has been asserted in accordance with the UK Copyright, Designs and Patents Act 1988.

First published in 2021 by Polity Press

Polity Press
65 Bridge Street
Cambridge CB2 1UR, UK

Polity Press
101 Station Landing
Suite 300
Medford, MA 02155, USA

All rights reserved. Except for the quotation of short passages for the purpose of criticism and review, no part of this publication may be reproduced, stored in a retrieval system or transmitted, in any form or by any means, electronic, mechanical, photocopying, recording or otherwise, without the prior permission of the publisher.

ISBN-13: 978-1-5095-3791-4
ISBN-13: 978-1-5095-3792-1 (pb)

A catalogue record for this book is available from the British Library.

Names: Myers, Joshua (Joshua C.), author.
Title: Cedric Robinson : the time of the Black radical tradition / Joshua Myers.
Description: Cambridge, UK ; Medford, MA : Polity Press, 2021. | Series: Black lives | Includes bibliographical references and index. | Summary: "The first account of the radical thought and life of the great Marxist critic of racial capitalism"-- Provided by publisher.
Identifiers: LCCN 2021002734 (print) | LCCN 2021002735 (ebook) | ISBN 9781509537914 (hardback) | ISBN 9781509537921 (paperback) | ISBN 9781509537938 (epub)
Subjects: LCSH: Robinson, Cedric J. | Communists--Biography. | African American communists--Biography.
Classification: LCC HX84.R576 M94 2021 (print) | LCC HX84.R576 (ebook) | DDC 335.4092 [B]--dc23
LC record available at https://lccn.loc.gov/2021002734
LC ebook record available at https://lccn.loc.gov/2021002735

Typeset in 10.75pt on 14pt Janson by
Servis Filmsetting Limited, Stockport, Cheshire
Printed and bound in Great Britain by TJ Books Ltd, Padstow, Cornwall

The publisher has used its best endeavours to ensure that the URLs for external websites referred to in this book are correct and active at the time of going to press. However, the publisher has no responsibility for the websites and can make no guarantee that a site will remain live or that the content is or will remain appropriate.

Every effort has been made to trace all copyright holders, but if any have been overlooked the publisher will be pleased to include any necessary credits in any subsequent reprint or edition.

For further information on Polity, visit our website: politybooks.com

Contents

Acknowledgments

The journey toward this book began with Robin D. G. Kelley, who has been instrumental both behind the scenes and in direct ways, in realizing its completion. Robin's initial work on many of the biographical details of Cedric J. Robinson's life was both inspiration and guide. His faith was also a steadying force. And his clearing of the way to Elizabeth Peters Robinson was indispensable. Without Elizabeth, this work would have never happened. She opened her home and heart to me in ways that I am still fully understanding. She provided not only access to an archive, she provided access to a way of feeling this life. I offer my unstinting gratitude to her and to the many people she placed before me as necessary witnesses to Cedric's life: Gerard Pigeon, Joanne Madison, Marisela Marquez, Avery Gordon, Gerardo "Gary" Colmenar, and Matthew Harris, among others. Gerard, Joanne, Marisela, and Avery stopped what they were doing and agreed to talk about their experiences with him. Gerard was Cedric's best friend and one of the most significant commenters on Cedric's character. My conversations with Avery proved to be very necessary in shaping aspects of the book. Gary was a remarkable help in securing necessary archives from the University of California, Santa Barbara campus during the coronavirus pandemic. I am grateful to him and Matt Stahl of the library for making a very large cache of materials available to me.

I am extremely indebted to Matthew's work in organizing and processing the Robinson papers, which are still held in private. Without that work, my task of engaging that bounty would have been next to impossible.

Cedric J. Robinson's students were a source of grace. I do not take their generosity for granted. I thank H. L. T. Quan for not only agreeing to an interview, but for graciously reading the manuscript and taking time to participate alongside Elizabeth, Robin, and me in a 2020 panel on Cedric that greatly impacted the book. My conversations with Tiffany Willoughby-Herard were deeply insightful. Not only did I find out that she was my South Carolina homegirl, but the care in which she outlined her memories of Cedric and what they mean for now, for the present, and the future of Black Studies will stay with me. Darryl C. Thomas gave me a clear picture of the earlier years and the important time the Robinsons spent in Michigan. I was also able to speak with Bruce Cosby, who took classes with Cedric at Binghamton. And Fred Moten who, though never a formal student of Cedric's, considered himself in this number as a younger colleague. All of these students and/or mentees are now scholars in their own right, a testament to Cedric's impact. There are many more whom I must thank, though we did not get a chance to speak about this project formally: Damien Sojoyner, Jordan Camp, Christina Heatherton, Greg Burris, Jonathan D. Gomez, Rovan Locke, Erica Edwards, and Ruth Wilson Gilmore.

Tracking down Cedric's comrades from his early years proved to be daunting. But I was thankful to find Ken Cloke, one of the organizers of the Berkeley Free Speech movement, who put me into contact with Mike Miller, an organizer of SLATE and eventually the Student Nonviolent Coordinating Committee. Miller remembered Cedric for, among other things, donating blood to him when he returned to the Bay Area after being injured in a car accident while organizing in Mississippi. He then connected me to Margot Dashiell, who was able to share with me her impressions of Cedric as a young activist who was connected to the UC chapter of the NAACP and to the emerging Afro-American Association. It was Dashiell who clarified so much about Berkeley history, Bay Area Black nationalism and radicalism, and other tidbits during those days, and I hope she is able to tell her story soon. She also graciously showed me letters that Cedric wrote her from Mexico, southern Africa, and Fort Sill, Oklahoma that she held onto for over fifty years. Others from that period in Cedric's life that I interviewed included Nell Irvin Painter and J. Herman Blake, two scholars whom I consider to be giants in their own right. Their recollections helped me properly paint a picture of his life during those formative moments. The oldest friend that I was able to speak to was Douglas Wachter, whose testimony before the House Un-American Activities Committee led to the events of May 1960. I am grateful to Douglas for his memories of Cedric's junior high years.

Though there were many collections held in private, I did have an opportunity to track Cedric and the larger movement to several formal holdings at the Bancroft Library, University of California, Berkeley, The Oakland Public Library, The African American Library Museum at Oakland, the Bentley Historical Library, Binghamton University's Special Collections, and the Schomburg Center for Research in Black Culture. I thank the many librarians and archivists who smoothed the way. I want to offer a brief note of thanks to Pendarvis Hardshaw, a true brother of the Town, who offered his help in connecting to Oakland sources. As far as libraries are concerned, I want to thank my cousin Dr Kayla Lee, who used her library access to help me secure some of Cedric's earliest articles when I first began to work on this text. Thankfully, some of those articles are now more widely available. Richard E. Lee, Resat Kasaba, and Beverly Silver directed me to several places to help me unpack Cedric's relationship to Terence Hopkins. Yousouf Al-Bulushi graciously sent over audio files digitized from Cedric's collection that proved necessary.

There are a number of scholars, activists, and organizers whom I spoke to about this project. Many of them read drafts, offered encouragements, and gave me directions that are reflected in the final project. These include Ava Wilson, Shauna Morgan, Ashon Crawley, Bedour Alagraa, Imani Perry, Alan Minor, Mario Beatty, Valethia Watkins, Greg Carr, Donna Murch, Chris Roberts, Stefan Bradley, Jesse Benjamin, Minkah Makalani, Baba Lumumba, Anyabwile Love, and Ashanté Reese. Shauna and Ashon read early drafts of the first words of this text and kept me encouraged. Bedour sent me periodic texts that betrayed an authentic and welcome excitement that I was writing this book. I began one of the chapters while sitting next to Ashanté, on a day where I felt stuck and did not feel like writing. By the end of that session, the rest of the book came rather easily. Finally, Greg Carr introduced me to Cedric J. Robinson in 2006. Though it would take several more years for me to actually read this work closely, it was his engagement with that work and its relationship to Africana Studies that started all of this so many years ago.

I have been privileged to bring Cedric's ideas into public spaces on several occasions. Conversations in new media helped propel my thinking a great deal before and while I was developing this text. I am grateful to Jared Ball, Jared Ware, and Joshua Briond for providing space to think in public with Cedric's work. Special thanks to Sankofa Video and Books' Haile Gerima and Addisalem Gebrekidan and the rest of the team who put together the "Critical Reading: How to

Read Cedric Robinson" series. Sitting with Acklyn Lynch and his tattered copy of *Black Marxism* months later was a revelation. Finally, thanks to Darrell Johnson, Chad Kehinde Graham, Aliah Hill, Ayanna Jackson, and Danita Florence Warmack who took my seminar on Cedric J. Robinson at Howard University. You, and all my other students, gave me the opportunity to really know and appreciate his work.

Thanks to Polity Press's George Owers and Julia Davies, who patiently shepherded this project through a very difficult time in human history. Thanks for believing in this project and for developing the Black Lives series.

A few final words for my friends: B. Nicole Triplett, who was with me when this work was at proposal stage and always provided space on my New York research trips. And to Chigozie Onyema whom I did not talk with a great deal about this project but who, when it comes to radicalism, was one of my first real interlocutors. Alexsandra Mitchell is always there, and when I first took this project on she said she cried. I feel her.

Introduction: Cedric's Time

The Bakongo peoples of West-Central Africa saw Life as a cycle. This was not merely the invocation of the idea that all time is the same, that all experience is constant. Rather, what is meant is that we experience time in ways that allow us to see how all other time was experienced, that our experiences of time are not without deep connections to the cosmological. Human life is mapped, spatially oriented in the Kongo cosmogram (*tendwa nza Kongo*) as a mode of realizing how "the four moments of the sun" mirror not only individual lives, but also communal existence. We live our lives as we experience *being* within the larger universe. Human existence is akin to bodies arranged about the sun: constant motion and movement, darkness and light. But the creation of society, of human relationships within and amid existence, is not mechanical. The cycles that the Bakongo observed did not produce natural laws that govern *our* interaction in space. To be human, for the Bakongo, is to seek to understand, grow, and mature in rhythm with ancestors and the natural world, and to align them with a vision of and for community. Yet there is no guarantee that simply being alive will produce such connections. The Bakongo believed that *tuzingu*, or "rolls of life," give us a record of what happened in the experiences of our ancestors, as we ourselves experience the cycles that mark our journeys around the sun. These records are required to pass down "lived accumulated experience-knowledge" to create social togetherness. They are there for us to see how it looked for others, so we can sense how it will be for us. Our lives are inherently linked, but they are our lives.[1] As Jacob Carruthers writes, time and eternity coexist and are in communion.[2]

Perhaps this is also a conceptual foundation for one definition of the Black Radical tradition found in the work of Cedric James Robinson. In the 2000 preface to his best-known text, *Black Marxism*, he describes that tradition as "an accretion, over generations, of collective intelligence gathered from struggle."[3] Enslavement, inasmuch as it provided the occasion for struggle over and within a particular kind of existence, was ultimately a challenge that required Africans to remain connected, to create the records – the collective intelligence – of those struggles and prior knowledges in order to continuously apply them to the realization of an otherwise to that existence and a more familiar mode of being *à la* Bakongo. Cedric's conception of the Black Radical tradition *as* that accretion, then, is consistent with the worldviews of our enslaved African ancestors. And we might easily find direct familial and ancestral ties between Cedric, an African with roots in Alabama, and the peoples of the region who conceived of the *tendwa nza Kongo*, who later found themselves in the western hemisphere in large numbers, helping to produce the artistic and spiritual cultures that have been collected under the designation, "black Atlantic."[4]

But, while interesting, an *immediate* genealogical relation is not required to reveal the greater insight: that these ways of seeing and imagining connections to each other across time and space were shared across Africana cultures. And so much so that what became the "deep thought" of the Bakongo might also be perceived as part of the *tuzingu* of countless other African intellectual traditions.[5] That it appeared among Africans in a space called "the Americas" at a particular point in time is, however, also deeply significant and consequential in its own right. For it was in this context, this moment of the sun, that the foundation for that accretion of intelligence – of which the genius of significant Black thinkers was derivative, of which the thought of Cedric Robinson was derivative – was necessarily realized.[6] This is to say, Cedric's time occasioned a unique vantage point for comprehending reality and questions of existence that were both exceptional and constitutive of the very traditions he named and narrated.

The construct of time is useful – as any among a range of possibilities, such as space, geography, race, class, sociality, or systems – for thinking the life of Cedric Robinson. If the method of his work is, as Erica R. Edwards describes it, "to carefully excavate the mechanisms of power and to just as meticulously, and with a singular determination that I think can only be called *faith*, detail the radical epistemologies and ontologies that those mechanisms have been erected to restrain," then we might use constructions of time as a route to understanding the ordering logic of those forces of restraint.[7] This is indeed the aim of Damien M. Sojoyner, who writes in *Futures of Black Radicalism* that time, as a mechanism of restraint, structures and utilizes difference while imposing ideological adherence to the regimes that require that structuration by instituting the "disciplinary mechanisms aimed at ideological positions that counter western notions of law and order." Resistance, then, if it is to be truly effective, requires us to initiate a "Black Radical time" – a time against the practices of difference making and othering.[8] And within such alternatives to time as imposition, we would also develop alternative modes of relating to each other and to the past. Cedric himself perhaps sums up the importance of this framing most effectively in *Black Marxism*, where at a pivotal point in the text he states:

> The point is that the construction of periods of time is only a sort of catchment for events. Their limited utility, though, is often abused when we turn from the ordering of things, that is chronological sequencings, to the order of things, that is the arrangement of their significances, meanings, and relations. Increments of time contoured to abstract measure rarely match the rhythms of human action.[9]

"Significances, meanings, and relations" are deeper than the order of time and are the points of departure that this text will take in thinking with the life of Cedric Robinson. As an intellectual biography, it speaks to and with the larger themes and considerations of his work, while thinking through the contexts that made the work, the moments that made the worker. It is chronological but also thematic. The first few chapters look at the foundation of Cedric's relations. They are followed by chapters that consider the meanings of his work. And a final chapter considers the significance of it all. This book is imagined as a contribution to the larger constellation of that work, an offering to future workers, an entry into Cedric's roll of life.

Western time was constructed to do more than serve as a "catchment" for events – it was an attempt to impose order on the rhythms of human action, rather than simply understand them. And, as such, intellectuals operating under these assumptions have maintained the useful fiction that Black Radicalism is at best derivative of western thought or western temporal systems. This is, as Cedric has maintained, an ordering conceit that made liberation from the terms of order unimaginable. But it had been imagined. As a tradition of seeking otherwise than what is assumed to be attainable or even desired – indeed as a tradition that calls into question normative assumptions around what liberation even entails – the Black Radical tradition emanates from thought that is "unthinkable."[10]

What *is* "thinkable" is that which is reasonable. The meaning of time as "measurable movement" in western civilization is a product of the conceptual architecture of Enlightenment, premised as it was on knowledge as the preserve of Man.[11] Though borrowing from such "classical" sources as Aristotle and St Augustine, much of what enters the western intellectual tradition owes its birth to the need to develop a form of measuring time that is ultimately about how patterns of human relationships with the natural environment can be understood. After all, if knowing through reason is a specifically human practice, then any attempt to naturalize humanity would have to also naturalize the environment in which such reasoning occurs. It is through a conception of human nature as naturally occurring that time as mathematical precision is assumed. But none of this is actually natural; it, too, is a conceit. Time's meaning is not given in nature, it is given in the human understanding of nature. It is a social affair. The attempt to naturalize time is the practice of "temporalizing," which requires also that human relationships to the past be imagined and narrated. And thus came the emergence of history as a conception for measuring and living with change.[12]

In order to understand what made human experiences

significant, conceptions of change that had existed prior to the elevation of reason as the foundation of knowing had to be extinguished. Cedric's work shows how incomplete this transition was, while also revealing that western thought attempted to achieve such a hegemonic disruption by imposing a logic of time, a historiographical tradition that imposed order on imagination, on the fantastic. The result was not only a theory of history but a theory of politics – a theory of reality that rendered the temporal scope of western civilization as the very meaning of what it is to be on and in time. From such distillations, notions of progress, momentum, and potential emanated to mark the physics and state of being. And it was this very arrangement of consciousness that could not incorporate "others" and their various accounts of what it means to live.[13]

This conception of time was also spatialized. Beyond the shifting time zones that mark different geographical locations, there also exist presumptions that "time is slower there," or "time is frozen there," which describe encounters with those who exist outside of "normal" time. These are, of course, premised upon colonial confrontations that gave birth to time-bound accounts of non-western life that sought to make their notions of life legible by presenting their ways of relating to each other as exotic or primitive. Much of this knowledge enters our consciousness through the domain of the social sciences, fabricated in often naive ways upon the philosophical assumptions of the natural sciences. Western time reads differences and imposes certain arrangements of other times and spaces, not necessarily to produce an account of universality or sameness, but to erect a knowledge useful for containing a threatening otherness. Time constructs a cartography of control.[14]

Part of what makes Cedric's work significant is that it is premised on not only understanding these arrangements but excavating the existence of these other arrangements – or even ways of being against arrangement – that characterize the lived histories of western thought's assumed others. It is work that covered an array of disciplines and deployed "what Michel Foucault called the 'counter-sciences,'" but it was not interdisciplinary as much as it was an attempt to think beyond discipline, toward the ways in which the disciplines of knowledge were in fact responsible for establishing order, establishing time.[15] Two of Cedric's collaborators in England, A. Sivanandan and Hazel Waters, capture the relationship precisely when they write that it was Cedric who asked a "question that scarcely even occurs within the academy." He questioned how our understandings of social "transformation" and "social justice" change when we acknowledge that the assumed foundations of knowledge of the world found in western thought – history, philosophy, and rhetoric – are themselves "stunted at birth, diminished in their capacities, crammed into spaces too small to contain them?"[16] Perhaps an answer lies in Black Study, a practice within Black Studies, a tradition Cedric would acknowledge as a "critique of western civilization."[17] But it was not an internal critique, one that sought to rescue that tradition. For it was not about its improvement as much as it was about "subverting" its particular ways "of realizing ourselves" – those ways practiced not only in the domains of the academy, but tantamount to the nature of western thought itself.[18] Such is one conception of Black Study, the practice of denaturalizing western disciplinary knowledges so that knowledges – ways of thinking and being – necessarily obscured by those projects can operate in spaces cleared of this debris. Though it was the original intent in many ways of the Black Studies movement, the existence of this approach to knowledge was never guaranteed, even in those spaces. In that sense, Cedric's work speaks to the ongoing crisis of Black Studies.[19]

In Cedric's practice of Black Study, we are offered the gift of seeing how those peoples who were excluded from history, and thus excluded from time, found ways to realize themselves. All time is not closure or management, reducible to spatial logics of colonialism and exploitation – all time is not order. As Sojoyner writes, time can be full of life, a shared construct of communal possibility; it is the collapse of the relationship to measurement as heard in the sounds of Ornette Coleman and Albert Ayler or Tyshawn Sorey and Esperanza Spalding, in the dance and play of Black girls around the diaspora, in the spaces created in the aisles of sanctuaries and the middle of the cipher – in the movements of cycles of life where we relate to each other, in, out, and around each other.[20] This is the Black Radical tradition, living beyond the order of time, finding ways to live again.

Cedric arrived onto the scene at perhaps one of the most critical junctures of western time: the mid-twentieth century. It was a moment where the hegemonic grip of western world order – the order that he would come to understand as constructed on a myth – was loosening thanks to the combined pressures of anticolonial and anti-imperialist movements across the globe. It was a freedom dream arrayed differently than the liberal model of political representation and economic ascendancy. And against an unsustainable market system underpinned by the violence of war and capitalist accumulation. In other words, it was a moment that saw revolution as a distinct possibility, even imperative to disrupting the time of western civilization permanently. In the wake of this moment in *Black Marxism*, Cedric wrote: "Everywhere one turns or cares to look, the signs of a collapsing world are evident; at the center, at its extremities, the systems of western power are fragmenting ... the characteristic tendency of capitalist societies to amass violence for domination and exploitation [created] a diminishing return, a dialectic, in its use. 'Things fall apart; the centre cannot hold.'"[21]

Cedric's sojourn through the conceptual worlds of Black Study began in earnest in the early 1960s in the Bay Area, continued through the Midwestern and Northeastern United States, and into the United Kingdom, before finding settlement in Santa Barbara, California, where he served as the director of the Center of Black Studies at the University of California, Santa Barbara. It was here where he and his partner Elizabeth, and daughter Najda, made their home, where all five of his books were released, and where the communities of struggle that would significantly mark their lives – both on and off campus – were based.

It would be impossible, however, to understand this intellectual journey by *solely* focusing upon the academic contexts of the work. This is a journey that must also take into account what it meant to be raised by Black folks from Alabama. It has to think through the meaning of the organizing tradition of 1960s Oakland and the larger momentum of Black revolutionary work that spawned networks of activists, thinkers, and artists in places like Detroit and New York. It has to search for meaning in the African-diasporic connections that were forged in travels to Mexico, southern Africa, and the United Kingdom. Black Study occurred here as well. And Cedric saw in real, Black space and in communal time the ways in which structures of thought that sought to understand and make realizable certain outcomes for Black peoples were deeply, even fatally, flawed. It was a form of study that was *with* rather than simply *of* Black peoples, a way of realizing that managed to offer more than the scientific veneer of objectivity in favor of a sort of rigor and deep thinking that was grounded in solidarity.[22] That mode of being with and for was necessarily a mode of being against the very structure of domination in even its most welcoming forms, and it inculcated a deep suspicion that Black people might be better off living, dying, and obtaining "freedom on their terms."[23]

This may indeed be a model for us in these ever dark times – this normal time of darkness. Thinking with Cedric and the contexts of his life then would reveal the particular sites of his epistemic rupture with western time and the premise of his quite prescient view that, at its heart, the Black Radical tradition was ultimately grounded in preserving the ontological totality of peoples whose lives were interdicted by the political and material requirements of the modern world and whose understanding of how to be free must now be our point of departure for thinking freedom. This is a text that exists to call attention to a life, and not merely narrate its details, in order that we do more than find in Cedric's work a subject to study. For, in calling attention to a life, we call attention to ourselves.[24]

Some believe now that western time is late, that capitalism is late. This idea of late capitalism is an attempt to name a moment where time had reached a moment of completion, a natural evolution toward an end – a teleological "end of history." Yet what actually attended late capitalism was a further deepening, an entrenchment of a violent logic of othering and weaponized difference-making that has produced an assault on the commons, a sensibility that renders everyone and everything in and as a market relation, as the new common sense of how to be in the world.[25] Cedric's intellectual work appeared at perhaps a critical inflection point in the making of this neoliberal set of arrangements, as the 1980s saw the coming together of both the discursive and political logic that attempted to stabilize order through the twinned tactics described by Edwards as "incorporate and incarcerate; co-opt and incapacitate; represent and destroy."[26]

Those signs of the collapsing world that occasioned the words and vantage point in 1983 have been exacerbated, as the "racial regimes" that Cedric wrote of in 2007 are constantly updating themselves, as they must if they are to continue.[27] Globally, the racist foundations of capitalism are evident; these "native racisms," responsible for death on a massive scale, have produced a moment where simply saying "Black lives matter" becomes an attempt to stave off the disavowal of Black humanity. And even such declarations are met with further utterances of contempt. Underneath those utterances are affirmations of the modes of living and the temporal and spatial constructs that have generated a newly energized racial capitalism that is supported and reified by a white nationalist consciousness where everyone is vulnerable, every day. One could easily identify the election of the forty-fifth US president and the subsequent right-wing and fascist efflorescence, the turmoil in Europe, Africa, South and Central America around migration, permanent war, the global pandemic, and the increasing fears around human planetary existence as realities that make the current moment a prime one for an initial engagement or reassessment of Cedric's work. And they would be correct. But western time has always produced the urgency we feel. It has never not been this late, this dark.

Black people, as Christina Sharpe has written, live in the wake of immanent and imminent death, which in the conception of western time is the erasure of life. We need Cedric Robinson's work, then, for it reminds us that there are ways of inhabiting these conditions and finding ways not to be reduced to them; or, in Sharpe's words, we need to find solace in "tracking the ways we resist, rupture, and disrupt that immanence and imminence."[28] We need Cedric Robinson's work because what we need in this moment are better ways of seeing and marking the limits of a conceptual project that renders so many of those who have been marked for death as having no rhythms of human action to speak of, who have been prevented from offering what they know about (an)other time.

It was Cedric, again in 2013, who reminded us that Black modes of living in the forms of spirituals were often dismissed as "noise," and that what was assumed as "noise" had evoked and invoked life. He told us to find that noise, to see the ways that this noise has been, at root, what we are.[29] For beyond these ideas of death is the mode for the very reproduction of Life, which is, after all, a cycle.

1

All Around Him

When he was asked, Cedric cited his maternal grandfather, Winston "Cap" Whiteside, who for much of his life worked as a janitor, as a primary intellectual influence.[1] Intellectual genealogies, like familial genealogies, evoke relationships across time, premised on cultural or philosophical ideals that determine the nature of those relations. In most academic treatments, conceptions of intellectual genealogies privilege intellectuals in the "formal" sense, even when those presences are not acknowledged or are obscured in the citation practices that accompany a text. But Black thought has always taken seriously the intellectual influences that exist beyond the patina of scholarly legitimacy and in locations that are unbound by relationships to conventional western educational environments. Blackness, insofar as it is a repository of African cultural meanings, produces another way to think genealogy, intellectual or otherwise.[2] In Cedric's case, there are many instances that point to the imprint that Cap – who never wrote an academic text – had upon his conception of Black being, his orientation toward the meaning of Black radicalism. And in one important case, a direct citation – a natural inclusion of Cap as part of that tradition – was present all along.

In *Black Movements in America*, a text that deftly traces the continuity of mass Black political action throughout the history of the American project, Cedric contextualizes the "push" factors of early twentieth-century Black migration in the United States with a story about his own grandfather. One day, sometime in 1927, the manager of the Battle House Hotel – a white elite enclave of Mobile, Alabama – attempted to "exercise his sexual privileges," with a maid named Cecilia, Cap's wife. According to Cedric's account, "When Cap was told, he returned to the Battle House that evening, beat the manager up, and hung him in the hotel's cold storage." A white hotel manager, heir to the long tradition of white sexual violence against Black women, was "chastened" by a Black man, heir to a tradition of resistance to that imposition. That tradition thrived among a significant segment of Black Alabama, as well as the Black South writ large, and through both word and deed asserted that white supremacist violence against Black women were terms of order that would not be accepted.[3] Resistance, however, also meant that Cap Whiteside could no longer stay in Mobile. Concluding the story, Robinson added: "In a few days, Whiteside headed for Oakland, California. When he earned their fare, he sent for his family: Cecilia and his daughters, Clara, Lillian, and Wilma."[4] It was in Oakland that one of those daughters, Clara, gave birth to Cedric a little over a decade later.

In retelling this story days after Robinson's transition, Robin D. G. Kelley reminded us that Cap's influence registered in Cedric's commitment to understanding not only the historical and political realities of the Black experience but also its spiritual meaning – for this is how he also under-

Figure 1.1 Cedric Robinson with Winston Whiteside

Image courtesy of Elizabeth Robinson

stood those conditions of Black existence. Kelley writes that it was Cap who represented the "personal dignity, discipline, quiet intelligence, spiritual grounding, courage, and commitment to family and community" that served as the foundation for that alternative tradition, what Cedric would characterize in his conception as "the Black Radical tradition."[5] What he would write of the radical intelligentsia was also true of his own life. This was a tradition that was "all around" him, present in the midst of his people – in their search for a level of autonomy in Mobile, in their migration to Oakland, in the community they forged in their churches and neighborhoods, in their common pursuit of knowing, and in the love they produced out of what may have seemed a kind of nothingness.[6] In times of trouble and in moments of joy, this was their ontological totality. The horizons of the possibility of a Black Radical tradition constituted a theme that Cedric would pursue throughout his intellectual work, but perhaps nowhere more beautifully than in the conclusion to *Black Movements in America*, where in a note of resolution he honors "the continuity of Afro-Christian belief and vision . . . with them it is always possible that the next Black social movement will obtain that distant land, perhaps even transporting America with it."[7]

All around him were these people, his people. They know that life, Black being, had required struggle. Their faith was the warrant for extending that tradition. One did not have to see what the end would be. One only had to believe in this collective intelligence that had been gathered from struggle.[8]

I can die, but I won't work

Before landing in Oakland, the Whitesides had already embarked upon a remarkable journey in the post-emancipation South. Cap's father, Benjamin Whiteside, was born enslaved in 1847 and had migrated to Mobile from Cooper's Gap, North Carolina after the Civil War.[9] Cap's mother, Clara Mercer, who had been enslaved in Virginia, had also managed to find a new beginning in Mobile, settling in a house with her widowed mother. We do not know the details of the circumstances that led either of them away from the only places they knew to a place that was the dreaded "deeper" South, the destination of many in the domestic slave trade. But Black migrations south after the war were not unheard of as many sought family members from whom they had been separated, while others merely wanted to test the meaning of freedom away from the familiar plantations that had been the source of their exploitation and their pain.[10] Mobile became such a space – with its Black population increasing by 65 percent in the years after the war – for many to practice these experiments in freedom. But such experiments were often fraught. In Mobile, as well as other recovering Southern cities, one would not have been able to escape the possibilities of violence and of a kind of class warfare that sought to control and manage the kind of militancy that might presage true societal transformation.[11]

In 1870, at the age of nineteen, Clara Mercer married Benjamin Whiteside. Twenty-three years later, Cap was born, becoming the youngest of seven children, amid the erosion of Reconstruction and at the height of Redemption – the *Plessy v. Ferguson* decision that solidified Jim Crow was handed down a month before his third birthday. Finding work as a drayman in industrial Mobile, Benjamin would soon put enough money aside to secure a family home and open a delivery business. Soon thereafter Clara became a restaurateur, serving home-cooked meals out of an adjacent property on N. Jackson Street. As Mobile's harbor activities recovered from the war, this growing Black population became a source of the necessary labor force required to make the port city attractive to international capital.

Throughout the 1870s, the Black population would struggle to consolidate the political power that manifested as a possibility during Reconstruction. In Mobile, this meant an intra-racial battle between an elite, moderate wing, often aligned with the "radical Republicans" and a mass-based militant assertion of self-determination that struggled to find a political footing within the Republican Party (which often meant alliances with the Democrats). This latter element included working-class freedmen, such as draymen like Benjamin Whiteside, who went on strike in 1867 to demand fairer treatment.[12] In cases where that militant segment did find its political voice in the Republican Party, with prominent personas like Lawrence Berry and Alexander Allen, their political maneuvering often went awry, with many living out their last years in public disgrace. Berry turned to alcohol, and committed suicide, with the encouragement of the white press, while Allen ended up in jail on murder charges after a mob descended upon a bar he owned. He would perish while incarcerated. Years of harassment and ridicule were the costs for advocating for the Black poor in Mobile.[13] Their deaths were part of a campaign of racial terror. It was defined by cases like that of elderly Black leader and minister Sam Gaillard who, after being sent to a chain gang for refusing to be degraded and referred to as "boy," subsequently refused to work and was shot down after uttering the last words, "I can die, but I won't work."[14] In response, other leaders counseled moderation, a tactic to defuse the situation. A Republican paternalism directed the city's part in Reconstruction. But it was, perhaps predictably, a moderation that was *still* too much for the white supremacist assumptions that informed Democratic power.

With Reconstruction and Black political leadership undermined through white violence and greed by the mid-1880s, a Black business class emerged situating itself along Davis Avenue in the Seventh Ward. A détente with Jim Crow, however, led some of them to adopt the self-help, apolitical posture of Booker T. Washington. But arguably this class – only representative of about 1 percent of the population – was not the true foundation of Black life in Mobile. The richer valences of Blackness resonated in the cultural and social lives of the masses who lived a rougher material existence that was nevertheless replenished by a deep spiritual well. On the occasion of a funeral, the community of Samaritans, a social order, would appear for the public ceremony in all-white, with "white broad-brimmed hats with long white veils," a rite reminiscent of African pasts not long past.[15] Death, even under the hard circumstances of life in the early days of Jim Crow, was a time to fortify bonds and togetherness. Like the churches and other social organizations, the creation of community-based and service-oriented businesses was also grounded in this pursuit of a measure of autonomy, care, and protection. It was necessary in conditions where the exploitative realm, the requirements of capital's expansion, was both grossly unfair and often deadly. While such a business class, even those who *were* political, could not fully negate the political and economic conditions that placed the vast majority at the behest of capital, they were part of a community ethic that was critical to the Black community's sense of order.[16]

Though not as financially successful as Washington acolyte, pastor, and insurance man Christopher First Johnson nor as well known as labor leader and store owner Ralph Clemmons, the Whitesides were a part of this economy which served Black Mobile, achieving, in fact, a semblance of economic independence. But, soon after, their failing health forced a primary school-educated Cap to emerge as the family's economic glue, a situation that was made more urgent after his older sister and mother passed in the first half of the 1910s. Facing the possibility of financial disaster, he sought and attained full-time employment at a cigar factory and would soon begin a family of his own, but not without further turmoil. Cap married Cedric's bloodline maternal grandmother, Corine Cunningham, in 1916. Their family apparently included some Native American and French ancestry. She had lived in Mobile with her mother and grandmother before moving into the Whiteside family house and caring for her father-in-law, Benjamin. After giving birth to Cap's three daughters in quick succession, the marriage abruptly ended and Cap later married Cecilia, whose assault would serve as the impetus for abandoning their lives in Mobile.

The rich textures of institutional and associational life in Black Mobile extended the militancy of the Reconstruction era to the period of the Nadir – often beyond and against the middle-class pretensions of Washington's followers. This political tradition was at once representative of Black resistance writ large and deeply connected to the contexts of Nadir-era Alabama. And Cap was its product. His generation, those who lived at a time in Alabama where the 1901 state constitution openly mandated segregation and disfranchisement, responded most famously with a street-car boycott, which was followed by a contentious strike of Mobile's back longshoremen, who were affiliated with the International Longshoremen's Association.[17] This threat of Black organizing and self-assertion led directly to a spike in racist violence, including a number of lynchings within the Mobile city limits. The Whitesides would have remembered the scene of Richard Robertson's 1909 extrajudicial murder by hanging, a violent spectacle that took place across the street from the historic Christ Episcopal Church in downtown Mobile. The Nadir was real in Mobile, even as the city fathers often brandished the city as a paragon of progress and a "new South."[18] But those labels, products of boosterish corporate imaginations, could not assuage the discontent that led to Black out-migration during the late 1910s and 1920s – a retreat northward and westward that the Whitesides would soon join.

Responsibilities of a community

The Oakland to which Cap arrived was not yet the space it would become after the wartime industrial transformation that preceded an influx of Black migrants from Texas, Louisiana, Arkansas, and other southern states. But it was not a culturally barren place either. By the late 1920s, many of the social and political institutions that would become the foundation for the new entrants were in place. They would soon remake Oakland.

But before that occurred, earlier migrants from the South, who had increased the Black population sixfold to over six thousand people from 1900 to 1920, were drawn to service jobs and opportunities associated with the three transcontinental rail lines for which the city served as a terminus, as well as eventually those within the shipbuilding industries. Almost immediately, they asserted what Dolores Nason McBroome described as an "economic militancy" that was largely framed within its religiosity and communal determination. Utilizing self-help organizations and a growing labor consciousness, these militant postures were desires to realize and live against the racial proscriptions that continued to set the political terms for their realities. At the apex of an organizing tradition that sought otherwise terms were organizations like the National Association of Colored Women, the National Association for the Advancement of Colored People, and Marcus Garvey's Universal Negro Improvement Association. Activists like C. L. Dellums, Tarea Hall Pittman, and Frances Albrier fought for employment opportunities and legal and civil rights on behalf of Black Oakland alongside religious leaders like John Snape and H. T. S. Johnson who joined their efforts by anchoring the community in the spiritual traditions they brought with them.[19]

As more jobs became available, the perennial challenge of housing shortages amid residential segregation reared its ugly head. Since the late nineteenth century, the neighborhoods of West Oakland had been a viable, but at times suboptimal, location for the Black community, given its close proximity to the rail lines and the requirements by some employers that workers be on call. In short order, a vibrant community of day laborers, factory workers, mechanics, and engineers had appeared. This community also included, perhaps most significantly, a large presence of Pullman porters, which by the mid-1920s under the leadership of A. Philip Randolph and Dellums was organized through the Brotherhood of Sleeping Car Porters and Chambermaids, becoming a critical force in Black working-class politics throughout the country.[20] It was also the community that Winston Whiteside would call home, living first at 1448 Jackson Street before renting a home at 34th and West Streets, and finally securing their permanent home at 3020 Adeline Street, just north of the McClymonds neighborhood.[21]

For those unable to hop aboard the Pullman cars, opportunities were relatively sparse. Laborers were subject to the whims of uncertain market conditions. But Cap was industrious and strong-willed. He would not be denied. After finding work in downtown Oakland, he found community and meaning in the spiritual traditions that had been deposited in West Oakland. Though the African Methodist Episcopal and Baptist churches were dominant, Cap converted to the Seventh Day Adventist Church, where he would have found a resonant, deep religious experience that bound him to a vision of a new land and world beyond, but also to a strict sense of moral uprightness in the here and now.[22] And he was a strict adherent to these views, eventually hosting Bible studies at his home. In their religious instruction, the Whitesides understood authority beyond earthly power, beyond our lesser human experiences. Though Cap was gentle, remembered for the power of his dignity and deep respect for others, this was a theology that could be wielded with a heavy hand. His ability to convey the necessity of moral control may have defined him more than any other set of attributes.[23] In 1933, after witnessing a store being held up at gunpoint (a toy gun, it was later discovered), Cap, who was all of 5 ft. 4 in., sprinted down the street to prevent the assailant from fleeing in a taxicab. Such an act garnered him a mention in the local papers.[24] He simply could not overlook a wrong. This would have meaning for Cedric's birth and childhood.

After a year of consistent work as a janitor downtown made it possible, Cap sent for Cecilia and the girls. It was the year before the stock market crash, and Black Oakland was growing and jobs were available, even as housing accommodations remained stagnant. And then the expansion suddenly ended. As elsewhere, in Oakland, the Great Depression meant a deepening of inequality in the Black community. With unemployment crippling the community, a mix of self-help voluntarism, "Don't Buy Where You Can't Work" campaigns, and labor agitation provided vehicles for activists to buoy West Oakland through the crisis.[25] And also, as elsewhere, the presence of radical forces provided an alternative analysis of "the problem" – one that saw it as a problem of racial capitalism.[26] But at the core of West Oakland during the Depression was a community, an attempt to forge togetherness in the face of hardship.

The community, the tradition that we are describing here, was not one without contradiction. Love transmitted through a "disciplinarian" ethic could at times be difficult for some to bear. Cap ran a tight ship. According to family lore, boys were not allowed near Cap's daughters – and the unlucky few who were caught were severely and violently punished for such an indiscretion. Whether it was a Christian morality or a fear of the possibility of what happened with Cecilia also happening with his daughters, we can only speculate.[27]

In Oakland and the region in general, a vibrant nightlife provided not an escape but a return to the worlds of meaning-making that industrial work tended to negate, a kind of joy and ecstasy that made sense of the realities of exploitation. And if that was not possible, they at least found – in what would soon become known as Baby Harlem – some peace of mind.[28] Much of what Cap had discovered in the church, Clara Whiteside likely realized in these spaces. She was constantly in search of a good time. Though she left Mobile when she was four, she would return yearly to attend Mardi Gras when she reached adulthood.[29] In more recent parlance, she might have been considered something of a socialite. She was beautiful, outgoing, and perhaps somewhat of a rebel to Cap's strict sense of control. After graduating from high school, she ventured out into the social worlds of Black Oakland. It was a world which also produced a class of leadership in both the business and politics that would also have consequences for the larger Black Bay Area society. It was here where Clara met one such leader, the San Francisco club owner Frederick Hill, and began an affair. Whether or not Cap knew about this dalliance, the fact would have deeply troubled, or likely angered, him. And that it produced a child born out of wedlock – who she named Cedric – certainly may have rubbed against his Seventh Day Adventist sensibilities. But none of this prevented Cap from showering the child with the love that would ultimately shape him. His other daughters, Wilma and Lillian, were also mothers, or soon to be, within a few years of moving out on their own. Whatever the circumstances surrounding their bringing of life into the world, its end result was a close-knit network of aunts, uncles, and cousins to which Cedric would become attached. Like all families, they were "full of imperfections and contradictions," but what their love of Cedric reveals was that it was an ethic also grounded in what Kelley describes as a kind of "holding on to each other because they had to and because their culture demanded it."[30]

Cedric James Hill was born on November 5, 1940.[31] Within a year, Clara married Dwight Robinson, from whom

Cedric took his surname. But their marriage was short-lived. Along with Clara, Cedric was cared for by his grandparents whom he called Daddy and Mama Do. They had just been contracted by the city to provide janitorial services to public buildings. They were continuing a Whiteside tradition of self-sustaining entrepreneurialism. There was also Cedric's father, Frederick Hill, who played a role in his son's life. There were some moments where he lived with him. His aunts Wilma and Lillian were a presence as well. Their children were like siblings to Cedric. They found much in common as young boys navigating life in West Oakland. Cedric's biological grandmother, Cap's first wife, Corine Cunningham, had even moved to Oakland. Though his family life was anything but the western sociological norm, Cedric had *people*.

And that is where "Ricky" – as Cedric was called – likely learned for the first time what it meant to live a Black existence, what it meant to confront the world that produced that existence with a Black ethic of confrontation. Cap instilled in Cedric a sense of patience and the necessity of rejecting impulsive thinking. When Cedric faced frustration, he was there to provide care and support.[32] But it was Aunt Wilma who was most interested in things Black. Working as a teacher's aide, she rejected the logic of white supremacy. She had no desires or plans to assimilate. She gave Cedric some of his earliest lessons in Black history and provided a sense of Black identity.[33] These were the settings that first showed Cedric that there was a depth to ways that Black people experienced these times. He would later recall that these early moments inculcated within him a certain pride in being Black.[34]

It occurred against a backdrop of Oakland's own transformation. In the year of Cedric's birth, Oakland experienced an injection of the faith of the Black Radical tradition that had for so long been planted in the rural cultures of the Deep

South. In the first half-decade of his life, it was rerooted in the East Bay in the very West Oakland neighborhood that his grandparents had been calling home since the late 1920s. Like other migrations, this was not simply a demographic transformation, a movement of just people, but as Robinson wrote of the Great Migration in *Black Movements in America*, it was a continuation of this search for a free space – a search begun by the maroons, by the emigrants, and other ancestors who knew freedom was rooted in flight.[35] It was a resituating of the spiritual core of African America in the West, a movement that presaged what Alain Locke called the New Negro, the creation of "a new vision of opportunity . . . a spirit to seize."[36]

And it was no mere trickle. From 1940 to 1945, the Black population in Oakland had almost tripled; by 1950, it had increased by a factor greater than five. Altogether, upward of fifty thousand Black folk came to the East Bay during the war, continuing their flight even after Potsdam.[37] This decade produced a monumental change in the character and tenor of the Black community, and thus the city. The material consequences were deeply meaningful for the Black migrants as the opportunity to participate in employment markets driven by the requirements of war was the ironic backdrop for all of this movement. When A. Philip Randolph threatened to march on Washington to force the hand of the United States to open the war industries to Black workers, Oakland became one place that directly benefited.[38] The older strongholds of rail-line work expanded, albeit temporarily, as did opportunities for Black workers to labor in the shipyards. But for Black people there was also an intense desire to start new lives. Unlike earlier migrations to the region, this movement was generated amid the hope and opportunities that arrived alongside an unprecedented industrial expansion. And maybe Oakland could be a new beginning. But they would soon realize that Oakland was still America.

Postwar reconversion meant another kind of (re)turn – to a racially ordered labor market that reserved the proverbial blessings of the prosperity of the 1950s for those who could claim property in whiteness. This made perfect sense, given that much of that prosperity was also extracted from the larger colonial theater, another racial order. Despite this, Black Oakland fought an extremely valiant fight for fairer employment – a fight that included activists from across the ideological range. Migration to Oakland from the South continued despite the decline in job opportunities for Black workers. Faced with a rising population that needed work, Black civil rights leaders addressed this question head on by seeking to end discrimination in the hiring process.

The year that Cedric was born, Clara was able to land a gig at the California Department of Unemployment. She stayed there for forty-four years.[39] For most, however, such opportunities were fleeting. Though we do not know for sure how Clara experienced workforce discrimination and whether or not she was approached by activists in her capacity in the department, there was much agitation among Black organizers with respect to city jobs. One of their targets was transportation. Oakland's Key System, which directly affected Black life, drew organizers and activists who sought to overturn the discriminatory methods it deployed when it came to staffing its operations. The labor militancy of earlier periods continued, with activists like Dellums, Albrier, and Pittman working to provide space for new migrants in the workplace as well as in the housing markets.[40] That militancy crossed racial lines in critical ways as well, despite the fact that unions did not have the best record when it came to Black membership and participation. When white workers executed a general strike in 1946, Black workers refused to cross the picket lines. It might have appeared to some that class solidarity and racial solidarity *could* in fact go hand in hand if the stakes were clarified – that it did not necessarily mean making a choice toward one end or another. But Oakland was not destined to become an interracial worker's utopia, as the next decade and a half demonstrated.[41]

Perhaps stewing from the fallout of Oakland's general strike of 1946, the city fathers – Republicans, all – made it their goal to extend a kind of growth liberalism toward a vision of what they called "an industrial garden."[42] In order to execute their vision, business-minded liberals, known as the downtown faction, had to unseat their main rivals for political power, ironically Oakland's chapter of the Ku Klux Klan.[43] In place of violent race hate as a modus operandi, the downtown faction imagined a political economy that realized racial capitalism through softer means: workplace and housing discrimination as requirements for capital growth. It was a vision of capitalism that connected development to a sense of the good life, with the garden metaphor representing both a real geographic location and the imagined idyll of the American dream. Tranquility meant the protection of middle-class status, a homeowner's liberalism. It drew resources from the state to support such development and in the end prefigured a neoliberal reality that was still decades away. The growth of the garden was a private affair, supported by a kind of state capitalism that privileged those white property holders as the citizens that mattered. This of course meant that prevention of Black access to the garden could have been easily predicted, as this very tactic was practiced nationwide. The industrial garden, however, was an apt metaphor. Access to the garden, as in all systems of private property, needed to be managed – it needed police. And in the Oakland metro area it came in the form of state-sanctioned housing segregation coupled with the surveillance of migrant communities and the repressive politics of juvenile delinquency.[44]

The children of the migrants were Cedric's classmates in

the public education systems in place in Oakland, where he thrived in a community of Black educators. But the further up one went within these systems, the inequalities emerged. Notorious for their "tracking" initiatives, these schools became incubators for what reformers would label in more recent years as the "school-to-prison" pipeline. They were tracked on a pyramidal basis with the majority of the children of migrants placed at the lower rung. They received an inferior education by design, and the expectation in many cases was that these students would merely drop out. For those who did not make it through an education system that denied Black capacity for thought, reform school became their fate.[45]

Clara had remarried and was living on Calmar Avenue in Berkeley. By using her address, Cedric was able to attend the nearly-all-Black Burbank Junior High School. During his junior high years, Cedric was remembered as popular, "a leading character," and in one instance he welcomed and befriended a Japanese student, a child whose family had experienced the internment camps. Years later, they remembered that Cedric was the only one that was willing to reach out to them, cultivating a relationship in what was for them a hostile environment. At Burbank, Cedric also nurtured his artistic side, taking up painting and photography lessons as well as portraying a "mystery" character in the yearbook, challenging students to identify him based on several clues; an act that endeared him to many of his classmates. He exerted a memorable presence among the adults at Burbank as well. More than fifty years later, Cedric's physical education teacher reached out to him to tell him how proud he was of the work he would come to do.[46]

That engaging and welcoming spirit followed Cedric to Berkeley High, a school notable for its legacy of student activism and engagement but also, as Kelley points out, for its racism. Nevertheless, Cedric's ever-present intellectual curiosity would again serve him well. This was all despite the fact that, like most migrant children, he experienced some level of "tracking" once he got there. In Cedric's case, he was encouraged to take a shop class, despite his high marks in college preparatory classes like English, mathematics, and foreign languages. Black students at Berkeley were often placed on a trajectory toward skilled labor, perhaps, or less. Even as jobs were disappearing, as discrimination toward Black working-class people was increasingly a problem, "tracking" prepared students like Cedric for jobs that might one day be obsolete or for more infamous destinations, like the California Youth Authority.[47]

Yet he seemed to evade these tracks, excelling in all of his academic work, as well as in leadership positions, serving as vice president of his class (for the H-11 semester), Bicycle Court Judge, and the Circle B society, while remaining active in the track team, the jazz club, and the Spanish club. He was a budding photographer and writer. In a short story he wrote for English V, "Joshua Fit De Battle," he told a tale of racist violence in the segregated South. A white man had murdered a ten-year-old Black boy for calling him "white trash." He was acquitted. And his grandfather, Joshua, who had been talked out of taking matters into his own hands, was left to surmise whether it was possible that God was really "gonna give the world to the meek . . ."[48] This story was written two years after the murder of Emmett Till, and one could see in its main character some shadows of Cap. It was also in his teenage years that Cedric would begin a lifelong love of music. Miles Davis was his favorite and, in what was a common experience of Black folk of this generation, sneaking into the clubs for Cedric was a rite of passage. He had even encountered Miles on one of those nights. Literally.

Miles, unaware of the teenager's presence, stepped on his foot. Cedric took it as a point of pride.[49]

For some who remembered those times, life at Berkeley, for a student like Cedric whose interests and friendships were eclectic, would have been alienating. Though he had developed relationships across racial lines, it would not have been enough to convert guidance counselors and administrators who would have categorized him as a Black student with West Oakland roots and thus relegated to a particular station in life. Despite these plans for him, Cedric lived on his own terms and shaped the educational vision that he required for himself, eventually graduating in 1958, ranking 95th in a class of 565, and deciding that he would continue his education, rather than function in and as what Berkeley schooling imagined for people like him.[50] Among those from his community who knew him, this was expected. In fact, many children from Seventh Day Adventist families excelled academically. The socialization of the youth within these settings prepared them for classroom instruction.[51] It was clear, however, that Cedric's desire to know guided him as well.

Though they might not have shared all of his political sensibilities, Cedric's family shaped him immeasurably. And they were proud of his achievements. He was his mother's favorite topic of conversation. They sent him off to college with a sense of self, a sense of purpose, and a sense of how that connected to his Blackness. Aunt Wilma's earliest lessons were the foundation for the intense library sessions that were to come. He saw models of what it is to be in community and to convene spaces for the purposes of learning and grounding. He saw it in how Daddy and Mama Do built spaces within their church groups' religious instruction which were also for each other, for community.

It does seem a cliché that scholars, whose politics align with the folk, are intimately influenced by elders in their family – elders who are without degree and without portfolio. But the prominence of a cliché does not mean the absence of a truth. In fact, it might contain an important lesson. We are not self-created, and our capacity for and recognition of genius exists in places where regard for our humanity is kept at the fore. This may be that lesson.

In a 1999 interview where he evoked Whiteside's influence, Cedric also framed the question of genealogy and political struggle within the deeper registers of African cultural traditions. He reminded us of the importance that enslaved Africans gave to a "world view in which the reiteration of names (an African convention in which the name of a recently deceased loved one is given to the next child born) reflected the conservatism and responsibilities of a community." As families grew, it was necessary to maintain "the resolve to value our historical and immediate interdependence."[52] The Whitesides had the ability to make Cedric Robinson, to inform his orientation, because he lived a life that tapped into an ongoing, living tradition of how to be in and beyond this anti-Black world – a tradition that would then be represented and made available to us. To reiterate their names within a project of and for Black Study is to remind ourselves that we too are interdependent. Our work is only possible when it is connected to communities of meaning that reside in spaces often held from view. It is an urgent and prescient meaning of intellectual genealogy.

2

The Town and Gown

"The Town" signifies a kind of collectivity structured by the boundaries of Oakland, yet also clearly inspired by a spiritual foundation that is unbounded by physical space. It is a way of marking a common experience, one rooted in both an older settler history but, more richly, a newer tradition of Black migration and resettlement – a convergence that generated the various social and revolutionary struggles that placed the city under an international spotlight during the height of Black Power. Today, that resettlement, of both geography and social relation, is most visible through cultural registers like Oakland's brand of hip-hop, a music and posture that is rooted in a sensibility endemic to the region, embodying a resistance to the normative logics of citizenship in the *polis*. "The Town" just rolls off the tongue differently when it is linked to the memory and possibility of Black life in the environs of the East Bay.[1] But it has older foundations and a longer history. When Black Power emerged within the region's colleges and universities throughout the decade of the 1960s – shaping a movement that was local, national, and global – it was set in motion by those cultural traditions that would later be described as "the Town."

"The Gown" denotes a distinction between the learned and the lay. Attached to a university idea exported from Europe, gowned intellectuals were those who lectured students and conducted "research." They were functionaries who preserved the political order and crafted new ways to rationalize it. And these were the terms and conditions under which American universities, like the University of California, were born in the nineteenth century, adopting and appropriating classical and research models that were newly imagined and updated for the American experience. By the turn of the twentieth century, rising populations and new market opportunities created the conditions for the idea of mass higher education, pursued under the assumption that a more skilled and competent populace might more efficiently create economic growth for American capital – their education construed as an initial investment traded in exchange for the financial security of middle-class life. And so birthed the idea of "Town and Gown," a concept that evoked a symbiotic relationship, between off-campus communities that existed to support and shape this practice of higher education and the maintenance of the good life under the logics of American nineteenth-century liberalism.[2] It was no shock then that under these formations, even of mass higher education, there existed a story of racist exclusion. One way to tell the story of the 1960s in the Bay Area is how an alternative conception of relationships to community – the specifically Oakland variant of "the Town" – intervened to disrupt this ordering principle of the university. It called for a new time.

A resident and relation of the Town, Cedric's journey would become a harbinger for those new times. But nothing was certain, nothing about this story inevitable. In fact, his arrival was peculiar. In the final years before the adoption of California's Master Plan, admission to UC was granted to the top 15 percent of students in the state. There were no standardized tests, but there was also no affirmative action – structural racism simply worked to deny Black folks' admission by placing the possibility beyond their reach through educational tracking.[3] Noted sociologists of the period even wrote that one of the issues of college preparatory secondary schooling was that many racial minorities lacked the "aspirations" for higher education.[4] These assumptions meant that Cedric received little to no guidance from his counselors at Berkeley High School regarding the process for applying and being admitted to college, despite his clear academic success. Thankfully, those closer to him knew that these racist expectations did not pertain at least to him. And it may have been one of Cedric's teachers, many of whom he remembered fondly, that ended up supporting his ambition to continue his education at UC.[5]

At the time, with a population of minorities that was in the lower hundreds, and a Black population (including continental Africans) of around two hundred, the presence of locally born Black students at UC in 1958 remained relatively minimal. On the day of registration, Cedric inadvertently joined a line for international students. While there, he met and chatted with a nineteen-year-old graduate student from India named Shyamala Gopalan, with whom he would soon become a committed confidante. And then, according to Cedric's version of events, the registrar took one look at him and asked if his country would also be paying his fees.[6]

While he had no country to pay his fees, thankfully there was no tuition to worry about for California residents. But there were costs. For most students, the yearly charge for incidentals was less than a hundred dollars and thus nominal. But Cedric would have to work. During his college years, he balanced his academic responsibilities while working as a dishwasher at the famous coffee house the Bear's Lair, as well as cleaning hotel rooms, working in a canning facility, and often filling in for his grandparents who had started a janitorial business.[7] There would soon be other work, and other time, for another education.

It is something to be Black

The University of California was chartered by the state of California in 1868 with the explicit mandate of making higher education available to residents of the state, regardless of socioeconomic status. The idea of creating a first-rate university, on much the same model as America's top eastern institutions, was grounded in the belief that what the state needed was an educated citizenry in order to strengthen and enliven the promises of the "California dream" of prosperity for all.[8] This egalitarian impulse was grounded in a liberalism that nevertheless did not preclude the university's pursuit of racist former general George McClellan for its presidency. Although he declined, the university did hire former Confederate Army scientists to become part of the project.[9] The United States was addicted to growth and expansion as a possible resolution to the economic costs of the Civil War; one might even argue that it was the reason *for* the war. And California, with its state creed of realizing "El Dorado," fitted nicely within this laissez-faire vision, which, as Reconstruction and its betrayal showed, had room enough for those who had started and perpetuated the rebellion but none in those spaces for those who had helped save the union.[10] Though nominally a state institution, capitalists, rather than statesmen, determined what happened at the new university.

Berkeley was based on the newer models of research-driven academic and pedagogic approaches that had been founded in Germany in the first half of the nineteenth century, which garnered interest in America, especially at Yale University, where many of UC's founding fathers had been educated. It was believed that research, new knowledge, could support innovation and further drive growth and societal flourishing. The state had a duty to allocate land and opportunity. It also had an interest in providing direct aid to these ventures. The elite financiers of the Gilded Age America, nineteenth-century liberals par excellence, found little in this vision to oppose, funding these new academic ventures with glee.[11] With the turn toward the progressive movement – and its concomitant belief in education as a guarantor of both reform and efficiency – the university would soon expand with the state's population and capital's needs, eventually creating what has become known as the University of California system, based on the "California idea" of mass education, which stood for many years as a model for state public higher education.[12]

Though the progressive movement was largely grounded in norms of social equality, the question of racism still remained prominent. Despite the often racist assumptions of nonwhites' educational capacity, a small number of Black students began to attend UC in the last decades of the nineteenth century, with the first Black graduate, Vivian Logan Rogers, receiving her degree in 1909. By the 1920s, many of the Bay Area's eventual leaders and activists were attending the university, including Tarea Hall, Byron Rumford, and Walter Gordon. Yet they all faced severe levels of discrimination. Their presence revealed a further limit to the egalitarian ideal that had so defined the university, as they were caricatured in racist cartoons in a student-run paper, *The California Pelican*, and openly excluded from the important campus social and community organizations. Given California's racial histories, it would have been expected.

In response, Black students developed their own organizations, both professional and social, and began to use important off-campus satellites, such as the all-important Stiles Hall, to engage questions of Black life in the progressive imagination.[13] But in other cases they utilized campus resources to their advantage. A young Louise Thompson – with whom Cedric would later make an important connection – majored in economics and literature at Berkeley and became a founding member of the first West Coast chapter of Delta Sigma Theta, which may have had a hand in bringing W. E. B. Du Bois to campus in 1923. That event had left her "feeling, well, it is something to be Black."[14] As much as Black matriculation at Berkeley was a "lonely endeavor," Black students during this era imagined it as a critical route to escape a kind of drudgery in these pre-migration East Bay labor environs, as well as perhaps, most importantly, a way to reach occupations in government service and politics, where they would work to expose and maybe overcome the racial seams of the California dream.[15]

The next wave of Black Berkeley students arrived amid an increase in the Black population in the Town during and after World War II and in a moment where UC, like many American universities, was becoming what future president Clark Kerr called a "multiversity" – a large organism designed to operate and serve as a multitudinous site of market exchanges under the guise of education. Trade relationships between industry and labor, commodities, and other instruments of value were guarded and controlled by an increasingly bureaucratic managerial class – an invention we now label "university administrators." Off campus, the erection of Cordonices Village was designed to house this growing Black population, and their presence elicited a negative reaction in the largely Republican town. This, too, would have been expected. But what these old guard leaders may not have expected was that Black students would make UC one site for launching a Black and liberal political coalition which sought to remove them from power. Yet it was also a moment in time that they sought to do and imagine much more.[16]

He said such wise things

Cedric spent his first two years at Berkeley as a pre-med student. Among the community of Black students, he would come to be known as relatively reserved. Perhaps he was concerned with the weighty matters of a strenuous academic program, possibly with matters much larger. Though quiet, he did use the few words he offered with great effect. He was known to punctuate silences with revelations that might not have been obvious to others in the circle. It could be that even then he was thinking about a way out or beyond the morass, the thickness of conformity that had no doubt been presented to Black students as the only possible or logical path.

On campus, Black students would congregate in the library or in the Bear's Lair, holding forth on a range of issues, these sessions becoming precursors to the more consequential study groups that would ultimately set the stage for the Black Power movement.[17] But for now, Cedric thought and observed, built relationships and asked questions. For instance, one very close friend remembers clearly the moment he lost his "religion," though not his deep respect for the Black religiosity and communitarianism that ran in his family. Asked what precipitated his questioning of the existence of God, Cedric muttered a one-word answer: "Sharpeville."[18]

The first year of the decade of the sixties was trying. And deeply transformative. It was part of a moment of Black students on campus moving toward a reckoning. They were being introduced not only to concepts of revolution and anti-capitalist thought, but to their very real application in "Third World" settings that were significant to them as nonwhite students, navigating a very elite white place. Cedric would experience this reckoning, at first personally, then, as they sought to study and organize, he would come to navigate its meaning collectively. On March 21, 1960, South African police had murdered more than sixty Africans in cold blood at Sharpeville. That, in tandem with rising liberation movements in Mexico, Cuba, and the growing US movement in the South, became important spaces to observe these unfolding moments. Then the House Un-American Activities Committee came to the Bay Area.

California had always been the site of intense Cold War activity. Its location in the Pacific theater was strategic, with critical defense outposts located all along the coast. The funding for defense industries dovetailed with the investment in basic and applied sciences at places like Berkeley, which intensified the support for American imperialism on campus and in the community. But it did not eliminate questions among progressives, especially those whose parents had come of age on the left. Only ten years earlier, the university, under president Robert Sproul, had forced faculty members to sign a loyalty oath, repudiating or disaffirming any connection to subversive activity. When several refused, there ensued a battle over questions of academic freedom that presaged the more famous, larger student battles to come in the 1960s. Though there were only three professed members of the Communist Party on campus, state leaders like Senator Hugh Burns, who ran California's Un-American Activities Committee, saw UC as a hotbed for radical activity. So when HUAC came, it trained its eyes, partly, on campus.[19]

Raised in the Communist Party USA, Douglas Wachter was a sophomore at Berkeley who was summoned to appear before the committee at City Hall in San Francisco. On May 12, 1960, the date of his appearance, hundreds of Berkeley students, organized by the Student Committee for Civil Liberties, arrived to protest. The following day, when some of them were refused entry, they protested, chanted, and held their ground in the rotunda. The San Francisco police drenched them with a fire hose, physically brutalized a number of them, before pushing them down the stairs and arresting the 64 protesting students who remained nonviolently asserting their right to witness the proceedings.[20] The media broadcast these images to the world, where they reached people like Bettina Aptheker, who came to Berkeley the next year inspired by the images of youth resistance she saw. They also inspired right-wing forces, who disingenuously framed police brutality as a "riot" precipitated by the students and utilized such framings to increase their surveillance of a growing body of students who were seen as a threat. The HUAC even produced a laughably cynical and inaccurate documentary to "warn" Middle America what these "privileged" students – supposed "dupes" of a communist conspiracy – were up to.[21]

Wachter had known Cedric since they were both students at Burbank Junior High School. He remembered that Cedric was "very easy to be around" and "clearly interested in socialism and Marxism," even at such an early age. And Wachter, who had spent part of his childhood living in Cordonices Village, developed an interest in issues of race and an appreciation of Black culture. He was no doubt among the circle of friends that Cedric attracted when they later matriculated through Berkeley High. But once at UC, they fell out of

touch.[22] However, none of this prevented Cedric from sup-
porting his friend when Berkeley students resisted at the
HUAC hearings. As a result of the protest, Cedric joined the
Bay Area Student Coalition against the House Un-American
Activities Committee, part of a growing number of student
organizations that were beginning to focus and confront Cold
War repression and global convulsions across the world.

Among those efforts was SLATE, a formation that was
created to break the hold on the imaginations of the student
government and larger student body at UC. Student government was dominated by Greek-letter organizations that were
concerned only with the on-campus "sandbox," whereas
SLATE pushed the needle to concerns beyond the ivory
tower.[23] SLATE was a response to the presumed apathy of
the "silent generation" – the group of students in the 1950s
that had been understood to have accepted the status quo
– and the harbinger of a generation that imagined itself as
connected to a revolutionary trajectory then being pursued
in the larger world. One of the first campus-based political
parties, SLATE would pioneer an approach to campus politics that sought to utilize student government as a means to
raise awareness and participate in ongoing struggles for justice, equality, and revolution.

Best known for its advocacy of free speech and academic
freedom through the movements of 1964, progressive and
radical movements associated with SLATE also participated in the peace and anti-nuclear weapons movement,
pro-Cuba advocacy, solidarity with farmworkers, anti-capital
punishment movements, and with the southern civil rights
struggles, launching the resultant sympathy marches and
direct action initiatives in the Bay Area. SLATE stood res-
olutely on the premise that Berkeley students must stake a
position on the side of justice, which, of course, caused the
university and its governing body to actively repress and

curtail the organization's moves, especially when it moved back *into* the sandbox, like in its campaign against mandatory ROTC.[24] Cedric joined SLATE, participating mostly in the background but, in some cases, out front and always present and bearing witness.[25]

It is unlikely that Black Berkeley students were present at the founding of SLATE. But this does not mean that there was an absence of concern or Black political activism on campus. In their sets on and off campus, Black students continued to pay close attention to the world around them. Cuba weighed heavily on their minds, as would have the happenings in the Congo, Kwame Nkrumah's political moves in Ghana, as well as the struggles of the Kenyan Land and Freedom Party in Eastern Africa, given that some Kennedy Airlift students also attended Berkeley. Much like the growing concern around the sit-in movements, Black self-defense in the South, and the work of the Nation of Islam, these questions of struggle and revolution were leading to critical conversations among young Black activists concerning what kinds of actions they might pursue.[26]

According to Margot Dashiell, several Black students had come to UC from Howard University with a consciousness and awareness of African anticolonial politics in tow. While she did not know him there, Dashiell was a year behind Cedric at Berkeley High and was one of five Black students who were discouraged to attend UC but came anyway. She quickly found herself engaged in these discussions of Pan-Africanism and decolonization. She remembered that before the arrival of Henry Ramsey, Donald Warden, Mary Agnes Lewis, and John J. Miller in the late 1950s, there was little sense of self-identification with Africa, despite an awareness of African decolonization movements. What they added to that awareness was a sensibility and a desire for Black folk in the Bay Area to also see themselves as African.[27] Likely inspired by these conversations, Cedric changed his major to anthropology in the fall semester of 1960, one of a number of Black students who felt that this particular social science was a place where they could encounter the nonwhite world academically. That semester, Cedric took classes on Africa, East Asia, and Indigenous America, and he chose Japanese for language study.[28]

That autumn also saw the arrival of a critical student organizer. Coming to Berkeley to pursue his PhD in sociology, J. Herman Blake brought a range of experiences with him. He had come from an impoverished background in Harlem – a "ghetto" experience that fascinated Cedric.[29] But he also brought life experiences as a military veteran and a full-time professional, as well as a family man, financially responsible for not only his wife and three children but his mother-in-law and her three children, *and* his sister-in-law and *her* three children. It is indeed shocking that he found time between classes, work, and family, to help revive the campus chapter of the National Association for the Advancement of Colored People (NAACP). Cedric ran against him for president, unsuccessfully, but quickly became a young understudy to the veteran organizer as vice president of the organization. More, Cedric pushed Blake in important and critical ways. Even in these settings, he remained a quiet but profound voice. Blake remembers: "He was not shy or in the background, but he didn't talk a lot. And when he talked he said such wise things ."[30]

At some point this group, which included Dashiell, Blake, as well as Ken Simmons and Sondra Robinson, put their proverbial boots on the ground in a Black community. Urban development had come to San Francisco, and the price, as it so often was, became Black removal. In order to justify "Negro removal," city planners, under the leadership of development czar Justin Herman, began to circulate the idea that Black people desired their own relocation. A Berkeley sociology student named Carl Werthman was working in a San Francisco community with a group known as Youth for Service that was involved in crime remediation, known then as "street work." The head of Youth for Service, Orville Luster, alongside the Crispus Attucks Club/ Bayview Hunters Point Citizens Committee led by Ardeth Nichols, knew the developers' narrative was false. So Luster approached Werthman with a proposal to help him prove it. And Werthman, along with a trio of sociology students, Howard Brill, Jerry Mandell, and SLATE veteran Mike Miller, prevailed on the campus NAACP to help. Together they participated in a Du Boisian style urban sociology project where they went door-to-door to develop a profile of the Bayview–Hunters Point community and its views on gentrification. There is no material trace of Cedric's feelings or experiences while interacting with these residents. But we do know that results of their survey revealed what everyone already knew: that Black residents wanted an improvement in their living conditions, not the razing of their communities.[31]

The movement against removal and job discrimination in this community was spearheaded by a collective known as the Bayview Big Five, a model of what some then called "matriarchal leadership."[32] Led by Nichols, Elouise Westbrook, Julia Commer, Oceola Washington, and Bertha Freeman, these women "became a virtual institution" making "sure the community would have a part" in decisions made by the developers and their mandarins in San Francisco. In time, the Housing Authority would yield to their influence, but at best this only slowed their plans.[33]

To have had any knowledge of or interactions with these women organizers would have been an impactful experience for Cedric as he had only experienced patriarchal organizations through both his religious and political affiliations.

These women's desire to "build a better future from the inside out" would have contributed to his growing belief that the people themselves might determine what was best for them in the face of capitalist exploitation.[34] He would later write of women like the NAACP's Septima Poinsette Clark in *Black Movements in America* who, like the Bayview Big Five, were organizers in the vanguard of social change during this era.[35] The NAACP's engagement with the community in San Francisco soon gave way to a formal program adopted by the university later that semester – much along the lines of the kinds of service learning that are now prevalent.[36] But by then other forms of community work had become more attractive to the group of NAACP students that conducted the survey.

You both make a truth

The spring semester of 1961 saw an escalation of activity, perhaps the most intense of Cedric's time at Berkeley. For Black students concerned about questions of "the movement" and larger global issues, the campus NAACP had become the place and setting for this work. Though they continued to organize and mount demonstrations, many in the group gravitated toward study and discussion as the grounds for their political consciousness. One consequence of this study was the welcoming of political thinkers to campus who had directly experienced and engaged the revolutionary alternatives being lived and practiced in the world. Revolution could not be simply theoretical; it lived and breathed. So these connections had to be made in real life, in real time.

On March 15, Cedric worked with the Fair Play for Cuba Committee to host perhaps the leading figure within the NAACP concerned with connections between local organizing and global revolutions: none other than Robert F. Williams, the leader of the Monroe, North Carolina chapter and the proverbial thorn in the side of both the local authorities and the executive committee of the NAACP. Williams was fresh off his visit to Cuba, so Cedric and others in the NAACP and Fair Play held fundraisers to make it possible for him to get to Berkeley.[37]

On the importance of the Cuban Revolution to Black America, Williams was unequivocal: "I had never known what it means to be free before I went to Cuba." Connecting the question of the Cuban struggle to the southern civil rights movement, he argued that his position as a southern-born African American allowed him the unique vantage to understand those humanitarian aspects of Fidel Castro's attempt to create an egalitarian society free of racism. Finally, Williams condemned the US media's coverage of Cuba's situation which was analogous to the "cotton curtain," constructed by southern media outlets, which offered a biased and untrue depiction of Black life in the American South.[38] Like Amiri Baraka, Harold Cruse, and others who visited revolutionary Cuba, Williams's visit had sharply intensified his understanding of the meaning and possibility of Black revolution.[39]

Joining Williams at the event was a graduate student in sociology from Stanford who offered the "liberal" and "civil libertarian" position on the Cuban situation. While conceding that Castro's initiatives had raised Cuban living standards, he asserted that such improvements came from what he considered a less than democratic project. Though Castro clearly had support, the student expressed some concern that Cuba did not seem an environment where dissenting opinions could be heard.[40] To these arguments, Cedric would offer a written response.

Published almost a week later, Cedric's *Daily Californian*

editorial began by championing the revolutionary move around the world to imagine a beyond to the western world, a world he characterized as an "anachronism." Williams's message of "militant self-defense" in the wake of that world's decline sounded "true and clear" to Cedric's ears, whose endorsement of Williams's program was shared by others in the audience. He then affirmed Williams's insistence that the posture of the "tolerant Black Christian has been too costly and a fool's errand." In such an environment, the application of Gandhism was a grave error "unless one happens to have four hundred million expendable individuals on hand." Moving to his central task of addressing the "so-called liberals in the audience who suddenly found themselves in the throes of confusion," Cedric argued that the difference between liberals and leftists was "the difference between those who want to change the world and those who simply wish to modify it." In light of the visions of freedom by "adherents of [both] Democracy and Communism," he emphasized the imperative to realize "that these peoples [the Cubans] do not wish to fit themselves into the neatly carved places defined for them." Self-determination truly meant that. And it meant understanding that freedom required a world free of human divisions wrought by "the ghetto, the nation, the race," stages that had to be passed through in order to realize the unity of humankind. What Cedric had gleaned was that Cuba's liberation struggle offered a vision of a future world not yet realized, and therein lay the fears of the West. But for those who saw in "the West" the source of their problems, that vision represented something to be embraced rather than feared.[41]

When news of the troubles that summer in Monroe reached the group, they quickly began to organize. Robert Williams, Mae Mallory, Julian Mayfield, and young people involved in the Monroe Nonviolent Action Committee had been involved in various efforts to picket the local swimming pool and support the efforts of the Freedom Riders. Those efforts were met with white violence. And in the wake of that violence, several members of the group were charged with kidnapping. These were the trumped-up charges that led to Robert and Mabel Williams's exile. In response, Cedric organized and became the chairman of the Bay Area Committee for the Monroe Defendants. Throughout November, they organized protests around the region to raise awareness about the case and its miscarriage of justice, at one point rubbing up against a city ordinance in order to do so.[42]

After having been electrified by Williams that spring, it was the least they could do. But they had also been shaped by other events during the semester. That April, Roy Nichols came to address the group. In many ways, he was woefully out of touch. The leader of the Berkeley NAACP and a staunch integrationist, Nichols was invited to speak on the burgeoning movement under the title "the New Negro." Instead, he offered the same *old* paradigm, and the campus NAACP ruffled the feathers of the local chapter when they dismissed these ideas.[43] The students had become to the local Berkeley chapter what Williams's Monroe chapter had been vis-à-vis the national. Signals came from New York to rein them in.[44] Especially after they drew closer to the Nation of Islam, a group that had also supported Williams in his program for self-defense. By the early 1960s, the Nation had begun to exert a critical influence in the Bay Area.[45]

The story of how all this unfolded on campus is interesting. On March 1, Donald Warden, supposedly inspired by the Nation, issued a challenge to the campus NAACP. In an editorial to the *Daily Californian*, he asserted that the student members had not only failed to commemorate Negro History Week but their focus on discrimination and segregation was less critical than the pressing questions of self-determination and national liberation. That ferment was evidenced in the UN demonstrations protesting the role of the United States in the assassination of Patrice Lumumba, in Fidel Castro's reception in Harlem, and in the rise of the Nation of Islam. The NAACP's narrow focus on "the securement of civil rights in this area" was evidence that it had "contributed nothing significant to our intellectual community."[46] It was almost as if Warden was describing the position of the national office – not the group that was then not only planning to bring Robert F. Williams to campus but also studying and debating the very movements he described. It seems Warden had not really engaged them on campus. Nevertheless, his missive endorsed the program of the Nation before extending an invitation to a representative of the NAACP to debate the merits of their approach.

The bombast present in this editorial might be attributed to Warden's personality. Graduating from Howard in 1958, Warden came to Berkeley as a law student. He was both brilliant and charismatic, and as a former child preacher and debate team champion, he had perfected the powers of persuasion. But as was often the case with great orators, sometimes the substantiation for many of his arguments was lacking. In the case of Warden, he was often accused of trading in outright fabrications that sounded good and moved the crowd.[47]

Responding to the editorial was Blake, who first refuted the idea that the campus NAACP, by its very existence, had limited the discourse concerning the best route to Black liberation. In fact, he reminded the public that it was the NAACP that had invited Black Muslim representatives to speak on campus. Many who were in the NAACP or close to the students involved were thinking about these questions and some even supported elements of the Nation's program.[48] A sophomore art student from Oakland named Nell Irvin had recently argued in the *Daily Californian* that if people were committed to "realizing that white supremacy has been an operating European policy since the fifteenth century, [and] realizing that his whole peculiar history has been one of separation and race before country, imposed by the white majority," they would see that for "this majority to criticize the Muslims is hypocrisy."[49] It was clear that many Black students were not only aware of ideological alternatives to civil rights, but that they were actively engaged in dialogues around these questions. Blake, who was well read and well studied, and in contrast to Warden spoke calmly and clearly, closed his reply by simply accepting Warden's invitation to debate.[50]

The public debate took place on April 13 in Benjamin Wheeler Hall. In presenting the Nation of Islam's views, Warden argued that the fatal flaw of the integrationist movement was the middle-class Negro, the Black bourgeoisie, that was alienated and disappointed, largely because integration would not and could not solve the basic issue of what racism attacked: their dignity. This psychological barrier to true equality would only be addressed through an affirmation, generated through separate Black institutions. Yet, for Blake, the larger question of economic and political rights was nevertheless a critical goal to be achieved. Grounding his argument in the Niagara Movement's declaration, Blake asserted that the fight was for nothing "less than our full manhood rights."[51] On the surface, it seemed to be the garden-variety debate around integration and assimilation versus separation and nationalism that often reappeared. But there also seemed to be something more at play. There was a clear concern and perhaps an anxiety around the question of how students situated at elite Berkeley could remain cognizant of issues in the larger world around them, to what

ideological and organizational tools were available to address
that world, and the obvious alienation that they felt.[52]

After the two presented their programs, Blake encouraged the Black students to join the work of the NAACP,
but Warden curiously urged them to join CORE, despite
the fact that initial impulse of the debate was the Nation of
Islam's program. CORE – the Congress of Racial Equality
– was largely populated by whites and had been active in
Berkeley in direct action work going back to 1959, but it
had almost certainly not pushed the nationalist sentiment
that characterized Warden's editorial. Ironically, it was the
NAACP that directly supported and enhanced the work of
CORE during these years. Though much of the activity in
Berkeley would greatly expand after the impact of Project
C in Birmingham, students involved in CORE had participated in sympathy marches and sit-ins throughout 1960 and
1961. In the wake of the birth of the Student Nonviolent
Coordinating Committee (SNCC), a formation calling itself
Students for Racial Equality found ways to directly support
this work financially alongside SLATE and the NAACP, possibly through Cedric's influence, although they encountered
struggles along the way.[53] Warden's endorsement of CORE
showed an interesting and confounding lack of awareness.
Even more interesting, members of the Nation of Islam
had actually attended the debate and were more impressed
with Blake than they were with Warden, the person that had
argued *their* position. As a result, Bernard X (Kushmeer),
leader of the Oakland Mosque, began to actively recruit
Blake into the Nation, setting in motion Malcolm X's visit
to Berkeley.[54]

The story, which has become legend, began in the wake
of the April debate. Soon after their connection, Blake was
approached by Bernard X with the idea of possibly hosting an event with Malcolm X later that May, to which he

agreed. About a week before the scheduled appearance, the NAACP picketed the university's placement office for allowing United Airlines to recruit on campus despite the fact that they refused to hire Black people for in-flight occupations. Blake suggested that this was the only reason that he, Cedric, and Warden found themselves in a meeting with Chief Campus Officer Edward Strong, days later, in a fight to reverse the administration's decision to rescind Malcolm's invitation. That it was retaliation for the protest might be validated by the fact that administrators had previously approved the event with no issues. But when the paperwork reached vice chancellor Adrian Kragen's office, a decision to revoke permission to host Malcolm was made.[55] It is also necessary, however, to understand the refusal amid the ongoing battles over speaker bans on campus.

One response by UC's administration to the Cold War environment was a revision to Rule 17, which essentially stipulated that speakers avowing political positions would not be allowed on campus. It was designed to protect the university's nonpartisanship, but it was also clearly designed to placate the Regents, as well as state assemblymen, who wanted to curtail any political radicalism or "subversive" activity on campus. They realized how draconian the rules were on paper when appearances by politically safe figures, such as Adlai Stevenson, fell under the speaker ban. Relaxed under Clark Kerr's administration, which coincided with Cedric's time, the rule was changed to allow speakers on certain conditions, including one that opposing views were also presented. Yet these latter stipulations maintained the ban on religious views and communists (up until June 1963).[56]

Though the controversial appearance of HUAC opponent Frank Wilkinson signaled that things were truly opening up, Kragen argued that it was Malcolm's status as a religious figure that warranted *his* ban.[57] The two leaders of the

NAACP, Blake and Cedric, along with Warden, retorted that this was of course inconsistent and unfair, given that the university had planned to host Bishop James Pike on the very same day – and had previously hosted Billy Graham and Rabbi Alvin Fine, not to mention Nichols, also a preacher, who had just been presented by the NAACP. While Blake felt that it was retaliation, Warden seized on the hypocrisy of the administration's insistence on the religious ban, arguing that if Malcolm's intention was not to proselytize, then he should be allowed to speak.[58] Though Malcolm had previously been identified by the FBI as a communist and was clearly inspired by the religious teachings of the Nation of Islam, it was of course his power as an orator and the growing community of Black nationalists that seemed to spook Kragen.[59] Years later, he admitted that what had guided his decision was the fear of "what his [Malcolm's] followers had done." What he was referring to here is unclear, but his comments suggest that wherever Malcolm spoke, violence followed. Edward Strong remembered it as a "courageous" decision.[60]

Once again, Cedric, as vice president, took the responsibility of issuing a statement of response on behalf of the NAACP. Appearing in the *Daily Californian* on May 8, the scheduled date of the event, the statement charged that the university's denial of Malcolm's visit was "invalid and indicated differential treatment." Rehashing many of the points raised privately, Cedric pointed out that, even if one accepted that Malcolm's intent was religious in nature, the university's allowance of other religious figures proved that their treatment was unfair. Cedric clarified that the NAACP's desire was to provide an educational forum for students to learn directly from Malcolm X – a privilege in many ways to witness one of the most well-known and eloquent representatives of the Nation – and as such the university's

denial was "fallacious." It was a university, after all. Speaking
for the group, and likely not for himself, he ended the statement by declaring: "The NAACP is opposed to the Black
Muslim brotherhood, but we can only express regret at the
University's denial of opportunity for dialog and discussion
in an effort at intelligent opposition."[61] The statement was
shrouded in the ongoing battles between student activists and
the university's preoccupation with surviving the Cold War
unscathed. These battles were inspired by a strong defense
of freedom of speech and for the expression of unique views,
but often came down to procedural and technical questions.
The university's rules and their enforcement were inconsistent because they were governed by the ideological excesses of
the era. Ironically, "free speech" was not meaningful enough
to protect students who wanted to discuss this very fact.

Losing their battle, the students retreated to the YMCA's
Stiles Hall, which continued its role as a safety valve for
student organizers, especially so during the speaker ban con-
troversies.[62] On May 8, Malcolm electrified an audience that
included the budding study group, the NAACP, and may
have even included a young Huey Newton, who had begun
to hang around these circles around this time. The campus
newspaper sent a reporter who framed Malcolm's message
as advocating "the complete separation of races." This idea
of "separation" was a preoccupation of liberals when it came
to understanding the Nation. But what could not be denied
was that at the root of the Nation's approach were both restoration and reparative justice, and the psychological healing
preparatory to self-determination. Malcolm made an important distinction between militant self-defense and violence,
and he asserted ultimately that Islam preferred peace.[63]
Blake remembers that he keyed in on the contradictions
of the students, including an interrogation of their appar-
ent preference for white romantic partners, helping them

to sharpen and refine their commitments to Black liberation.[64] What would become the Afro-American Association
was indelibly shaped by this moment, particularly Malcolm's
disavowal of the term "Negro." Warden, by all accounts,
was never the same. But in many ways that became true of
the entire group.[65] The NAACP statement notwithstanding,
it was clear that Cedric, too, was moving closer to a deep
appreciation of Malcolm's ideas, if he was not already there.
About a decade later, Malcolm would become the subject of
his first scholarly article.[66]

While helping to bring Malcolm to campus, Cedric was
also facing his own future at UC. A few weeks earlier, a
US-supported operation intending to overthrow the government of Cuba had been launched. The Bay of Pigs invasion
was widely condemned among radicals who felt that the
Cuban Revolution was righteous. The presence of the Fair
Play for Cuba Committee had initiated widespread support
of Fidel Castro's project among many students in the Bay,
and those who were skeptical at least felt that the United
States should respect Cuba's sovereignty.[67] Among Black
students, there was a growing respect for Castro. In addition
to the connection to Robert F. Williams, Castro's Harlem
meeting with Malcolm X and engagement with the very critical and diverse wings of the movement was inspirational.[68]
So it was no surprise that Cedric helped plan a protest of
the invasion on campus. He belonged to a movement that
went beyond just UC, which had convened a major rally
held in Union Square in San Francisco. Alongside activists
like Robert Scheer, Cedric was on the executive committee of the Bay Area Student Ad Hoc Committee Against
US Intervention in Cuba, which tried to raise support for
their position against intervention by appealing to faculty at
both Berkeley and Stanford.[69] But they ran into resistance.
The university's Regents, the state assembly, and traditional

media viewed support for Castro as *ipso facto* evidence of subversion.[70]

The rally at UC took place on April 18, a day after the invasion. Speaking at the occasion were Warden and Maurice Zeitlin, a graduate student in sociology, who spoke on behalf of the Ad Hoc Committee. But the protest was "unauthorized"; university regulations required a week's notice to hold rallies.[71] Cedric remembered that his response to this guideline was that the United States did not give Cuba a week's notice, so they could not have possibly been expected to do the same.[72] Zeitlin and Warden were both given a formal reprimand. For his troubles, Cedric remembered, he was given a suspension.

According to his transcript, he applied for and was granted a formal withdrawal around this time. But while the *Daily Californian* reported on Zeitlin and Warden's disciplining, it was silent on Cedric.[73] Was this another case of differential treatment? Did the university treat Cedric differently because he was an undergraduate student with at least another year to go, while Warden was a law student on his way out? It is hard to know what went on behind closed doors. Though he rarely talked about it, he revealed to those close to him that he had been dismissed. Unable to complete his studies that spring, he dashed off to Mexico.[74]

During this period, Cedric had begun a long-term relationship with Margot Dashiell, who remembered that the Mexican retreat had deeply struck him. This visit was facilitated by Kenny Freeman, who was then taking graduate courses in Mexico but was destined to come back to the Bay Area and initiate work foundational to West Coast radicalism. While engaging Freeman and the people of Mexico, he witnessed suffering firsthand and learned what it was to live under the thumb of capitalist *and* imperialist exploitation. And it sensitized him. Mere days after seeing Malcolm speak

in Stiles Hall, Cedric, from the rural outskirts of Mexico
City, wrote "a letter of love and despair" to Dashiell:

> I have seen in four days more poverty, deprivation and
> practical deformity of the human condition than I thought
> possible. The villagers of the western coast are not indo-
> lent or inferior but have been simply defiled to the point
> of becoming pitiful robots, mechanized to their expectant
> duties and roles. The blind beg, not because it is the natural
> condition of the blind to beg, but it is expected and no other
> role has been assigned or defined for them.[75]

He wrote again a few weeks later to tell her a story of a young
boy and his sister, both of them poor, cold, their clothes
soiled, their eyes desperate. They approached Cedric to sell
him chocolate. Of them, he wrote to Dashiell: "You remember the eyes, I have had to remember too many little wanting
eyes – demanding the luxury of survival. If your God exists,
tell him for me and everyone like me, there is something
rotten in this world."

In this recollection, he also spoke glowingly of his conversations with people there about Cuba. He became deeply
interested in visiting the island with Freeman during his
dismissal and hoped to conduct a comparative analysis of
the Cuban situation with what he found in the Mexican
countryside, but he never made it. We can only speculate
how that might have furthered his critique, his commitment
to understanding this world. Dashiell notes that this was
also a moment where Cedric was becoming clearer, exhib-
iting a "low tolerance for ambiguity."[76] Liberation was no
plaything, and it had to be seriously and rigorously pursued.
He wanted her to know that the work that they were doing
was meaningful, urgent, and necessary. If it felt like woe, it
must have also felt like an invocation to one's purpose. After

describing the political scene in Latin America, he brought it all home:

> And yet all these things, and more; seem unreal because of [a] little boy, a little ray who is being told every day in almost every way: "We don't want you and we don't need you." The marvelous and yet sometimes sad fact is that he doesn't seem to understand or hear even.
>
> He is reality and together you both make a truth.[77]

Cedric returned to Berkeley that summer to address SLATE's summer conference. These meetings were developed to allow SLATE members to conduct workshops on pressing matters, both inside and outside the Berkeley campus "sandbox." Cedric presented a paper entitled, "Campus Civil Rights Groups and the Administration," which argued that groups that had been organized to support and protest questions of civil rights faced an ironic attack on their civil liberties through administrative repression. Its thesis was that university administrators, perhaps keen to protect the university from the "inevitable pressures of the conservative and reactionary pressure groups in the state," had resorted to measures that attacked the very ability of student groups to conduct their affairs, and these administrative restrictions affected the very survival of this organization whose chief job of organizing the student body was compromised if they could not hold space on campus. His case studies were of course three of the actions that he had participated in that previous spring: the work of the Students for Racial Equality, the United Airlines protest, and the Malcolm X event.[78] In the wake of the revocation of SLATE's own official recognition that summer, as well as in foreseeing the events of the fall of 1964 on campus, Cedric's insight about the ways in which the university utilized procedural legalese to conceal its politics was indeed prescient.[79]

Black dignity could be achieved

Malcolm's visit generated more energy among the Black students who were searching for spaces that might act as a respite as well as something larger than the campus NAACP could provide. Thinking with each other, building community, and camaraderie were precious, which does not mean these times did not produce severe disagreements. Passionate exchange foregrounded the intellectual transformations that made each of them who they became. This is what made it precious. The work that those in the study groups would accomplish was a consequence of the space they made for each other.

In early 1961, a study group had begun to convene in the home of Mary Agnes Lewis, a philosophy transfer from Howard University and ultimately a major intellectual influence on Cedric. Along with Shyamala Gopalan, she became one of his closest friends.[80] Lewis's salons were hosted with her roommate, a schoolteacher named Ann Cook. She was also an activist who in a few years' time found herself in Guyana, married to Eusi Kwayana and committed to a long life in the Pan-Africanist movement, taking the name Tchaiko. Their house became the site where the group studied and debated not only Malcolm X but also important works like E. Franklin Frazier's *Black Bourgeoisie*, Melville Herskovits's *Myth of the Negro Past*, the classic works of W. E. B. Du Bois and Carter G. Woodson, and secondary studies on critical figures like Marcus Garvey and Kwame Nkrumah.[81]

With their sharp focus on Africa, the group began to develop what Donna Murch called a fusion of "the opposing views of Herskovits and Frazier to fashion" an "antiassimilationist ideology."[82] Engagement with Kenyan students on campus as well as the thriving independence struggles on the continent no doubt cultivated an identification with Africa that readings of Herskovits only buttressed, creating an appreciation for the power of cultural retentions in liberation struggles. There was also an animus toward middle-class Black politics, one that could be traced to the group's disavowal of the gradualism of the local NAACP chapter, which was deepened through their explorations of Frazier's and Woodson's work on the middle class. Cedric's later work repeated and extended these dual themes consistently. While study was sharpening their analysis, it was also making the group restless – the question of whether it would be enough was vigorously raised.

With the off-campus conversations thriving, Cedric and the others in the NAACP broke from Blake's leadership and moved toward Warden. Eventually, the core of the campus NAACP sort of dissolved into what became known as the Afro-American Association. That Berkeley core included Warden, Lewis, Henry Ramsey, Donald Hopkins, Donald Harris, James Lacy, Otho Green, and those who had been in the NAACP with Cedric, like Margot Dashiell and Ken Simmons. Cedric's friend Shyamala Gopalan would also begin to attend meetings off campus.[83]

Free of the NAACP's oversight, they became nationalist in orientation. In a *Root and Branch* essay on the group's philosophy, to which Cedric likely provided assistance, Warden outlined what he called the emergence of "the Black Negro."[84] Warden's major argument was that the position of Black folk in the United States required a deeper understanding of both the material and psychological requirements of subjugation, and that these deeper elements would not be solvable under the logics of the movement toward integration. Synthesizing the Herskovits and Frazier debate, he asserted that the African cultural retentions were increasingly compromised by an assimilationist ethic grounded in the American tradition of anti-Black racism, the creation of the Negro. Repeatedly, throughout the piece, he lamented the failures of American solutions to this Negro problem, which emanated from an inability to see Black people as human – and that this was not a matter that a movement for civil rights might resolve. Instead, Warden ultimately called for a shift, asserting that Black people must "break down attitudes ... in themselves, and then in their oppressors." And what might precipitate that shift was Black people's desire to come together, to establish and live on their own terms, to reject identification as Negroes. But this, he warned, was not a possibility that oppressors were simply going to allow.[85]

To develop this argument, Warden relied on Cedric's research on the founding creed of America as read through the ideas of Thomas Jefferson and others, showing that in works like *Notes on the State of Virginia*, the framers of the American project had revealed that they never indeed intended for this country and its definition of citizenship to include Black folk. But he did not stop with America. Warden's piece also included both Karl Marx's statement about the centrality of enslaved Africans in the emancipation of the working class and his private letters, where he, too, succumbed to the racial thinking of the day with racist dismissals of the "Negro type."[86] It was not just an American cancer; what Cedric would later call the conceit of race pervaded the whole of western civilization.

Meetings often moved from Lewis and Cook's house to Donald Hopkins's apartment, sometimes hosting fifty or more students. As they continued to weigh whether or not to move their work to the streets, they looked toward the Town. Making use of the vortex of activity along Telegraph Avenue into West Oakland, they saw in the Black non-campus community an additional base for their ideas – or at least a way to spread them. They affirmatively decided to become a "street" organization, bringing the stepladder tradition to places all throughout the Bay Area. In these settings, they preached the importance of embracing a Black identity, grounded in African cultural awareness with a strong thrust of self-reliance as central to liberation. Warden emerged as their charismatic leader.[87]

When Leslie Lacy encountered Warden and Ramsey during this period, the influence of Malcolm was evident. Writing in his 1970 memoir, Lacy stated: "Donald and Ramsey had already formed the Afro-American Association, and he now reminded the five hundred people listening that it was only through groups like this that Black dignity could be achieved."[88] In presenting a Black nationalist argument, "Donald was respected by the sometimes embarrassed Blacks he lectured to because he had the courage to say publicly things they felt privately."[89]

Officially chartered in March 1962, the Association mounted protests, built Black institutions and businesses, supported Black Studies, and preached the four tenets of "unity, self-help, education, and dignity" throughout their roughly one decade of existence.[90] It was during this period that a range of figures expanded the core to Paul Cobb, Ronald Dellums, Willie Brown, Bobby Seale, Huey Newton, Ann Williams, Carol and Kenny Freeman, and Maulana Karenga, all of whom used these Black nationalist beginnings as a point of departure for the political work that they would eventually accomplish. Indeed, one could tell the story of each of the central organizations and elements of Bay Area Black Power radicalism through the lens of the work of the early 1960s iterations of the Afro-American Association. The contributions of Cobb in community organizing, Dellums and Brown in electoral politics, the Freemans with the Black Arts movement through *Soulbook*, and later revolutionary nationalism with the Revolutionary Action Movement and the Black Panther Party of Northern California, Newton and Seale with the Black Panther Party for Self-Defense, and Maulana Karenga with the US organization are all notable for having been grounded in the work of the Association.[91] Warden himself would change his name to Khalid Abdullah Tariq Al Mansour and continue to advocate for a "Pan-African republic." This was, in his view, the only logical conclusion for Black America to the West's system of racism and white supremacy, a system which revealed that "the African American has no permanent future in America."[92] Lacy is undoubtedly correct in his assessment that the Afro-American Association "helped the alienated Black students feel a part of the stagnant intellectual community" they encountered in the academy, and "when the history of Black protest is accurately written, the members of the Association will have an important place in it."[93]

Cedric, however, did not stay around for all of this evolution. At some point in 1962, he stopped regularly attending the sessions. While the reasons are unclear, we should take into account the whirlwind of events of the previous year. Also, the fact that he *still* worked and that it was time to think about graduation might be possible factors. It is likely he just needed a break. Another, more likely, possibility is that Warden's approach to movement work could have begun to grate on his sensibilities. Both the overbearing charismatic personality and the growing dogmatism of the Association and its eventual adoption of a Black enterprise-oriented nationalism that was pushing "Black capitalism," rather than an internationalist critique of imperialist exploitation, could have been too much for Cedric. Perhaps his reasons were similar to Leslie Lacy's, who also eventually left the group but remembered that "like so many radicals fresh out of the womb of enlightenment, they unfortunately thought that history began when they became aware. You were either 'together' or 'shaky,' there was no real place for stumblers like me."[94] Cedric was no stumbler, but he was also clear in his own convictions, which often went against the grain.

When the Association mounted its Mind of the Negro Conference and supported the student movement at Merritt College, Cedric was less involved, if at all. But all it takes is one look at the last few lines of the original preface to *Black Marxism* to realize that their provocations remained with him, as they did with others who had been in those study circles at Berkeley. He wrote that it was they, members of the Association and others from that Berkeley orbit – "Mary Agnes Lewis, Margot Dashiell, Frederick Douglas Lewis, Welton Smith, Sherman Williams, Nebby-Lou Crawford, Jim Lacy, Gopalan Shyamala, Jay Wright, J. Herman Blake, Don Hopkins, Henry Ramsey, [and] Donald Warden" – "with whom the project had its beginnings."[95] And, years later, in a return to campus he would recall that this group was "one of the beginnings of Black Studies at Berkeley." Its "foundation" was "critique," for they had found the academy to be inadequate. In reinventing Black Studies for their time, the group created vital intellectual experiences "on the Terrace, outside the Reserved Books Room of the main library, in the music booths in the Student Union, in Stiles Hall, in one or two coffee houses on Telegraph Ave., and in our rooms."[96] He was, in effect, describing an undercommons. In the first years of the sixties, they had produced a subversive tradition.

A tremendous effect to be in Africa

Throughout the fall of 1961, events in Africa had captured the attention of Berkeley students. Along with the discernible presence of continental Africans enrolling as students, the era of "flag independence" had raised considerable debate and engendered important conversations. Whether it was attending sessions of Operation Understanding at Stiles Hall, where Cedric often got into heated debates, listening to political scientists lecture about Pan-Africanism, or attending a garden party at Margot Dashiell's parents' house for Kenyan students, Cedric's ideas were sharpened in these discussions.[97] The assassination of Patrice Lumumba earlier that year and the persecution of Robert F. Williams had likely soured him toward US foreign policy and its relationship to Africa and the larger Black freedom struggle.[98]

So it is curious, then, that when the State Department-endorsed Operation Crossroads Africa (OCA) came to Stiles Hall late that fall to recruit UC students, Cedric attended and applied the following February for an opportunity to spend two months with the group in Africa.[99] The history of OCA is connected to US anxiety about the future of Africa amid the anticolonial movement and the Cold War. The program was the brainchild of James Herman Robinson. He was a Black minister that had attended Lincoln University and even took classes there, taught by a Penn graduate student named Nnamdi Azikiwe, the eventual prime minister of Nigeria. After a 1954 trip to India and along the west coast of Africa, where he met with Jawaharlal Nehru and Kwame Nkrumah, James Herman Robinson was inspired to create a program to increase knowledge about Africa among college students and to give them an opportunity to participate in something concrete toward the development of these countries, some of which had not yet achieved independence. But independence leaders like Azikiwe, Nehru, and Nkrumah were not his primary intellectual influences, nor was his politics theirs. In fact, settler colonial regimes welcomed James Herman Robinson's OCA. Just as he had done in similar circumstances in New Hampshire, Robinson worked with African governments to identify infrastructural needs in rural locations, where the students would participate in various projects during their visits. It was a kind of service learning. But like the Peace Corps, which was later modeled on Robinson's approach, it also advanced US interests in the region.[100]

In the year of Cedric's trip to Africa, James Herman Robinson published *Africa at the Crossroads*, part of a series on Christian perspectives on world events, edited by the emerging liberation theologian Gayraud Wilmore. But Robinson's views were more convergent with the Washington consensus. Distancing true "Africa work" from initiatives like those of Marcus Garvey or the Council of African Affairs, Robinson's "Christian" perspective sought to protect American foreign policy and economic interests by calling for an increased awareness of the national liberation struggles and Africa's role in the global sphere, even issuing the de rigueur warning against communist influence on the continent, which he characterized as a "threat to the United States."[101] It was akin to the same rationales for the creation of African Studies, which Robinson pointed to as critical to US interests. It was also the basis for the work of OCA, which was partially funded by US corporations, though the students raised money independently as well. That spring Cedric was accepted into the program and, though he went along, Cedric would have strongly disagreed with this Cold War approach to Africa. It would be clear soon that he had his own ideas, his own plans.

Cedric learned that he would be assigned to Tshabalala Township, outside of Bulawayo in Southern Rhodesia, with ten other group members whose task was to build a school. After orientation and training in DC, they left from New York en route to Paris, where they spent the day before landing in Nairobi on June 26.[102] That he was thinking critically about African self-determination and the liberation struggle was once again revealed in letters written to Margot. Because of the nature of politics in southern Africa, Cedric knew that he would have to hide his true thoughts: "Southern Rhodesia is the most complex state anywhere, in Africa . . . because of the acute situation of the present time." He then added the disclaimer: "Our mail will be read, so most of my impressions will have to wait."[103] But we do get a sense of Cedric's feelings as soon as he arrived in Kenya. He wrote of feeling as if he were indeed home, a common first impression of Africans from the diaspora who returned to the continent. But amid the turmoil of his life and the world around him, it was important that he found solace. His words are beautiful.

> In Nairobi, we saw our first African air hostesses and as a symbol for what is happening even in Central Africa, I feel warm inside for the first time in a very long time[.] Slowly, each Negro in our group has seen himself and his people in an authoritatively different role. It is a tremendous effect to be in Africa and I was intoxicated by the coming home and it is a home.[104]

Moving from Nairobi to Blantyre that day, they spent the next few days across the Zambezi in Salisbury at the University College of Rhodesia and Nyasaland for orientation. There they learned of the basic rudiments of life in the Central African Federation, the semi-dominion, which included the future independent states of Zambia, Zimbabwe, and Malawi. But those winds of change had not yet reached the settler colonial project when Cedric arrived. The complex politics that he wrote about to Margot, however, were in plain view. Their orientation included a lecture by Terence O. Ranger, the British historian of Africa, who was considered then to be "controversial" because of his leadership in "integrative activities." And then, on June 28, they received a deeper education as the four major political parties addressed the group. They instantly fell under the spell of the last of the four, the Zimbabwe African People's Union (ZAPU), represented by Rev. Ndabaningi Sithole who spoke and signed copies of his *African Nationalism.*

ZAPU was widely popular, the latest iteration of the self-determining impulse among native Africans to white settler rule. Cedric wanted to know more about this group but also about the lives of the people that they sought to represent. In addition to letters he sent to Margot and to his Aunt Lillian and Uncle William, we have impressions of Cedric's time in a collective journal where each member of the team took turns documenting the entire group's daily activities. From this precious source we learn that during downtime the following day, Cedric and three other group members visited the local school at Highfield Township.[105] It would be a pattern that Cedric repeated throughout the summer.

By the first of July, the group was on its way to Bulawayo and then to Tshabalala, starting construction work on the school under the tutelage of their foreman, Tembyai Sithole, and their OCA group leader, Duncan Edmunds. Within the group, a conflict emerged on the third night. It was a heated debate concerning how much time should be spent engaging native Africans versus the settlers, as the latter were likely responsible for OCA's presence. Whether or not it was Cedric who prevailed on the group, it was clear where he stood on the issue.[106] For the rest of the trip, the group would maintain a close connection to the African masses – so much so that the local newspapers reported that white elites had begun to grow suspicious of them. In the Bulawayo *Chronicle*, local "industrialists, business men and members of leading organizations" told reporters that they were angry because the volunteers had "refused to listen to the Europeans' point of view and sided with African nationalists." In addition to blowing off such "big men" of the settler colonial project, they committed the crime of meeting with and learning from members of ZAPU.[107]

They worked six days a week. But on the seventh, Cedric, often with other members of the group, took the time to venture and behold a Southern Rhodesia, beset by settler colonialism but filled with beauty. Cedric wrote Margot that at night he could hear drumming and chanting, recalling Thomas Wentworth Higginson's experiences of hearing the ring shout in South Carolina during the Civil War.[108] So he began to venture into those spaces. On July 7, Cedric wrote in the group's collective journal: "Charles, Dave, and I, left the bulk of the group to witness tribal dancing by Kalanga people under a shed amidst a scene reminiscent of a French landscapist." He learned as much as he could of their languages, the Shona and Sendebele tongues, and of the history of the Ndebele and Matabele, their migratory patterns, the process of peopling the region – the legacies of Shaka Zulu and Mzilikazi.[109] And he continuously visited schools, "as was his custom," listening and often lecturing to students on topics as diverse as the origin of humanity and the Angolan conflict.[110] They continued to wander, "determined to see THE Africa [so they] followed their noses . . . and the sound of drums to a small campfire about 1/8th mile off . . . to meet Africans of the first 'genuine' reserve and to what local singing and dancing [sic]."[111] Africa had to be witnessed.

As he wandered, he wrote. In his letters to Margot, he noted the progress of the school that they were building. But he took care to regale her with stories of their appreciation for the people and the countryside, including the journey the group took to ancient Zimbabwe. He marveled at structures he thought "viable and vital." He also sent updates on the political situation, revealed plans to venture to Bechuanaland

Figure 2.1 Cedric Robinson in Southern Rhodesia, 1962

Image courtesy of Elizabeth Robinson

Figure 2.2 Cedric Robinson (center) dancing in a Kalanga village, 1962

Image courtesy of Elizabeth Robinson

and meet with a traditional chief, as well as to Kenya with the group to meet with Jomo Kenyatta and Tom Mboya.[112] On August 5, the group attended a ZAPU rally and finally witnessed a speech by "the Old Lion," Joshua Nkomo, along with a crowd of 25,000. Entranced by Nkomo's words, they would spend the remainder of the trip acquiring ZAPU caps, which they proudly wore, much to the chagrin of the white business leaders.[113] In the final letter to Margot, he offered that he was impressed by ZAPU but not optimistic, predicting that they would be "banned before he got back to the states."[114] He knew that radical groups faced repression – and in the case of ZAPU, whose national liberation struggle had been supported by Russia, Cuba, Egypt, as well as Ethiopia, its days were numbered. Cedric's prediction was off, but only by several weeks.[115]

Over the next week they completed the school, spent their final moments in Southern Rhodesia – where Cedric again wandered to museums and the offices of local newspapers, seemingly on a perpetual search for information – before the final debrief in Nairobi. There the group met with Cedric's Berkeley friend, Gikonyo Kiano, attended a Kenyan African National Union rally, which Cedric secretly taped, and spent time with the other Crossroaders on Jomo Kenyatta's farm, where the national liberation leader spoke to them about their struggle.[116] By the end of August, the Operation Crossroads Africa summer experience was over and Cedric was back in New York, but he was far from done with Africa.

That December, Cedric penned an article recounting his experience for Carlton Goodlett's *Sun-Reporter*, the most important Black newspaper in the Bay Area and a space where he did not have to worry about the colonial censors. Titled, "How is it in So. Rhodesia?," the article began with a declaration that the peoples of southern Africa, through their anthem "Nkosi Sikelel' iAfrika," had issued a call for "brotherhood and peace in Africa among all peoples." It was a "song of people building, sweating, and toiling for a new world." And yet, this call "frightens the white man. Why?" Because of the land question. And that question was intimately tied to questions of freedom. Black freedom would mean the loss of the "privilege and power to direct another man's life." And this the settler regime would not and could not countenance.

Cedric wrote of the idea of tribalism and how the settler colonial project and its maneuvers of divide and conquer were quickly being subsumed by the unity represented by African nationalism, which led to the banning of ZAPU the previous September. It was part of a long history of repression: "Many Africans have lost their lives, hundreds have been detained, exiled to the Native Reserves, many of them for months, some for years." Yet, "still, they protest." Tied to their pursuit of freedom was the idea of "one man, one vote" which meant "power for Africans" – a demand for political equality, tied to radical decolonization, and in some cases the last resort before an armed confrontation.[117] The article closed with a brief summary of Cedric's interview with an African student who had worked with OCA on the school they built in Tshabalala. His question was simple but profound. Cedric asked the student what he would say if he were returning to the United States in his place: "He spoke very slowly with a quiet and sad emotion: 'My people are not happy, they want to be happy . . . to be free.'" Foreshadowing themes he would cover in later treatments of southern Africa, Cedric's article ended with a warning:

Now the African can no longer fight with words only, as he has tried to do in the last ten years, he has had to begin to fight with the same weapons like Europeans have used so effectively against him for nearly a century: terror and intimidation. Terror and intimidation are now words which come easily to Americans because they are cruel and harsh, but they do not come easily to the Africans, despite the image made popular by the white press and film industries of Europe and the United States of the African savage.[118]

It was but an echo of an idea that he was to stridently engage and rethink. But here it was, in print, in 1962: Under what terms would Africans free themselves?

When you introduced me to the Crawfords

After completing his studies the following summer, the next phase of Cedric's life seemed unclear. When he deplaned in New York, after his trip to southern Africa the previous summer, Cedric actually took a moment to visit Nebby Lou Crawford, a friend who was close to Margot, whom he had met after he returned from Mexico. She was an East Bay native who had moved to New York to pursue graduate study at Columbia.[119] Her parents, Matt and Evelyn Crawford, were stalwarts in the earlier phases of Bay Area Black left radicalism. Their friends in New York were William and Louise Thompson Patterson, the latter being the Berkeley graduate mentioned earlier.[120] By 1962, the Pattersons, as well as the Crawfords for that matter, had accomplished much in the tradition of Black revolutionary organizing, focusing their work in the landscape of the Communist Party and human rights. It is likely here in this precious time spent with these elders that Cedric began to ponder what his contribution might ultimately become.[121] During these years, William Patterson would serve as a quiet mentor to SNCC, as well as other Black Power formations, reminding them of the international dimensions of their struggle.[122] We can only wonder what exactly the Crawfords and the Pattersons bequeathed to Cedric. We do not have to wonder, however, if it was significant because he carried these encounters with him. Two years later, in the throes of postgraduate life, he gave his regards to Patterson through Nebby Lou, hopeful that "he remembers [him]."[123] And regarding Matt and Evelyn Crawford's influence, he reminded Margot in a 1983 letter accompanying a copy of *Black Marxism*: "This book began long ago when you introduced me to the Crawfords."[124]

Having met and engaged Robert F. Williams, Malcolm X, Jomo Kenyatta, the Crawfords, and the Pattersons, and having organized within the NAACP and the Afro-American Association in its early phases, it would appear that now was a moment to deepen his commitment to the movement. Black Power was on the horizon, in the Town as well as Gown. But before he could make his next move, Cedric's path was interrupted.

3

Authority and Order

Cedric's first encounters with the meaning of authority and order would have come in his grandparents' home. But the protection that they provided would not have been able to shield him from other meanings of authority, other senses of order. Consciousness of this social reality was soon to occur in both his understanding of the explicit arrogation of authority by the political system as well as in his witnessing of the disciplinary force of order in the context of the movement years. Even in times when he was alienated from the movement by larger circumstances, Cedric continued to study. And then there were those direct experiences with state and imperial power which were mere moments of the larger unfolding of the time of western civilization.

I can fight with my own tools

After graduating from Berkeley, Cedric decided to take a job at the Alameda County Probation Office. It was a moment where gross job discrimination was still in force – even among Black middle-class college graduates – though movements to force the Bay Area's businesses to hire across the color line were to soon intensify.[1] So Cedric, with his opportunities limited, joined the office's officer trainee program and in the meantime worked as a youth counselor. He was only there one month when he received a call informing him that he had been drafted. On November 1, 1963, Cedric was inducted into the United States Army at Fort Ord, California.[2]

The draft had remained a fact of life since close of World War II. Though the United States was heavily involved in Southeast Asia at the moment, no one could have predicted the shift in attitudes toward the draft that was to come in the wake of the intensification of America's invasion of Viet Nam.[3] Even fewer would have been able to foresee the ways that the draft would be used to ensure that more than a fair share of poorer, nonwhite men would be forced into the service of American imperialism – with more draftees than enlisted personnel losing their lives by the latter part of the decade. An unpopular war meant more Black folk would have to fight in it, an unfortunate reversal of the military's history of exclusion and/or segregation.[4]

But in 1963 the draft was not yet what it would be, with the numbers inducted that year among the lower figures in that history of American conscription. Concerned with the threat of Soviet influence, the army desired seasoned troops over young and inexperienced draftees. There was during these years no real crisis, no real need for soldiers.[5] Yet, for

Cedric, the draft remained a disruption. Military service
was not his idea of upward mobility. Becoming a soldier of
misfortune in the United States' ill-fated Cold War was not
an option he would have pursued without being coerced. It
is, however, interesting to speculate how time in the military in the drum-up to war in Viet Nam might have given
him a front row seat to matters of "authority and order," to
real-time instances of how "the political" asserted itself as
powerful, or to "leadership" as the "mythic paradigm" – all
questions to which he would come to devote the first half-
decade of his formal intellectual work in the academy.

Within a month of being drafted and inducted, Cedric
was assigned to the United States Army Artillery and Missile
School in the United States Army Training Center at Fort
Sill, Oklahoma. He reported on January 16, 1964, unsure of
what awaited him.[6] The Army had established the fortifica-
tion near the end of the Civil War to serve as a base for its
campaigns against several groups of First Nations in Texas
and Mexico – part of the United States' drive to protect
capital's westward expansion into the final decades of the
century. It was here that Geronimo lived his final years in
captivity. Not only had the Buffalo Soldiers who participated
in these missions called Fort Sill home, but long after the
closing of the Frontier, the base was home to 350 imprisoned
Japanese Americans during World War II. Cedric's personal and political histories then were part of the soil of Fort
Sill. Spending his tour in this setting might have provided
moments for him to recall the meaning of his family's possible Indigenous connections, his people's roots in the United
States South, and their relationship to settler colonialism.[7]

Within four months of his arrival, Cedric applied to
Officer Candidate School. It is not clear whether he was
encouraged to do so or whether the desire stemmed from
his own ambition. But college graduates were one pipe-

line for entrants into the school – which might also explain how, two years after Cedric's application, only 0.4 percent of the army's officer corps were Black.[8] During his first two years at Berkeley, he had taken four semesters of military science, likely part of the mandatory ROTC programs then in the curriculum.[9] Perhaps these credentials helped secure his initial acceptance into the program. But Cedric had also acquitted himself well during his first few months of training. His commanding officers praised his "exceptional leadership ability for an individual of his grade and military experience," and characterized him as "highly motivated . . . ambitious, intelligent, and eager to succeed."[10]

Before enrolling in officer candidate school, Cedric took a course at nearby Cameron College in English literature.[11] While taking this course, he maintained a general awareness of what was happening in the civil rights movement, particularly the growing movement in San Francisco opposing job discrimination on Auto Row. The movement combined both grassroots organizing and moderate civil rights leadership. The students were led by the Ad Hoc Committee's Tracy Sims, who often forced the issue, much to the chagrin of elders who counseled negotiations and patience. In a letter to Nebby Lou Crawford, Cedric lamented some of these conciliatory gestures: "It seems we will go to an extreme to prove (or better said assure) to white folks that we want something which only they can give us." He was also critical of NAACP organizer Anthony Burbridge's leadership, despite the fact that the movement would come to embrace him (and just as much Burbridge would be moved by them to embrace direct action). For Cedric, these protests amounted to a conflation of "Cadillac and their properties on the *market* with *people* and their properties in the society."[12] His criticism revealed that Cedric's political priorities were driven by human needs, rather than the movement's potential interest convergence with American capital. The two were often mistaken for each other. He was thinking about liberation beyond anti-discrimination in a moment where the struggle for civil rights dominated the headlines.

In another letter to Margot Dashiell, from whom he had then become estranged, he dreamed of life after his service: "My ambitions were to work until I could return to school, an American institution, receive a higher degree and then settle down to teaching and writing and perhaps, in strength, forsaking my enemy to his own devilry." These were plans he had also revealed to his mother, who longed for his return from Oklahoma so that he could begin work on a Master's and a PhD.[13] It was a dream shrouded in his discomfort with a movement he felt needed to fight differently. He perceived that the main lines of the civil rights movement had adopted a posture that was difficult for him to follow:

> If I attach my future to the people who I have been taught to love and understand, I must stand, as they, inextricably bound to their own sensuous nihilism, we all die building our pathetically ethereal towers. Since only messiahs take up the challenge, thrown by [E. Franklin] Frazier and [W. E. B.] Du Bois, those same challenges have become themselves tools of the selfsame precepts that they sought so deftly.[14]

In these words, we find an ambivalence toward the dominant threads of movement leadership and messianic transformation, a topic he would soon address in scholarship. "The people" he had been "taught to love" lived lives too circumscribed by the enormity of oppression to be simply swayed or moved by a great leader, some great moment, some great purpose, so long as that greatness was defined within the normative language of the "devilry" they all faced.

If they desired a messiah, it would not be one wielding the American Constitution. Bemused by the ironies of having to fight under that flag, Cedric came to a conclusion:

> I know now what I once could only believe: I am merely a conscripted alien. I know that soon I will have to fight on other than personal criteria for what I believe in but I will also do whatever I can morally assume to see that I can fight with my own tools and in my own arena simply because I want to win. I could not win by using moral or political intimidation ... because I could not ever understand the adulteration of preeminence inherent in that argument – that is a concession to political and social illegitimacy, it is also what all the appropriate pathos and indignation of the "movement" distills to.
>
> I am no longer ambiguous about what I want, I am no longer afraid to admit its impossibility or more reasonably its improbability, I still want it.[15]

There is both a kind of clarity and abstruseness in the statement. What, after all, did he want? What was winning? That is not altogether clear. But, with hindsight, we might read this moment as one where Cedric's sense of purpose was indeed coming into sharper focus. The years of Berkeley activism coupled with the months spent at Fort Sill were pushing him in a particular direction. It was the precursor to a period of intense study of radicalisms of all sorts. Military service had given him the occasion to reflect on what was being done, and what was to be done. Much of what had been percolating in the movement had struck him as inadequate. But it should not be read as rejection of solidarity or a disavowal of that work – sometimes one had to build political community despite one's "personal criteria." Yet there also had to be more. What might these other "tools," this other "arena," produce? There is a resolve to do battle with a radical imagination, with an awareness not simply of what was being done but of what *could* be done. Cedric's desire was for those forms of liberation thought impossible or improbable within the given terms of order.

While Officer Training School did not prove to be difficult, clearance was another matter. According to Cedric, military intelligence had raised issues largely because of his previous support of Douglas Wachter and his other Berkeley activities.[16] Nevertheless, on October 28, 1964 he received his clearance. A little under six months later, on April 13, 1965, he completed his training at the US Army Artillery and Missile School and was officially appointed as a reserved commission officer at the rank of second lieutenant.[17] With another six months left on his initial two-year tour and the United States figuring out how to "stabilize" an increasingly volatile situation in Indochina, these must have been nervous moments.

After years of supporting the French and installing a puppet government in the southern part of the country, the United States was moving toward a declaration of open hostilities with the Vietcong, especially so after August 1964's Gulf of Tonkin incident. As 1965 approached, Lyndon B. Johnson managed an intensifying conflict that United States leaders assumed would be quickly resolved – their army was superior, after all. As Cedric was completing officer candidate school, Operation Rolling Thunder, a vigorous air assault, sought to destroy the North Vietnamese capacity to intervene in the South. But it did not produce the swift results the United States desired. A week after Cedric graduated, Johnson authorized some 80,000 ground troops to support the forces in South Viet Nam. Johnson and his advisors felt that the best way to save face in the region was to support flagging air assault efforts by securing the airfields with foot soldiers.[18] But as the Vietcong maintained the initiative, the United States decided against withdrawal and doubled down. The new tactic became the vaunted "search and destroy" maneuver, which would require additional troops. That July, the United States called in 50,000 troops – a call that it would issue over and over, as it repeatedly failed to produce the victory thought to be imminent. In the three years before the turning point of the Tet Offensive, American military leaders had requested as many as half a million troops to ensure that elusive victory.[19] The violent and destructive quagmire of US involvement had reached its peak. Though many people who shared his race and class background were sent to fight this war, Cedric was never deployed. Had he been drafted a year later, as the buildup of ground forces intensified, the story might have been different. But as it was on October 31, Cedric's tour ended and, after three years as a reservist, so did his military career. He made his way back to Oakland.

Elizabeth

When he returned, Cedric resumed his work at the Alameda County Probation Office. He completed his training and worked primarily as the summer boys' camp counselor for high schoolers. He was only back a few months when he met Elizabeth Peters, a recent Berkeley graduate, who had majored in criminology and worked as a counselor for child protective services. She recalls that when he walked in the room, "he looked as serious as a heart attack." Two years behind Cedric at UC, Elizabeth seemed called to do this sort of work. Born in Oakridge, Tennessee to Lebanese-American parents with east Texas roots, her family moved frequently throughout her childhood. By the 1950s, her father, an engineer, found work in Southern California where Elizabeth would be educated primarily in parochial schools. There, she met many kids who ended up on the wrong side of the youth authority, which instilled within her a desire to address these problems. At Berkeley, she studied the problem of "juvenile delinquency," but from a radical perspective. Scholars like Anthony Platt – a graduate student at the time – were then beginning to set the grounds for studies of the carceral state. Elizabeth remembers him as "the first person I ever heard talk about people in prison as [being] there for political reasons." It was "the beginning of insistence on the recognition of the social and political inequities that went into being in prison."[20] Platt's eventual 1969 text, *The Child Savers*, explored the political contexts and the assumptions structuring the "social problem" of delinquency.[21] But Elizabeth was among a group of Berkeley graduates that were practitioners.

Often crossing paths as they worked together with the same families, Cedric and Elizabeth practiced what Robin D. G. Kelley characterized as a precursor to "restorative justice," where "they embraced effective, transactional methods to reach young people."[22] Elizabeth described their work as existing in tension with the police department, many of whom were directly recruited to Oakland from the Deep South, bringing southern-style racism with them. But somehow the probation office had cultivated what Elizabeth described as "a humanized environment." They sought real connections, particularly with the women. They practiced therapeutic techniques that sought to relieve the pressures many of them faced. At one point, Elizabeth and other counselors converted the basement of the office into what we would now call a "safe space" for these purposes. Though they were civil servants, they did not appear to these folk as the face of the state. It was community.

For Cedric, both study and political work continued

during the almost two years he spent at the probation office. Though he remembers being intimidated by her presence – and she his – love would soon blossom between Cedric and Elizabeth. On August 17, 1967, they were married before a small gathering in Elizabeth's apartment. Oakland activist and childhood friend, Harold Wilson, officiated at their ceremony. By the time of the marriage, Cedric had begun to move toward a break from his work at the probation office. Elizabeth recalls that this work had always been "an interim stop" in his life's journey.[23] It would serve its purpose as another moment to observe in an intimate way an arm of the state's authority, its order.

Figure 3.1 Cedric and Elizabeth Robinson at their wedding, 1967
Image courtesy of Elizabeth Robinson

He made the correct choice

In the fall of 1966, Cedric began this new path backward
to the academy, enrolling in a Master's program in political science at San Francisco State College. He arrived
during an explosive period. That year saw former Afro-
American Association member Aubrey Labrie introduce
one of the earliest Black Studies courses in the country. It
was part of SFSC's Experimental College. The following
spring, Jimmy Garrett, a seasoned activist, had submitted a
proposal to establish a Black Studies program formally on
campus. This proposal embodied many of the elements of
study and practice that were foundational to aspects of the
Association and the larger Black Power movement that had
been gaining steam. And it was preparatory to what would
become the Third World Strike, a Black Student Union-led
effort to ensure that the creation of Black Studies, as well
as other demands, would be supported and protected. Over
five months, students shut down the college to reimagine
it, actions resulting in an often bloody confrontation with
the police. Affirmed by a supportive community, they faced
off with the repressive S. I. Hayakawa, president of the college and future icon of Republican politics. This struggle for
liberated space within San Francisco State was perhaps one
of the more significant of the confrontations that led to the
creation of Black Studies, involving at times critical figures
like Garrett, Nathan Hare, Sonia Sanchez, Askia Toure, and
Amiri Baraka.[24]

In the political science department, Cedric's advisor was
John Bunzel, a scholar who had researched small business
development and electoral politics. Broadening his concerns
to civil rights and higher education, he eventually became
a college president and would go on to serve as a Ronald

Reagan appointee to the US Civil Rights Committee. In the wake of the movement at San Francisco State, he became a notorious critic of Black Studies director Nathan Hare's proposal for Black Studies. As a political project, Bunzel argued, the proposal seemed fine, but it raised questions regarding academic standards.[25] He would raise similar issues of academic and scholarly propriety in Cedric's graduate school papers, but in ways that demonstrated that he supported his work.[26]

Yet as the student movement gained momentum, Cedric did not participate. According to Garrett, who met him around the time he was discharged from the army, he was more into "debating ideology rather than 'street fight/organizing.'" By the time the events of 1967 were taking place, Cedric had made a decision to lay low, to "get his political worldview together." From Jimmy Garrett's view of things over fifty years later, "he made the correct choice."[27] The decision remains curious, especially given his background in the movement at Berkeley. Those past events and future episodes would seem to indicate that the decision to recede to the background during the buildup to Third World Strike was not the result of a lack of courage. It was more about Cedric's commitment to study. Through silent witness, he might make a different kind of contribution. By clearing space to think, he would offer something beyond the rush and excitement of direct action, as critical as it was. Activism also required clarity. He poured whatever desires for radical change he harbored into understanding political theory. The question of the nature of the political systems under which Black people were oppressed beckoned.

For his thesis, Cedric decided to focus on the "relationship between man's thought and his action." He was "enamored with the areas of political theory, political philosophy, epistemology, and the sociology of knowledge" as avenues to consider such questions. Radicalism, he believed, might best be understood as one's personal confrontation with "the order complex." It was a certain "distrust of order and fear of authority" that produced radical responses. From here, Cedric reviewed the literature to test political science's saliency in understanding these issues. In their descriptions of "society," theorists from Aristotle to Thomas Hobbes to John Stuart Mill had bequeathed an understanding too limited to account for twentieth-century "mass" society. Also limited was contemporary political scientist Gabriel Almond's conception of political culture, which relied too heavily on those aspects of political action which were merely "functional" within the political system.[28] Months after completing the proposal, Cedric was working out many of these ideas with Almond himself.

Cedric was recruited to Stanford's PhD program before even completing his thesis at San Francisco State and arrived with these questions unresolved. However, what *was* becoming clear was that the process of addressing the links between radical action and the nature of political order would not mean opening new vistas within political science or anything resembling an ultimate reaffirmation of liberal democracy, which happened to be the *raison d'être* of the discipline. Those trained in American political science during this era were taught under the assumption that the American political tradition was the norm, and even that this liberal structure was superior and should become universal to the benefit of humanity. As a discipline, political science would and could not step outside of these assumptions. It was structurally impossible.[29] Even as this discipline was born under the racist logics of white supremacy, this seeming contradiction was thought solvable *within* the tradition.[30] If political science had racist antecedents, a "truer" science of politics – that supposed legacy of a distinctly American approach to

problem solving – could chart the way to a pluralist democratic future.[31]

Cedric rejected this out of hand. At a minimum, all of
the central assumptions of political science would have to
be questioned in order to truly uncover the contradictions
of American governance – the gap between those who were
in power and those who were living under power's thumb
– whether they be racialized, gendered, or classed. The discipline's pretense toward measurement, control, and even
improvement of the political process was not simply a failure
of scientific method,[32] it was a conceit derived from a conception of rationality at odds with how the vast majority of
humanity conceived of life. Cedric's task would be to under-
mine the tenets and logic of the discipline to truly unmask
its role in reifying American institutions of governance.
Before enrolling, he issued a warning to the department that
he intended to challenge the discipline of political science.
They may have heard him, but they certainly did not listen.[33]

It was an interesting period to be at Stanford. Cedric was
likely recruited as part of an initiative to address the woeful
numbers of Black students there. Four days after Martin
Luther King's assassination, 70 members of the Black
Students Union rushed the university's convocation on race
to demand the admission and hiring of more Black students,
staff, and faculty. The plan called for the doubling of the
Black population to 350 students.[34] A year later, catalyzed by
a racist incident during an admissions interview, angry students ransacked the university's bookstore on their way to
demanding swift action on twelve new, but related, demands
which now included increased attention to the fledgling
African American Studies program and a strengthening of
the relationship to the Black East Palo Alto community. In
the midst of this action was an Afro-American Association
veteran, Leo Bazile, among many others who represented

the energy and verve of the Black Power movement. Their faculty mentor, the anthropologist James Gibbs, was the only permanent Black faculty in the university. By March, he would be joined by St Clair Drake.[35]

Although he was on the downswing of a brilliant career as a scholar and activist, Drake was brought in as the first director of African American Studies. A pioneering social scientist and movement stalwart, he offered consistent and critical advice to the growing discipline, arguing in part that it represented a "counter-ideology" to the truth claims of western knowledge, or "white studies."[36] Yet it was also the "utopian vision of a constant stream of young Black people from the college and the universities helping ghetto dwellers to achieve Black Power."[37] For Drake, though, this vision should not and could not mean to "impose ideologies," but rather "to expand consciousness and to present alternatives to action."[38] African American Studies at Stanford would be drawn into these questions, as it, like the movement in general, would experience levels of "polarization between Black Nationalists and pan-African Marxists."[39] Many members of the Black Student Union during this era – some who became prominent figures like john a. powell, Robert O'Meally, Charles Ogletree, Dolores King, and Michael Dawson – either shared space with or were directly mentored by both Drake and Gibbs.[40] And though there was no Black Studies PhD program, Black scholars like Ronald Bailey, who would write on the convergences of slavery and capitalism in the United States and produce a K-12 Black Studies curriculum guide, as well as twin brothers and philosophy graduate students Johnny and George Gregory Washington and literature student Nathaniel Mackey were at Stanford or would soon be.[41]

But much like at San Francisco State, Cedric stayed aloof from this activity. Between his commute from Palo Alto to

Oakland and his studies, he chose not to engage. About a decade later, there was a tinge of regret at not having at least made a connection to Drake at this juncture. In a letter to Drake, he lamented: "My short time at Stanford would have been immeasurably enriched if I had had the courage to look you up then." From a distance, Cedric had developed a considerable respect for Drake, who was one among the Black Radical intelligentsia he would soon describe. In this letter, Cedric stated that "thinkers like Du Bois, [George] Padmore, [Oliver] Cox, C. L. R. James, Wright, and yourself found it necessary to proceed beyond Marxian boundaries." Drake, not quite surprisingly, did not agree, writing in the margins that he should not be included since he had "never taken a position."[42]

But there would be other kinds of encounters. At the annual meeting of the American Political Science Association (APSA) in New York City in 1969, Black scholars primarily working at Black colleges would raise the issue of Black representation within the discipline, leading to the creation of the Committee on the Status of Blacks in the Profession. But there were also those who desired a full break, creating a separate organization, the National Conference of Black Political Scientists (NCOBPS), rather than a caucus-like formation. When the APSA met the following year in Los Angeles, members of NCOBPS, again dissatisfied with the response to demands made upon the APSA, had staged a boycott.[43] Cedric had been scheduled to present for the first time. Arriving at the hotel, he and Elizabeth were greeted by protesting scholars, who essentially told them what was going on. Cedric agreed to support their efforts. Elizabeth delivered the paper on his behalf.[44] According to Mack Jones, a young scholar then at Atlanta University, NCOBPS was founded to develop a "new, different political science," one less moored in the "self-serving, Eurocentric, parochial

view of political life" that characterized American political
science.[45]

Cedric was already headed there. His APSA paper,
"Malcolm Little as Charismatic Leader," argued that the
question of leadership exhibited by Malcolm X was grounded
firstly in the requirements of those who "followed." It was
an argument sharpened in graduate seminars at Stanford and
first read in 1969 at San Francisco Psychoanalytic Institute
with the encouragement of Alexander George. Cedric read
The Autobiography of Malcolm X as a "psychoanalytic interview," which he brought to bear on the question of the
charismatic leader.[46] Yes, Malcolm had desired a mode of
being that displaced his earlier descent into "his own personal
hell" – a path toward "righteousness" which propelled him
to his role within the Nation of Islam.[47] But it was also the
"migrant communes" in the Black ghettos of northern cities
who required a kind of leadership that was "charismatic," a
light that "lit the darkest recess of the ghetto experience."[48]
Normative readings of charismatic authority focused more
on the leader's psychic dimensions than on the worldviews of
their followers. Cedric sought to balance this account: "The
leader's search for resolution of this identity crisis *and* his
community's search for another meaning system result in the
charismatic situation."[49] If Malcolm's ascent had a lesson,
it was that in order to truly transform themselves and the
world around them, "to become one," leaders would also be
constituted by the led.[50] Cedric would soon enlarge upon
these themes.

While some in NCOBPS were attempting to open the
door to think through Black subject matters in the study
of American politics, Cedric's ideas included but exceeded
these goals.[51] It was one thing to suggest that Malcolm X was
a subject for political science, but wholly another to critique
how the concept of leadership itself might be understood

or rethought through his example, through the Black experience. Two years later, this paper would become his first scholarly publication, appearing in the Richard Trent-edited journal, *Afro-American Studies.*

Realizing ourselves

By the time Cedric entered graduate school, behavioralism had conquered political science. Much like the approaches of the past, behavioralists endeavored to understand how politics functioned. But they abandoned the value-laden idealism of generations past. Reform politics gave way to scholarly supports for mechanisms for social control. Democracy was now working fine. Adopting scientific methods that intended to offer the discipline a source of scientific legitimacy, political scientists addressed research problems related to the normative functioning of governance. The political system, this thinking went, was rationally constructed, and if there were any flaws, they could be addressed through more effective rationalization.[52]

Stanford's department had been among the most well regarded in the country as the discipline grew in the twentieth century. During Cedric's tenure, it featured as chairman one of the most respected behavioralists in the field in Heinz Eulau. And during the sixties it expanded, attracting a faculty focused on the field of comparative politics, a subfield that explored both western and non-western political systems, in order to flesh out the dynamics that revealed the true advantages of liberal democracy.[53] Those attracted to the Cold War era exceptionalism would hope to find in the study of comparative politics confirmation of the superiority of western systems of governance. Within Stanford's department were scholars like Gabriel Almond, a prominent behavioralist involved in comparative study; Alexander George, who had recently come from the RAND Corporation and was preparing a study on Southeast Asia; David Abernethy, whose work considered the development of education in Africa; Hans Weiler, a German scholar who also had a background in African Studies; and Richard Fagen, a Latin Americanist and rare sympathizer with the Cuban Revolution. Cedric's graduate seminar papers in courses with these instructors demonstrated considerable range – from theoretical considerations of revolution and social action, to concrete concerns about the liberal state, the Cold War, and the post-independence political situation in Africa. There was a clear interest in the ways theory showed up in our lives.

The late sixties saw a breakdown in many of the behavioralist articles of faith. The turmoil across the globe had caused a reckoning. Radical political scientists suddenly emerged, calling for a "new political science."[54] Probably the lone true theorist on Stanford's political science faculty was Charles Drekmeier, who, much like Fagen, was firmly in this camp. Drekmeier had supported students in the antiwar movement and was planning to take students to attend the Poor People's Campaign before things at Stanford got dicey in 1968. An interdisciplinary scholar, whose focus had been on India, Drekmeier and his wife Margot, a historian of European thought, had developed a program called the Committee on Social Thought and Institutions, an undergraduate seminar that encouraged thinking beyond disciplines.[55] Both Cedric and Elizabeth would spend quite a bit of time thinking with the Drekmeiers, often at salons in the latter's home. Margot supported Elizabeth's intellectual ambitions. And since he was the only political theorist, Charles naturally became Cedric's dissertation advisor. Elizabeth remembered that Drekmeier had been considered an outlier among his colleagues in political science. So in Cedric he found someone to mentor, perhaps because Cedric too was, in Elizabeth's words, considered a "curiosity" when it came to the other graduate students in the department. A disciplinary rebel, Drekmeier read widely and often pointed Cedric to work in fields that ranged beyond the normative categories of political science.[56]

After completing his coursework, Cedric began pondering the dissertation. His original intent was to focus on Africa and study with the Africanist historian George Shepperson, then at the University of Edinburgh. So Richard Brody and Alexander George assisted him in obtaining a Leverhulme Grant which would enable him to spend a year in England. In order to make ends meet, Elizabeth returned to work at the probation office after a brief stint doing custody investigations, and Cedric continued to work as a lecturer of anthropology at the City College of San Francisco. After their stop at APSA in September and with funds from the sale of Elizabeth's car, they left the Bay Area, never to return as residents.[57]

Unfortunately, Shepperson was not available to work with Cedric, so the Robinsons had to make alternative arrangements. Their destination was the town of Brighton, the vibrant university town that was home to the University of Sussex, where Zevedei Barbu would serve as his advisor at the Institute for the Study of Collective Psychopathology. Armed with the contact information for Dominic Sankey, an Irish-Nigerian resident, the Robinsons immersed themselves in the social scene which was then filled with students from the Third World. With the money from the fellowship, they rented a house, where gatherings with these students created a generative social milieu. Among the topics that guided discussions was the ongoing labor unrest in England, as well as the series of commemorations celebrating the centennial of the Paris Commune. Marxist thought and thinking pervaded the air.[58]

Cedric's interests in "revolutionary followership" and its relationship to hierarchal systems of power eventually became the basis of his proposed dissertation.[59] At Sussex, he studied with Barbu, a social psychologist, and Norman Cohn, a historian of radical millenarian movements, whose most well-known study, *The Pursuit of the Millennium*, traced the evolution of charismatic movements in medieval Europe, linking these heresies to peasant movements as much as to powerful messianic figures, many of whom emerged from the middle and upper strata.[60] Barbu's focus was on the modern period, yet as a psychologist, he employed the disciplines of sociology and history to explain the emergence of the rationalist personality. Though it was based on ancient precursors in Greece, this pretense toward rationalization found its full flowering in liberal society. Barbu, who lived under both "totalitarian" Nazi and communist regimes before landing at Sussex, exhibited an intellectual bias to the liberal-democratic form of society, arguing that it was the form most conducive to the project of freedom.[61] So neither thinker could be said to have shared the intellectual objectives that Cedric carried with him to England, but in their documentation and analysis of western cultures – Cohn's in particular – he would gain much from an engagement with their work. For Cedric was searching for the foundations of political theory in western religious history and in their relationship to psychologies of domination. Authority and the presumption of order, and their mythic nature and qualities, became subjects of intense study during this year abroad.

The first draft of "Leadership: A Mythic Paradigm" was completed at Sussex in 1971. The dissertation was a perceptive distillation of the meaning of political order. Among other tasks, the study clarified how both order and authority combined with "the political" to produce conceptions of leadership that never truly transcended – in fact, appropriated

– non-secular, "irrational" traditions in the process. In myth and legend, in the psychoanalytical and the charismatic event, lay the foundations of the political in western consciousness. Developing a methodological alternative to the then normative practice of behavioralism, Cedric deployed what he called "the counter-sciences" to "abuse the political consciousness."[62]

By 1973, the final version was ready to be submitted to his committee. And when it was finally published as *The Terms of Order* in 1980, he attached a preface revealing that the source of his critique was "inherited from a people only marginally integrated into western institutions and intellectual streams."[63] In a work that offers among other considerations that "one cannot resolve the question of the nature of the political by the process of distilling it from a science of politics," Cedric instead privileged the "vantage point" of the marginalized and excluded – indeed, those dismissed as irrational.[64] Writing at a time of a general disillusionment that had followed decades of a self-confident practice of that science of politics, his framing was different from what David Ricci labels and ultimately dismisses as "critical theory."[65] The declaration of the preface presaged what we might call Black Study and its critique of the question of disciplinarity and of western knowing in general. The knowledge systems of the West were replete with "contradictions" that "have been conserved at the cost of analytical coherence."[66] More, he would explore those whose marginality produced otherwise modes of existing – modes other than the political. Though conversant with the basic themes of critical theory, Cedric's work resolved itself differently.

At the outset of the text, he engaged Karl Popper and Thomas Kuhn, two theorists whose conceptions of scientific change had influenced the direction of the American science of politics. Popper's idea of scientific development through method and Kuhn's notion of paradigmatic evolution provided political scientists with ways to structure their claims to objective knowledge.[67] Though Kuhn's idea of progress through the replacement of normal science with revolutionary science might have cleared certain spaces for novel understandings in the history of science, Cedric found that it could not uncover the "ideological function" of the political – a claim he tested with an exploration of the concept of democracy. Moving from its Greek and Christian foundations to something we have called "the state," democracy was a system where "the people" ruled. Yet, if the *demos* were the people, it was not "all the people." In the modern world, democracy meant exclusion: "the people are those for whom the state services the necessary preconditions for the good life (that is satisfaction of happiness, its more primitive and crude equivalent). The architectonics of the state refers then to a spiritual and material well-being which precludes concern for the poor or slaves."[68] As the discipline evolved, more and more people were disappeared in the "puzzle solving" practices of "normal" political science and the "disciplinary matrix" it found in the idea of democracy.[69] But as these anomalies were rationalized, its "metaphysical and sociological" aspects persisted. Political science, Cedric concluded, was an "arrested" discipline. It possessed "artifactual innovations" deposited in the soil of political thought from pre-political sources.[70] To understand it all, Cedric would need "metatheoretic and epistemological materials," some of which were still resonant in those societies that demonstrated that humans had alternative conceptions of society that did not conform to western notions of the political, and some of which were also resident in western societies themselves. By way of the "primal" predecessors of the political, that is, in "authority and order," Cedric began to address the phenomenon of political leadership.[71]

The ancient idea of authority was not synonymous with the idea of modern political authority, which was a consequence of the modern state and the Machiavellian distortion of the Greek and Roman notions of authority – its reimagining simply as power and force. In its ancient form, the concept signified a sense of reality, of the ideal that existed "beyond human affairs or intervention, but inevitably reflected in the human."[72] The absence of a connection to power in the Greek and Roman formulation indicated that authority was a province of knowing and seeing reality that was preparatory to life and living – it was a fount of wisdom. And yet, with their experiences of empire and othering, the Romans began to corrupt and confuse the idea of authority with power, eventually leading to the Christian era, and then to Machiavelli, who bequeathed to political societies authority in its modern incarnation. But, as Cedric shows, the force of authority was ultimately a question of consciousness.[73]

As was order. Cedric argued that order constituted one's particular way of arranging reality, a conversation he traced to Gestalt psychology, which purported to demonstrate "the relationship between the eye, the brain, and the mind, culminating in, for the individual, the experience or insight of objectness, the figure or order against a backdrop of randomness."[74] The order of politics, it followed, was as perceptible as the biological mechanism of perceiving an object. Society, therefore, could be understood, its parameters and boundaries revealed. But to manage and distinguish that which was orderly about social order, one required political authority. On the relationship between the two, Cedric writes:

> So social order must consist of integrations, institutions, and patterns in order to satisfy the images of the mind and the skills of the brain and eye. And the coherence, the certainty of that coherence in western political thought, is obtained

by one object, political authority, acting on the others and corresponding as such to another dictate of the perceptual experience, movement, and thus causation.[75]

Such notions of political order were linked to Aristotle, just as they have been linked to Edmund Burke, G. W. F. Hegel, and Karl Marx. The preference for order appeared to be a civilizational question after all.[76] The political could only operate within that civilization. Its handmaiden, political science, is a discipline that thinks alongside and practices within the bounds of political authority, a form of knowledge production that Cedric, quoting the paleontologist George Gaylord Simpson, characterizes as "'the perceptual reduction of chaos,' the ensuring of the existence of an identifiable, objective reality."[77] It encounters a world in need of a measure of social control that only a science of politics can provide.[78] So it is authority that produces the terms of order, the basis of modern life under the civilizational project of the West, otherwise known as "the political." And it is authority that shapes what can be known about that project, as well as what kinds of remedies might be pursued, otherwise known as the discipline of political science.

Yet if all of this was possible, how did it work? For Cedric, the political, in its subsumption of alternative ways of thinking through authority, relied on myth. And it was leadership which made it all possible. In the second chapter entitled "Parameters of Leadership," he asserted that the myth and legend, or "social ideology," collected under the sign of "leadership," constructed an authoritative view of order that corresponded to the "crisis experiences" of a certain moment. It is the leader who guides humanity through these moments of chaos. It is the leader who makes decisions and who reduces chaos through rational means. In the case of the modern world, those crisis experiences were "the developments of industrial capitalism, the State and the liberal theory of democracy."[79] Leaders, the myth went, were necessary for ensuring the good life.

But leadership, which was the highest expression of political authority and political order, also demonstrated the contradictions of the political. For all of the associations of the idea of leadership as the province of exceptional decision makers who are able to shape the good of society, many who have occupied the mantle of leadership could only have been able to do so because of their very ordinariness. Leaders are supposedly "deviant" – that is, different from the mass – but somehow also subject to the prevailing "processes of ideology, socialization, and rationalization."[80] Somehow leaders were unique, yet the terms of their leadership were routine. For Cedric, this meant, obviously, that the idea of leadership as the special property of a select few had to be abandoned. His work also signified, however, that we might perhaps need to critique the very idea of political leadership. The problem was not simply bad leaders. It was leadership.[81]

For leaders were beholden to regimes of force and violence.[82] Leadership directly caused harm. Their processes for making decisions were grounded in the dictates of "market society," a theater of violence. It was this space that set the grounds for modern articulations of political authority, its "conceptual imprint."[83] The premise, issuing from theorists like Carl Schmitt, that the concept of political leadership was a response to the inherent friend-and-enemy distinction in human nature, is for Cedric more evidently connected to the particular evolution of western civilization, and the power relations and psychic energies linked to the modern world: "The market society informs the political authority of Western society. It is at its roots. The constructs of the market or economic society are one set of the material factors which service the political authority *episteme*."[84] The implications of this are plain. The same capitalist-imperialist system, which provided the occasion for African existence in the New World, for settler dispossession of the Indigenous, for the ongoing pillage of the Third World, required leaders and leadership. Those leaders were the fount of the terms of order. And their status as "the elect" had no basis in any sort of natural skill, and the idea of leadership no basis in human nature.

But how might we explain the persistence of the leader and of leadership? It was as the title of the following chapter indicated, "a question of rationality." More aptly, it was leadership's appropriation of "the irrational" desire for order and authority among those who had experienced a kind of terror; "those who would know order through terror and realize terror in order."[85] Though the argument critiqued the irrational, it was not a discarding or a dismissal of its explanatory power in service to the assumed primacy of rational thought in western social science: "Western peoples did not have to relinquish their beliefs in other than scientific laws but many of their intellectuals did." And "bourgeois social and scientific thought" had "monopolized and dominated the definition of knowledge."[86] Within political science, it was the rational actors, those with "the ability to reason," who stabilized the liberal order.[87] But Cedric's analysis searched for those elements of irrationality that might be juxtaposed to the perceived rationality of social order, which might give us a fuller picture of how the myth of leadership prevails. He argued that the "irrationalists" – those scholars who sought to understand the irrational in either its ecclesiastical, psychological, or historical materialist continuities – had demonstrated its durability without fully describing it on its own terms.[88] They had sought explanations for the desire of ecclesiastical or fascist order by simply arguing that these irrational systems replaced one another, or "by either changing the phenomenon into something else or redirecting attention away from it."[89] They would describe how eschatological terror would lead to the establishment of ecclesiastical order, the terror of capitalist society to fascist order. But what actually explained the phenomenon that transmuted that fear into obedience and submission?

Understanding this particular evolution of political leadership called for what Cedric described as a "mixed paradigm." This vehicle allowed him to juxtapose the supposedly rational system of politics with its irrational traditions, indeed its irrational foundations, to expose how pre-political myths were subsumed by political authority, ultimately creating the violent force of the market society. One such mixed paradigm combining these elements was the idea of charisma in both its "historical *and conceptual*" emergences.[90] As a "holdover from a prescientific past," charisma held the key to understanding the process through which leadership was constituted by followership even as it represented a form of authority that sought to obliterate the liberatory visions of mass society.[91]

To understand charisma, one had to understand concepts of time. Cedric worked through linear time, regarded as the serial nature of periodization as well as cyclical conceptions of time that cohered around traditions that emphasized the infinite rather than individuated experiences. But ultimately it was through eschatological time – the notion that Time could end, producing the withering away of the world and its replacement with another – where one could begin to see the role of charisma as a way of coping with and understanding large-scale, cosmological change. For this "new world" was a Divine promise, a messianic event.[92] This episteme found its way from the mass psychologies of Judaic and Christian traditions to the thought of G. W. F. Hegel and his "actualization of the Spirit in process of Being,"[93] and finally to Max Weber, who brought charisma into western social science as part of the legitimating process for leadership. Charisma could operate in secular worlds with no less power. In Cedric's formulation, "Weber borrows from the eschatological tradition the notion of the messiah and seeks to rationalize (systematize) it in the concept of charisma by reversing and as well particularizing the eschatological sequence."[94] Through effective leadership, Time might become History, become rational, become ordered.

From concepts of time, Cedric moves to myth, for here is where eschatological expectation was often contained. Through an exploration of Claude Levi-Strauss and Michel Foucault on the structuralism of myths in human consciousness, he demonstrates how myth pervades ostensibly rational systems, such as the human sciences. This was especially so in political theory, which sought to analogize the Greek *polis*, a society which also sought without success to suppress the irrational. By the time "rationalist" Greek ideas were becoming widely translated into Latin in the twelfth century, the messianic ideal had widely circulated within Western European societies before it "suddenly became both more numerous and important."[95] For Weber, though, it was the rigid order of ancient thought in the first place that had produced the attraction to Christianity and the "chaos" of salvation, messianic expectation, and the charismatic event.[96] But while Weber's analysis of this attraction would venture into psychopathology – much like the "irrationalists" who utilized this framing to explain the folk attraction to fascism – Cedric argues that "the charismatic phenomenon is, at base, one of liberation rather than one of totalitarianism."[97] Notwithstanding their appropriation, "political society and political order cannot logically locate their foundations, structurally, in the charismatic phenomenon for the substance of that relationship is fundamentally different from what can be achieved in a rationally related society."[98] Weber could only find psychopathology in messianic expectation because his work viewed order as the effective rationalization of charisma – a project of political leadership. But, for Cedric, this was a perversion of charisma.

Given the force of charisma in structuring political leadership, Cedric moved toward excavating the nature of anti-political or non-political traditions. But in the final chapter of the dissertation Cedric showed that these radical traditions in the West were similarly bound. Of these traditions, he explored anarchism, a "specific negation to the evolution of political authority."[99] Anarchism, too, was a product of Enlightenment rationality and its ensuing debates over the question of human nature. So in tracing its genealogy, beginning with Jean-Jacques Rousseau and William Godwin and continuing through the more recent theorists categorized as either "egoist" or "social revolutionist," Cedric found that their thought could not imagine an anti-political reality outside the conceptual logic of the political.[100] And not for a lack of attempting to theorize or organize them. For the problem was epistemic.

Though anarchist theorists attempted to reconstruct social order mainly on the basis of economic authority, their conceptualizations of social order had identical epistemological and metaphysical foundations to that which they sought to oppose. Anarchism became a *political* force against the state, a *political* force in opposition to political authority. Such a contradiction anticipated the degeneration of anarchism into tragic idealisms and conspiracies of terror and assassination. The root of that contradiction lies in a consciousness dominated by political authority.[101]

For Cedric, it would appear that in the West the only solution would be in those traditions that preceded the political, rather than those radical traditions that arose in response.

Simply put, "political freedom is only prior to political organization and experience, never following out of it."[102]

Or one could simply look elsewhere. The second half of the chapter takes us to southern Africa. Here Cedric takes a critical look at "the anthropological literature" and finds that perhaps stateless societies could provide examples of non-political authority.[103] That literature, however, had to be handled with care. Cedric's background as an anthropology major at Berkeley and instructor at San Francisco City College, as well as his time spent in Southern Rhodesia, likely caused him to draw upon the example of the Ila-Tonga with some awareness of the fact that much of anthropological theory reduced their ways of knowing to categories commensurable with western experience, including the political.[104] This bit of intuition was not a part of anthropological discourse until the mid-seventies. Cedric would later comment that the "behemoth of race" was largely absent from his prior anthropological training.[105] And even as anthropologists attempted to scale back from these colonial frames during the seventies, there was still the residue of rationalist bias lurking in this body of literature. Despite these limitations, Cedric was able to find that the Ila-Tonga, of what is now Zambia, had lived in societies that were simultaneously "successful," that is, continuous, but also incomprehensible to the colonialists. They were able to found life on a broad notion of kinship that structured both relationships and reality in the *mukowa*, or clan. The *mukowa* served as the basis for social relationships, which lacked a clear hierarchy yet was not devoid of authority. It was simply that the latter was structured through kinship, togetherness, a desire "to remain one with all."[106]

These were a people and a society that privileged what Cedric called "the principle of incompleteness" – the idea that "*all are equally incomplete*."[107] It was altogether distinct from practices of social science that vainly pursued "complete" understandings of the basis for social interactions of other populations (read: social control).[108] Social and intellectual practices within these societies did not seek rational closure. Moreover, if we were all incomplete, it also meant that we were one.

Yet questions remained. How were differences addressed? How did this principle translate into ways resolving disputes or conflict? Among the Ila-Tonga, these were handled through "shame, rather than guilt" via the "joke."[109] The jokester was responsible for protecting "the exchange from becoming violent while relieving it of the underlying tension."[110] And importantly, these graces extended to "strangers" or "enemies" who lived outside of these social relationships. For strangers were no threat, they too could be part of the community.[111] While this engagement with the Ila-Tonga was only suggestive, it demonstrated that perhaps methods for addressing the political were lodged within systems that could act as its "perceptional and conceptual negation,"[112] as "an alternative epistemology and a postrevolutionary system of integration."[113]

Cedric's concern with the overdetermination of the political in revolutionary or radical struggle might be the true purpose for undertaking this study. After all, it was written at a moment where the Black Power movement, Paris 1968, and a range of revolutionary struggles in the Third World were taking root. So he concluded his dissertation by stating it was crucial that we understand how these anti-political traditions, which included not only anarchism but Marxism, also revolved around the political. In their search for "a more rational expression" of society, they "were alternatives *of* social order, rather than *to* it."[114] As he would argue in later texts, our struggles must acknowledge the validities of these traditions, while requiring more. It must also be a struggle to conceive of who we are, and what we must be, in different terms than the political. The implication of revealing the political as "a temporarily, convenient illusion" was that it was contingent, and therefore replaceable, and that we could in the end "subvert that way of realizing ourselves."[115] We could realize ourselves anew.

The Robinsons returned to the States and to a move to Ann Arbor, Michigan in 1971. For the next few years, Cedric revised the dissertation. By the mid-seventies, it was clear that it would be a struggle. Alexander George was said to have remarked that this work was almost illegible as "political science." Along with Gabriel Almond, he was one of many members of Stanford's department who dropped out of Cedric's committee, one after another. In the end, Drekmeier prevailed on a younger scholar, Nannerl Keohane, new to Stanford, and with Richard Brody the three constituted the committee that approved the dissertation in 1975.

After its publication in 1980, *The Terms of Order* was met with silence. The only extant review of the text was written by Cedric's friend and accomplice, Mary Agnes Lewis. By then, Lewis had entered the academy herself, writing a dissertation on Ghanaian market women, and was well on her way to playing a role in building the Black Studies department at Laney College in the Bay Area. Of Cedric's work, she would remark that its purpose was to "instruct, as it becomes increasingly evident that the oppression of African peoples is intellectual as well as physical."[116] Ultimately, the analysis of the political revealed "how the separation of knowledge into various disciplines has encouraged and perpetuates the fragmentation and distortion of social reality."[117] As the cliché went, "everything is political," yet "the political" could not reveal everything.

Cedric's ability to critique the dominant frames given for

understanding reality called for a thinking beyond them. In the struggle for space to think and organize, Black students forced open the academy. Black Studies provided the occasion for such thinking and such thought. It would become the next step in his journey.

4

Beyond Racial Capitalism

It was a moment of economic uncertainty and unrest in Brighton, and indeed throughout the country. The historical celebration of the Paris Commune had brought discussions of radicalism to the fore. But when the United Kingdom's postal workers went on strike, disrupting the country's already fragile economy, revolution may have seemed imminent in the winter of 1971.[1] Unable and unwilling to use the British post, Elizabeth traveled to Paris for a week to mail job applications for Cedric. For while the working class in England struggled, the Black Studies movement stateside needed scholars. Cedric would eventually receive four offers and returned briefly to the United States to visit three of the campuses. But after he had settled on his choice, Cedric took a call from the Trinidadian political scientist Archie Singham which convinced him to change his mind. After returning to England to complete his fellowship, Cedric joined Elizabeth on her second trip to Paris. And then she traveled to her ancestral home of Lebanon, while Cedric prepared for his first full-time teaching gig at the University of Michigan. Appointed as lecturer in political science, Cedric would also teach in the newly formed Black Studies unit on campus. When she returned, Elizabeth began graduate work in Michigan's anthropology program. The Robinsons were now ensconced for the first time in the environs of the Midwest.[2]

We must in fact be different

The Black Action Movement (BAM) at the University of Michigan was a coalition of Black students which arose to challenge the university's record of recruiting of minority students. If the university was to be representative of Michigan, it was failing tremendously in reflecting the racial makeup of the state. In the spring of 1970, BAM called on the university to commit to increasing the proportion of Black students on campus to 10 percent of the whole. Drawn from students in psychology, education, social work, law, and the undergraduate Black Student Union, this coalition was also diverse ideologically, with many students coming from socialist and/or nationalist persuasions. Yet they all agreed, as organizer Cynthia Stephens asserted, that Black students had a right to the university.[3]

Along with the demand for more Black students, BAM also called for community engagement with the budding Black Studies program. This necessitated a related demand for more Black faculty across the university. And this is how Cedric ended up there. Unhappy with the progress of the university, BAM engineered a strike which lasted for weeks in late March. When it was over, they declared victory. But as subsequent years revealed, it appears the administration was simply biding its time, seeking to contain the more radical edges of Black student activism on campus. By the time the university exploded again, with second and third iterations of BAM, in 1975 and 1987 respectively, the Robinsons and several others who had been brought in were long gone.[4]

Yet their time here was productive. Among the people recruited to address the racial imbalances on campus was Harold Cruse, who had just written *The Crisis of the Negro Intellectual* in 1967. It was the text that in many ways threw down the gauntlet to Black radicals and critics for that period. A veteran of radical movements by that time, Cruse's 1962 essay "Revolutionary Nationalism and the Afro-American" had circulated widely among students who had developed the Black Power formations which had preceded the more well-known explosion of the second half of the 1960s. This was likely Cedric's first encounter with Cruse, as this article had been required reading for members of the Afro-American Association and the Revolutionary Action Movement, groups connected to his earlier activism.[5]

But in *The Crisis of the Negro Intellectual*, Cruse would change his focus to cultural revolution, arguing that some measure of autonomy was necessary for Black cultural production if it was to be liberatory. He maintained that an association with organized Marxism diluted the power of Black cultural work and political independence, and thus the kind of autonomy and self-determination that was a precondition for freedom.[6] But it was not a text without controversy, as it often overemphasized the extent to which white institutions influenced Black art and was often overly critical of the artists working within these spaces.[7] Cedric offered another level of criticism. In Cruse's recovery of a history of Black Radical thought, he assumed an identification of radicalism with the intelligentsia, rather than the folk. *Black Marxism* was in many ways a response to this "conceit."[8]

While at Michigan, Cedric would encounter other prominent figures. Perhaps none more well known than Walter Rodney, who was also invited to spend a semester on campus during Cedric's first year. On leave from the University of Dar es Salaam in Tanzania, Rodney was soon to publish his *How Europe Underdeveloped Africa*, to which Cedric would author a review. But even before the appearance of his magnum opus, the Guyanese radical had already been a crucial voice in the revolutionary Pan-Africanist movement – a tradition that Cedric first encountered in 1962, and one whose particulars formed the basis of much of his teaching while at Michigan. As Cedric jostled with Cruse over the question of the revolutionary intelligentsia, he critiqued Rodney's emphasis on the structure of political economy in his histories. In his review of *How Europe Underdeveloped Africa*, Cedric argued that the appearance of the text was "of signal importance." Yet he lamented its inattention to "the thought, consciousness, and the social organizations of African peoples," arguing that as a general history of the political economy of colonial Africa, its "true value" would emerge upon the appearance of studies understanding what the "African masses" were "doing and have done."[9]

The decade of the seventies was a vibrant time for Black Radical thought. Revolution was real. And it was global, occasioned by the predicament of military aggression and imperialist exploitation. The Black scholarship of this period spoke to these realities, these possibilities. A signal moment of these times was Cedric's ability to help convene a remarkable collection of thinkers to ponder the "revolutionary legacy of C. L. R. James" in the winter of 1972. Co-organized by the Center for Afro-American and African Studies and an organization called the Black Matters Committee, the conference featured Cruse, Rodney, Robert Hill, Donald Harris, Trevor Munroe, and Sylvia Wynter, among others, despite every attempt by the state department to prevent the attendance of radicals from Jamaica. Archie Singham, a member of the Black Matters Committee and professor of political science, would have to work behind the scenes to secure a visa for Munroe. Through the intervention of Congressman John Conyers, he would make it to Ann Arbor. Wynter needed the intervention of a well-positioned comrade in the Kingston Embassy to secure her attendance. It recalled the repression of the McCarran Act, which was of course entirely consistent, given the history of US repression visited upon the conference's honoree.[10]

A long-distance runner in both the theory and practice of revolution, C. L. R. James's thought was both the occasion as well as a call to arms. Opening the conference on behalf of the Black Matters Committee, Cedric explained the stakes in these terms:

> ... that group which we call the Black Matters Committee ... we've taken it upon ourselves the task of developing a community of Black and Brown scholars who will and do see their task [as] developing a revolutionary understanding of the world. A revolutionary understanding of the world's history, of its present, of the world proletariat. We mean by that last term the revolutionary instrument of history. C. L. R. James has repeatedly instructed us, all of us, that we must be smart, we must be intelligent. He has also warned us that in being smart and being intelligent, our categories must change, must constantly change ... we need categories that move and do not stay put. Now one resultant insight for us is that we must take on new identities, we must see ourselves differently, we must in fact be different.[11]

Along with Singham, and other leftist faculty members like William Ellis, Joel Samoff, Nancy Hartsock, and Nellie Varner, the Black Matters Committee (BMC) was comprised of graduate students in Michigan's department of political science. Its purpose was the recruitment of Black, Chicano, and women students, helping them to "navigate the academic terrain," and also the assembly of "a new curriculum in which the political economy of race, gender, ethnicity, and development ran alongside behavioural and quantitative approaches" in the discipline.[12] It was not simply a diversity initiative. Cedric asserted:

> Since we are here at the university, for a moment at least, our first efforts have been to and should be to breach the stranglehold of bourgeois thought on ourselves. We as students, we as professors, we as the first born – we must, then, and we have decided to generate new calculus, new rationale, new visions, new perspectives – that is, we've decided to be free. Now the revolutionary legacy of James which is the title of this conference is one of the foundations of our work and our lives.[13]

C. L. R. James, who by then had been living and working in Washington DC, was a fixture in Black radical thinking and organizing in the twentieth century. James's name had appeared as one of Cedric's "greatest" influences in the 1999 interview, where he had cited his grandfather.[14] But Cedric was never one to shy away from legitimate critiques of James's work. We see in their relationship a clear demonstration of critique from within a tradition of radicalism and struggle. Still, it was James's insistence on the revolutionary potential of the masses to unleash "the germ, the force, the organism, of the new society" which would prove instrumental for Cedric's understanding of revolution.[15] That this potential for transformation resided in Black working-class life – as demonstrated so profoundly in texts like *A History of Negro Revolt* (1938) and *The Black Jacobins* (1938) – was the historical trace pointing Cedric to a conception of the Black Radical tradition that was at once part of, but larger than, the canvas on which James painted.

In his seventies, James had remained active, convening working groups in major cities across the African diaspora. In 1969, he was recruited to Federal City College by young Black radicals, and from there he participated along with younger Pan-Africanists in the planning of the Sixth Pan-African Congress to take place in Tanzania. Elizabeth remembered that Cedric took a trip or two to Washington, DC during the years leading up to the Congress, a fact confirmed by Jimmy Garrett, one of those younger activists who had helped bring James to DC. From his apartment at the Chastleton on 16th Street, as well as in radical spaces like Drum and Spear Bookstore and the Center for Black Education, artists, organizers, and students would seek James's counsel and often critique and nudge him on certain ideas.[16]

So Ann Arbor was merely another setting for this work. On the first night of the conference, Rodney's keynote set the ground of the conversation, asserting that it was James's participation in Pan-Africanist movements in London that drove his intellectual work. Speaking on the theme of his relationship to the ongoing African revolution, Rodney found in his *A History of Negro Revolt* a search for a model of Black revolutionary self-activity in Africa; it "intended to stress that continuity of a historical tradition of resistance." Against the historical error or erasure of most commentators, James's study reminded us that "from the very beginning, the intrusion was resisted and that this resistance has taken several forms."[17]

In her comments, Sylvia Wynter also seized on the import of cultural traditions and the activity of the masses as distinct from and more critical than the selfish delusions of the Black middle classes. Her prepared paper was revised to include a response to Cedric's student, Rovan Locke, a Jamaican who questioned the ability of middle-class scholars like James to truly understand peasant and ghetto life as it was. But James's own journey was instructive on such matters.

Entitled "C. L. R. James and the Cultural Revolution," Wynter wrestled with the meaning of James's attempt to break free from the grip of the colonial expectations of his class in order to truly envision Black proletarian struggle. It was "this great refusal of James, his great refusal to take his place in the system," which produced this opening. "So, therefore his own life begins the concrete embodiment of his own initiation of a cultural revolution, which embodies all other times." It was this, Wynter argued, that remained for Black intellectuals to imitate. For there was something to the cultural authority of the people that remained open and available for study and for realization: "You will see that he insists, over and over again, that the people lead themselves ... Over and over again, this spontaneity of the masses is what leads and creates revolutions."[18]

If this is what radical intellectuals gleaned from James's works, then one can also see connections to many of the ideas that Cedric was working through at the same time. To close the conference, James offered remarks that were ultimately more forward-looking than a retrospective on his life. Framing his comments on the Hegelian idea that the "negation contains its own affirmation," James saw nothing but revolutionary potential in the movements of Black and poor peoples around the world at that moment.[19] Whether in the sugarcane fields of Jamaica and Barbados, the jungles of Southeast Asia, in the struggles in Bangladesh, or among the British miners, the conclusions he drew were the same: that capitalist society was "doomed to destruction."[20] And echoing remarks he had earlier made in 1948, the seventies would usher in a revolution that was led by peasants, by students, by the Black masses:

But over the past fifteen or twenty years, I have seen that the peasants, first of all, who formerly we paid little attention to, number two, the students in the universities who we looked upon as people whom the proletariat had to teach; and today the Black people in the world have taken the lead. We live in a different political world in which I was educated, and which I knew up to fifteen years ago. Today it is certain that peasants and students and Black people, wherever they are, are taking the lead in the overthrow of the capitalist society. Maybe as in France, when the students fought De Gaulle's army and police and beat them, the proletariat came on to it. I believe at the present time, it is the underdeveloped people who will play the advanced role. The proletariat has to come in at the end, but we haven't to wait on them to go our way.[21]

This question of the Black peasantry would have to be addressed.

Two weeks after the conference, the BMC penned a tribute to James in the *Michigan Daily* which, while providing a brief biography, covered his conference address, highlighting his assertion of "the urgent need for a theoretical framework for all aspects of the struggle to humanize the world through the material and cultural liberation of its peoples." It was clear from the story that one objective of the conference was to introduce Black university students to this revolutionary persona. Cedric had even suggested a resolution to have the university award him an honorary degree – admittedly a "contradiction," but nevertheless important – "to emphasize to Black and oppressed people that Black intellectuals have a long and honorable tradition."[22] The conference itself was historic, if for no other reason for the people it convened. It was so important to Cedric that he sought for several years to get these proceedings published. That sadly never came to pass.[23]

Yet as important as James was, he was not alone among the radicals that Cedric introduced, engaged, and critiqued alongside the BMC. Darryl C. Thomas, who was one of the students recruited to join the department, arrived in the summer of 1972 to a department struggling to live up to its new mandate. Both Ellis and Singham had left for the greener pastures of Howard University. As a result, the task of providing a hospitable home for these new students became that of the Robinsons. Thomas identified their home as one of the spaces that rescued them from the alienation of Michigan. Despite the fact that Cedric was still revising his dissertation and Elizabeth was working and taking classes, every Friday night over "red beans and rice, cornbread and Stroh's beer" they built a community. And on weekends, somewhere between thirty and fifty graduate students across various disciplines attended weekend seminars where Cedric walked them through "issues related to Marxism, anarchism, radical Black politics, political theory, gender and feminism, and Black nationalism." Importantly, these seminars also featured guest lecturers, including "C. L. R. James, Robert Williams, James and Grace Lee Boggs, as well as political and social activists from the area or further afield."[24] The Robinsons had modeled and produced a Black Studies practice that intersected with but was much larger than the university setting.

In so doing, they participated in a dynamic interchange with activists and intellectuals on campus and the revolutionary movements taking place a few miles away in the metropolitan center of Detroit. Ernest Mkalimoto Allen, a former member of the Revolutionary Action Movement, who moved to Detroit in 1970 to organize alongside radical autoworkers, recounts briefly meeting Cedric as there was "a fair amount of traffic of Black radicals between Detroit (League of Revolutionary Black Workers) and the U. of

Michigan's Ann Arbor campus."[25] Alongside the impact of C. L. R. James, the emergence of the League was influenced by an important history of radicalism in Detroit: James and Grace Lee Boggs; the Group on Advanced Leadership, headed by Albert Cleage and Milton and Richard Henry; and the local Freedom Now Party. Much like in the Bay Area, the early sixties' iteration of Black Power in Detroit was rooted in a convergence of working-class and student-based movements.[26]

After the rebellion of 1967, the revolutionary union movements that developed among the autoworkers merged with organizing work outside the plants, resulting in what Muhammad Ahmad calls the "most advanced African American workers organization to emerge" during the period.[27] Where C. L. R. James served as an ideological influence, James and Grace Lee Boggs offered their homes and organizing experiences to young radicals as a base to think and imagine their revolution. As longtime organizers, the early sixties became for the Boggses an opportunity to develop a theory and practice of "American revolution." They were especially important to that younger genera-tion, given that much of their revolutionary imagination was generated both from deep study of radical philosophy and perhaps more importantly an appreciation for the ways people actually lived their lives amid the forces of exploita-tion. It was all about living differently.[28] This was what the League believed could be achieved through the revolution-ary activity of workers. Before its infamous split, radicals like General Baker, Ken Cockrel, Marian Kramer, Luke Tripp, Cassandra Smith, Mike Hamlin, John Watson, and Chuck and Gracie Wooten had contributed to this splendid attempt to foment a revolution from a working-class base, that is, at the point of production.

By the time the Robinsons arrived in Ann Arbor, the

League had begun its rapid decline, rent by internal contradictions. But being within earshot of Detroit Black radicalism provided important examples to study and engage. Black Studies scholars could not afford to ignore this movement as it provided direct answers to questions of revolutionary organization. It was an instance and example of praxis.[29] Cedric arranged for Allen, by then a part-time lecturer in Afro-American and African Studies, to appear over five weeks in a 1973 course entitled "Problems of Political Development in Black Radical Thought." In fact, as an early example of Black Studies practice, the entire semester featured both former and current organizers as presenters, with Cruse, James, the Boggses, and Nellie Varner rounding out the semester. Cedric's engagement with Detroit activists would continue after moving on from Ann Arbor. In 1976, he appeared in a United Auto Workers-sponsored television series at Wayne State, giving a talk on "Imperialism and the Making of the Third World."[30] In both content and form it foretold work still to come.

Teaching at the University of Michigan in both political science and Afro-American and African Studies gave Cedric necessary classroom experience. But as already stated, such practices were critical and nontraditional. He was among the faculty members that gave space in his syllabus to the Program for Educational and Social Change, an experimental initiative that sought to broaden the reach of the university. It offered the community the opportunity to audit courses for free, and in some cases guest lecturers would teach some of the sessions. Though the university tried to stop the practice, Cedric's Winter 1972 political science course featured a segment called "Community Control of Prisons" that was taught by John Sinclair, then an organizer of the Rainbow People's Party. Sinclair's activism stemmed from his incarceration and the burgeoning resistance to the state's "war on drugs." Inspired by the Black Panther Party, he founded the White Panther Party in the late sixties to bring a measure of political relevance to the counterculture after being sentenced to ten years in prison on marijuana possession. The focus on prisons at this juncture was equally intellectually stimulating and politically urgent with the emergence and assassination of George Jackson and the Attica rebellion that had occurred months before.[31]

The course reframed the meaning of criminality through the lens of a structural critique of an unequal society. It was those who society deemed "less than," those "minority groups" that were framed as criminal, whose "normal activity" was "subject to the consequences" of the prison system.[32] Positive law was generated to regulate their activity:

> By defining crime in this way, one can put aside the more important question of why some things are crimes and other things are not – that is, why some things are against the law and other things are not. Positive theories of the law act to keep us from discussing questions of justice. In fact, the explicit purpose of some of these theories of law is to offer a "neutral" concept of law that will not bring in any particular idea of substantive justice.[33]

With Sinclair as a lecturer, Cedric sought to pierce through the conceits of criminology and penology, which reduced the prison to "an interesting subject."[34] The authority of the prisoner was the perspective that would reveal the prison as a site of oppression and brutality. Perhaps remembering his own experiences working for Alameda County, Cedric's discussions closely resembled those we would later describe as "prison abolitionist." The course raised the question of whether simply reforming the prison system could actually shift things if the "fundamental presumptions grounding the way we live are wrong, are twisted and perverted." Moving beyond prisons toward real change required revolution "encompassing everything."[35] In defending the course and Sinclair's right to lecture, Cedric would write: "It is my basic belief and opinion that prisons are obscene."[36] For their students, it was a necessary rejoinder to the traditional views of the social scientist.

In order to boost awareness of the course offerings, faculty in the Center for Afro-American and African Studies created videos which featured instructors explaining the scope of their courses. In the winter term of 1973, Cedric taught two courses entitled "Charisma and the African Diaspora" and "Anarchism and Violence." These courses were both connected to his dissertation work as well as to questions and concerns that animated movements in the streets and beyond. The videos are windows into his thinking during the period. In "Charisma and the African Diaspora," Cedric's intent was to "reverse the emphasis that [Max] Weber puts on social movements by arguing that it is not the leader but the followers who are significant. In fact it is the followers who construct the very basis for the leadership, the followers who construct the ideology, the followers who construct the fundamental organization." Further, foundation for these ideas was to be found in the charismatic traditions of the African diaspora, in the movements "led" by Dona Beatriz and John Chilembwe on the African continent, the Haitian revolution in the Caribbean, by Denmark Vesey and Nat Turner in the United States, by Marcus Garvey and Malcolm X in the twentieth century. Through it all, the focus remained "with the followers, with the mass of people" and the ways that they created movements, how they created ideology "through spirituals, through folk songs" and the larger materials of the charismatic expectation. In "Anarchism and Violence," Cedric stated his objective was to create "a course in changing one's mind, and I don't mean that in terms of attitudes, I mean that in terms of fundamental ways of thinking." It was both an examination of what he would later write in his dissertation concerning the political character of supposedly anti-political traditions and an exploration of how "the kind of violence that people engendered, people generated in order to produce a difference in the world that they had to live in."[37]

These were to be the last of Cedric's courses at Michigan. Elizabeth finished up her degree and was accepted to the doctoral program. The anthropology department at the time featured a number of thinkers like Michael Taussig, Niara Sudarkasa, and Marshall Sahlins doing critical work that would have also resonated with Cedric. But it was not to be. Michigan had provided the Robinsons with an opportunity to think about the nature of capitalist exploitation with similarly minded radical intellectuals and organizers. It was a time of debate, of sharpening. Yet the space became hostile. The work of the Black Matters Committee and its challenge to the disciplinary norms of political science created havoc in the department for both graduate students and Cedric. Internal squabbles over the direction of the curriculum and the matriculation of Black graduate students some deemed incapable of high-level academic work, in Darryl Thomas's words, were attempts by the old guard to make the lives of Black folk and their allies in the department "miserable." Cedric was targeted particularly because of his predilection for theory over the quantitative-driven methods of the majority of the professors. And there was also the pressure they applied because he was still fighting Stanford to obtain his PhD.[38] Like others, the Robinsons joined the exodus for greener pastures. In the era of early Black Studies, opportunities for thinking the nature of the beast, for thinking the meaning of Black resistance, were fortunately not in short supply.

He never had to be

Despite persistent narratives of decline, Black radical movements remained energized by anticolonial struggles waged around the world throughout the 1970s, especially those on the continent of Africa. During this period, Black Studies scholars and organizers in Black Power organizations learned from and shifted their thinking in response to and in concert with the struggle against Portuguese and settler colonialism in Guinea-Bissau, Mozambique, Zimbabwe, and South Africa. Though often reduced to a "race versus class" debate, these discussions were crucial for conceptions of the nation, of national liberation, of independence, of a truer manifestation of decolonization – for the very definition of freedom, its mode and meaning.[39] It was in this intellectual and political moment that the Robinsons arrived at the State University of New York (SUNY) at Binghamton, where Cedric would eventually serve as the chair of the Afro-American and African Studies department.

Black students at Binghamton were organizing. Constituting less than 1 percent of the student body, they formed a Black Student Union in 1968. Like Black students at institutions across the country, they demanded increased support for the university's special admissions program and classes in Black Studies – taught by Black faculty, which in 1968 was "almost non-existent" and under the "direct influence" of the students. The department was renamed "Afro-American Studies" and approved in the fall of 1969.[40] Amid the many expectations that were foisted on Black scholars and students alike, some insisted on deeper questions about vocation and their role in the liberation struggle beyond campus.

Student activists, like Kassahun Checole, brought

experiences from the wider Black world. Checole was an Eritrean student activist involved in the struggle against the Ethiopian monarchy. He had arrived on campus in 1971, escaping the violent repression of the movement. He would use his American platform to raise awareness about those struggles back home, developing several publishing vehicles for that purpose.[41] It was in his *Third World Coalition Newsletter* that Cedric would publish his review of *How Europe Underdeveloped Africa* in 1975. And their families grew close. In addition, Checole, the Robinsons, and many others participated in Binghamton's Off-Campus college. It was a flexible setting wherein they produced innovative course material and applied knowledge – an example of which was a course taught by Checole in the spring of 1974 entitled, "Revolution in Africa: The Cases of Angola, Mozambique, and Guinea-Bissau."[42] About a decade later, he would establish Africa World Press, a critical extension of the Black radical publishing movement. Elizabeth worked for the press as an editor.

As Cedric's dissertation went through its final approval process, the summer after their first year in Binghamton found the Robinsons in Nigeria. Part of an initiative started by theater professor Percival Borde, they joined twenty-four students from various New York universities for a West African Summer Seminar at the University of Ife. Experiencing Africa for a second time – this time in the wake of a civil war – was critical for Cedric's conception of the politics of the Third World. In addition to studying politics, he told a journalist of Binghamton's *Press and Sun-Bulletin* about the power of Yoruba culture through the language of the talking drum – something he and Elizabeth picked up from connecting with the art historian Rowland Abiodun. It was a special year for another reason. That December, Najda Ife Robinson was born, her middle name a reflection of the Robinsons' sojourn through Yorubaland.[43]

Back in Binghamton, Cedric continued his teaching, even adding classes in the sociology department. A recent arrival to that department was Terence Hopkins – the last member of the trio of intellectual influences that Cedric cited in the 1999 interview. A Euro-American scholar, Hopkins was, like Charles Drekmeier, a disciplinary rebel. Having spent time in Uganda and Trinidad, Hopkins arrived from Columbia University with a deep awareness of the material conditions of the Third World. A protégé of Karl Polanyi, Hopkins created a model of graduate education in sociology at Binghamton that was based on his radical view that major fields and core curricula were unnecessary. Instead, Hopkins cultivated a standard that required that students demonstrate competence by constructing their own "fields" of research.[44] It was a kind of openness that simultaneously inculcated a seriousness of rigor, of purpose. It was a constructive project that Hopkins felt was necessary in building a historical sociology that could be for and with radical movements, rather than misunderstand and misname them in service to the status quo. It was also a reaction to the discipline of sociology's inability to truly conceptualize the modern world-system – the name that Hopkins and close colleague Immanuel Wallerstein would give to the "time" they were living, that we are still living.[45]

The modern world-system was the idea that capitalism's ascendancy was the project of a single, unitary economy rather than of separate national units. And if the economy was singular, and if it was the engine behind so much of the movement of peoples and material resources, then the idea of national development as the proper "unit of analysis" would not provide clarity as to how the world operated. Society had to be reconceived. World-systems theorists, however, wanted to do more than rewrite the world. Changing it was also a priority. It was a "transgressing" project.[46] As the methodologist of the modern world-system, Hopkins wrote a series of articles in the mid-to-late seventies that encapsulated a set of considerations for achieving the promise of this thesis. Chief among these was how to think the traditional division of labor within Marxian thought, given that the ideal bourgeoisie–proletariat dyad did not explain the "unequal exchange" which characterized capital's expansion beyond Europe. Of the relational pairs that would prove critical was the relation between the *core* of capitalist production to the *peripheries* – the places where both extraction of resources and labor took place.[47]

The core–periphery relation, in addition to transforming how we might understand capitalism as a system, also produced a different sort of proletariat. Though Black scholars had preceded world-systems scholars in pointing these issues out – a point world-systems scholars readily conceded[48] – Hopkins and others seemed to focus squarely on the material processes of capital accumulation. And even then, rarely were considerations of race and gender understood as constitutive of the division of labor so critical to the formulation.[49] It is clear that Africa and Latin America were critical sites to the theorists of the modern world-system,[50] but the consciousness of the proletariat was both a matter of material relations *and* a question of culture. In Hopkins's oft-cited article on the concept of the modern world-system, he raises concerns about studies on the formation of consciousness and revolutionary ideology: "For aside from general observations . . . there are no studies of a conventionally sociological nature on the *theory* of the formation and development of social consciousness and ideologies that bear even in an involuted way on the matters at issue here."[51] But there, within Black intellectual traditions and within larger movements toward decolonization, was work that converged upon this critical question. In a footnote, Hopkins noted that, "Work in progress by Cedric Robinson on the black Marxists elucidates the originality and continuity of many of the ideas defining the black intellectual tradition within and against western social thought and demonstrates their theoretical scope and coherence with such creativity that his study will in all likelihood be received as a major theoretical contribution in its own right."[52] When those words were written in 1977, it remained to be seen if world-systems theory would accommodate both Black thought and/or the idea that race was central to any theory of accumulation and expansion, any conception of the state, any idea of the division of labor.

Sometime in 1975, Terence Hopkins's comrade and colleague Immanuel Wallerstein was recruited to Binghamton as director of the Center for the Historical Study of Society (CHSS). He had been one year behind Hopkins in graduate school and they had worked together at Columbia during the heady days of the student movement. He was the logical choice to lead the Center, which was in disarray. Founded by Hopkins, it was imagined as a place where scholars would come together to work to theorize the inner workings of the modern world-system.[53] Having authored his *The Modern World System* a year earlier, Wallerstein was on the way to becoming perhaps the most prolific scholar demonstrating the concept through historical-sociological example, rather than only theorizing it.[54] By the time of his appointment in 1976, however, the reimagining of the CHSS as the Fernand Braudel Center for the Study of Economies, Historical Systems, and Civilizations was complete. That story enveloped both Cedric and Elizabeth in interesting ways.

Her work as an assistant at the CHSS gave Elizabeth a front-row seat for its operations and potential. It had been mired in several difficulties. In an external review, scholars had argued the perspectives were perhaps too radical. According to historian Juan Andres Bresciano, this was one reason that Fernand Braudel was chosen as the namesake of the later iteration. He was considered safer.[55] Yet there were also internal tensions. In a letter to Wallerstein, Elizabeth characterized the CHSS as "in need of dire revitalization, or more concretely, vitalization."[56] In gathering together research proposals to be discussed for an August 1975 meeting, she included a statement from Cedric that might in fact be his most direct written commentary on the saliency of world-systems theory. And indeed, how it might be vitalized.

In this proposal, Cedric began by declaring that the idea of the "relational pair" of core and periphery so germinal to world-systems theory could not provide the authority to understand the "totalities" *of* the peripheries and those "contemporaneous structures" not yet subsumed by the system. In other words, as a method for understanding the world historical process, the modern world-system was somewhat well equipped, but there was more to be understood. Cedric argued that there were "critical social phenomena" such as "cultures, languages, historical and social consciousnesses to which the formation of the world-system is an external dynamic." In these beginnings of what would become a major thesis in *Black Marxism*, he resisted the notion that oppression was total and totalizing – that Black consciousness was limited to a "negation of the oppressive presence." He writes that it was Karl Marx who "can be credited with having established some of the philosophical and analytical tenets which betray a deep understanding of exploited and oppressed peoples." Insofar as world-systems theory repeated this "historicist error," it would prove to be at best a partial assessment of the ways in which the world was ordered and understood by people caught up in the capitalist division of labor.[57]

From this orientation, Cedric proposed two research projects that the Center might support. The first had to do with

Black organizing within the communist movement in the early 1930s. There was a need to consider the successes and failures of the organizing efforts of the Communist Party in order to truly ascertain the "authority that Marxist theory possesses with regard to American racialism." What explained the acceptance as well as the rejection of organized Marxism within the folk cultures – what Cedric called "the radical Blacks (the rank and file)" – of Black America as opposed to the intelligentsia? It also proposed studying the dynamics of organizing among that intelligentsia within *and outside* the Party. What were the differences between independent Black Marxists and those subject to "party discipline?"[58] We now know much more about this era, thanks to numerous historical studies, including the dissertation research of Robin D. G. Kelley, on whose committee Cedric sat.[59] It is interesting, however, to speculate what may have come from a research project supported by the Center along those lines and its potential impact on the debates of the seventies. Commenting on Kelley's dissertation in 1985, Cedric argued that the basis of the Communist Party's leadership's dogma was its envelopment in Eurocentrism and its lack of familiarity with American social reality. Though "essentially correct" about the Black petit bourgeoisie, the leadership of the Party lacked the "probity" of the Black Radical intelligentsia.[60]

The second project was more analytical. Cedric proposed research into the nature of class formation and class consciousness in the Black community. In a series of questions, he probed whether racial consciousness and class consciousness operated together in the consciousness of Black folk in the same ways that it operated in the materialist processes of capitalist production. More importantly, he raised again the question that theories of class formation often ignored, especially so within world-systems theory, and this was whether or not materialist approaches could truly uncover the nature of ideas, consciousness, and ideology.[61] The social history of race and the nature of resistance to racialization as it manifested in Black thought and movement could help clarify ideas about the nature of cultural hegemony as well as provide direction to radical organizing efforts on the ground. And what Cedric's engagement with thinkers in what would become the Braudel Center reveals is that he was not only aware of the grand arguments taking place in the Marxist world, but he actively contributed to thinking through the logics set forth in that intellectual genealogy. It was a continuation of the engagement he began in the Bay Area and continued in Ann Arbor. But here he was thinking together with a group of mostly white radicals in the academy who were rebels to their class and profession.

The ill fate of these proposals notwithstanding, Cedric continued a dialogue with the group of thinkers around the Braudel Center after it was formally launched in the fall of 1976. Despite suggestions that it be named for Walter Rodney or Frantz Fanon, the Center was reborn as the Fernand Braudel Center, after the Annales school historian who took the approach of understanding the formation of historical systems and structures through the *longue durée*.[62] Its major thrusts were the development of publishing vehicles like its journal, *Review*, and the creation of working groups. The Robinsons participated in both efforts. In 1977, Cedric had joined its executive committee, *Review*'s editorial board, and served as the coordinator of the working group charged with developing a "historical glossary of concepts related to world-system." In a precis of their work, Cedric argued for the importance in clarifying the history of the "concept-complex, the alternative classifications or categories found within each concept-complex, and the range of possibilities for translation" for "concept-complexes" such as "bourgeoisie," "imperialism," and "national liberation." And as a doctoral student, Elizabeth participated in working group seminars, along with a coterie of scholars from around the region.[63]

It was during these early moments of its existence that Cedric presented another proposal to the executive committee of the Braudel Center. This time, it directly impinged upon the nature of Black Studies and its approach to the questions which guided the Center's concerns. Insofar as the scholarship that the Center wanted to promote was truly transgressive, it is clear that it shared some elements with Black Studies, which was founded to transgress. Cedric's proposal called for both a deepening of that transgression as well as an unthinking of the disciplinarity which had up until that point held Black Studies together.

In "Social Movements and the African Diaspora," he recounted the need for Black Studies to continue to give attention to questions of Black material reality. For it had been the "exploitation of the labor of African peoples, the imaginations of African intellects, and material resources of the African continent" that had "been integral to the contemporary world's development."[64] Helping to contextualize that reality in the nineteenth and twentieth centuries was a series of unique "transformations which have occurred in social organization and political structures." The expansion of the modern world-system had become "mammoth in effect," creating the conditions for "wars, depressions, and revolutions." These were concerns that were also within the Braudel Center's scope. Yet there were others such as the role of culture and consciousness, as Cedric had earlier emphasized, that were also important to Black Studies work: "Little in the twentieth century, with respect to the ideational and ideological orderings of everyday life as well as its historical meaning, replicates the verities extant at the beginnings of the modern era."[65] And if this temporal dynamic was to be fully appreciated, so too were spatial ones. Black Studies could not be limited to any singular location. For Cedric, the question of the influence of the social and political movements in the diaspora on the continent, as well as the continent on the diaspora, were equally critical for Black Studies thinking. That these issues, which demonstrated the vast complexity of Black Studies, were not pursued and understood together were for Cedric "ultimately" at their roots "epistemological questions."[66]

They required a rethinking of what some continue to believe is the "inherent interdisciplinarity" of Black Studies.[67] From his perch as the chair of Black Studies at Binghamton in 1977, his words are instructive. While it was true that in its early moments, a solution to the problem of constructing Black Studies was "to construct this new discipline along multidisciplinary, or further, interdisciplinary lines," he writes that this was "not, however, a definitive nor ultimately a satisfactory solution":

Such a procedure could not address in powerful, authentic terms the social and historical ordering, the cultural sensibilities which were concomitants in ideological and sociological form to the persistence of African peoples beyond the advent of modern industrial systems of production and social organization. Too much depended upon the sensibilities, the conceptualizations, the categories of experience, and the perceptions of African peoples being similar to those of non-African (specifically, European and Euro-American) peoples. African notions of time, space, explanation, and the order of things, that is rationality, had to resemble enough what is made of them in western experience in order to be submitted to treatment according to the peculiar organization of knowledge which westerners now think of as universal. This was the epistemological thrust which accompanied the early development of Black Studies and which contributed some misdirection.[68]

Though important work on individual intellects and the historical nature of slavery and resistance had emerged from this basis of the orders of western knowledge, they could not and would not be synonymous with Black Studies. They could not deal with the fact that "it was neither a sense of racial oppression nor a sense of surplus value which propelled Blacks into revolution and rebellion in the eighteenth and nineteenth centuries." It was rather a worldview that tended to escape the "intellectual structures of western thought." The task remained instead to understand this history differently, "to construct a Black Studies which contains the terms and reflects the internal ordering of the Black experience."[69]

It was only from these foundations that Black anti-systemic movements could be understood within Black Studies. Though Hopkins and Wallerstein had evinced similar protestations regarding the organization of disciplinary knowledge, it is unclear what became of Cedric's proposal. But this powerful statement was an early window into how Cedric understood questions of Black Studies and methodology. Yet it was not the only such foray into these matters.

Two years later, in an article entitled "Historical Consciousness and the Development of Revolutionary Ideology," Cedric extended his thoughts concerning ways of studying and understanding Black social movements. The piece proceeds from the premise that western historiography, inasmuch as it is grounded in a scientism that removes other ways of knowing from its project, could not provide us with the understanding we might desire. It was not simply enough to add new subjects to an already developed or developing field. One had to recognize that scientism has "disrupted the meanings ascribed to the notion of culture."[70]

In fact, the very term "modernity" was merely cover for a European experience masquerading as universal. This technology of materialism was a proxy for European culture, a highly rationalized form of power and conquest. It was both the means of colonial subjugation and its intellectual context, "the criteria for perception, analysis, and judgment."[71]

More people had myths than had historians. And, for Cedric, this was not a problem or a gap to be filled. For these very myths provided a means for conceptualizing new experiences, even those signified under the rubric of progress and technology – experienced by Africans and others as settler terror. He learned from African thinkers like John Mbiti, whose study of African religious traditions uncovered that there was no concept of progress as such, an idea so vital to historical thought in consequence of and beholden to modernization. But it was his engagement with Amilcar Cabral that drove Cedric's point home. Cabral's revision of Marxism enabled a different kind of vision. What Cedric saw was not something as simple as incommensurability – for Europe also had myths – but a kind of incompleteness when it came to western scientific thought and Black experience. If class struggle, as Cabral wrote, did not unfold in the same way across time and space, it might be also true that class struggle was not the dominant mode of human experience across time and space. And if human beings bring their previous universe to bear upon the contradictions of the "relational pair" of the modern world-system, then their ideas of revolution cannot be understood by those contradictions alone. Western radicalism then is limited. For Cabral, "revolution" was "the organized political expression *of a culture*."[72]

Yet another intervention appeared in the pages of the Braudel Center's *Review*, which, according to Elizabeth, was one of the few places willing to publish Cedric's work. Published two years after the Robinsons left Binghamton,

"Notes Toward a 'Native' Theory of History" is the most well known of his examinations of this question of historiography, western thought, and Black experience that Cedric developed during this period. However, it is criminally underread. If it was true that Black social movements deserved to be studied – in fact, needed to be studied – to understand the modern world, then it was necessary that such studies be approached on their own terms. Colonialism implied that "the first attack was an attack on culture."[73] Therefore, Black consciousness was a project of recovery, which required a "new and different philosophy of history." And not merely what he termed "Black scholasticism" – a form of mimicry (and theft). What was required was a new form altogether. Quoting Cabral yet again – "it is generally within culture that we find the seed of opposition, which leads to the structuring and development of the liberation movement" – Cedric showed that the stakes were high, the revolution was imminent. This recovery was urgent.[74]

The remainder of the article is a critique of George Shepperson's treatment of the 1915 Nyasaland uprising in his *Independent African* (1958), co-authored with Thomas Price. Both Robinson and Shepperson shared an interest in British Central Africa, with the latter connected to the region by dint of his Scottish heritage. Yet Shepperson's interest was not exactly of a piece with the sort of colonial knowledge production that had animated histories of African resistance. His intent, as Cedric characterized it, was to give the African "a little dignity."[75] In his hands, the revolt, led by John Chilembwe and the African church movement, intended "to create a new theocratic order. He was a revolutionary nationalist founding and developing a political tradition out of which mid-twentieth century Malawi would emerge."[76] But having studied movements like these for over a decade, Cedric was not comfortable with Shepperson's characterization of John Chilembwe as an African version of Oliver Cromwell. Instead, looking to another account, that of George Mwase, he offered an alternative interpretation concerning the motivations of African leaders and those who participated in charismatic movements. What did it really mean to follow the slogan of the uprising, "strike a blow and die"? Mwase's account relied on the memories of Wallace Kampingo, a participant in the struggle. They would provide Chilembwe with a "very different sort of dignity":

> Absent from the Mwase–Kampingo account are the frustration of a desperate attempt to reconcile his Africanness with his European identification; his pride, ambivalence, and fear. Chilembwe's revolt is a gesture of love not hatred, though it is consummated in blood. He and his people must kill the love–hate object – the white man – in order to celebrate their Christian spirit, in order to establish their right and duty not to kill.[77]

In his response to the piece, published alongside the critique, Shepperson remarked that to tell the kinds of stories that Cedric evoked would have required documentation that had not been available.[78] This of course was a perennial problem of historiography. Yet the epistemological issue remained: "Chilembwe was not a Cromwell; he never could be. But most importantly he never had to be. His movement had its own quite special and remarkable integrity."[79] It was not necessarily about archives, though these were often implicated. Cedric's critique ultimately revolved around the necessity of the "recreation of Black life," an imperative that could not be sustained by the European intellectual tradition, no matter how sympathetic.[80]

The approach of Cedric's writing during these years explains much. They are an extension of the heretical approach to the disciplines that were present in his dissertation. This time, however, the target was the disciplines of history and historical sociology. The Braudel Center's radical approach to history was a significant intervention in how we conceive of the world. Hopkins and Wallerstein believed that the modern world-system functioned "*through* time." It did not "have a history or a set of histories" so much as it *was* history.[81] But the promise of Cedric's approach was to insist on a history of radicalism that was seemingly far beyond the temporal scope of world-systems methodologies. He later explained that "no coherent order, no singular whole, has ever been forged under the authority of capital and the unifying language of world-systems theory simply does not capture the chaos of capitalism." So it would be necessary for a tradition of radicalism to "remain focused upon the cultural legacies that have provided for its strengths" which have been "most powerful when it draws on its own historical experiences while resisting the simplifications of Black nationalism." Rather than shadow or reiterate the "centralism" of world-systems theory, alternative sites of radicalism were necessary for undoing capitalist oppressions and for underscoring that there were other times, other histories, other realities.[82] *Black Marxism*, which Cedric began writing while working out these critiques in Binghamton, would continue this line of questioning.

We are strangers

In December 1978, the family of three began moving across the country to Santa Barbara, where Cedric had taken a job as Director of the Center of Black Studies at the University of California, Santa Barbara (UCSB). This time the move was difficult. Najda was four years old. Elizabeth was ABD

Figure 4.1 Cedric Robinson with his daughter, Najda
Image courtesy of Elizabeth Robinson

(all but dissertation) in her doctoral program. They had forged a community in Binghamton. But Santa Barbara was also much closer to family. And Cedric's academic status at SUNY-Binghamton was less than certain. In addition, with the new position at UCSB, he would have the opportunity to oversee a research agenda. So the Robinson family decided to make the move. It would be their last such move.

The state college in Santa Barbara was absorbed into

the University of California in 1944 with the intention of some to create a "Williams College of the West." But the pressures of postwar higher education finance led to its birth as a major research university in the late 1950s. It was a thriving campus soon after.[83] But in 1960 there was only one Black student and one Black faculty member. By the time of the explosion of the student movement in 1968, there were between forty and sixty students.[84] And many of these were athletes, who were subject to racist treatment by their coaches. Portraying this moment years later, Cedric lectured:

> On our campus, it was the football team. Blacks who were part of the football team, who revolted against their coaches . . . they also said: "Look, you recruit Blacks to play football, but not to play anthropology, play chemistry. Why is that?" Because we are strangers. We are strangers who have been inferiorized. You imagine us as those inferior slaves, who were never inferior, just simply victims. You imagined that we cannot wrestle with difficult questions . . .[85]

When the international wave of rebellions took place in the spring of 1968, students at UCSB began to organize. As they returned to classes after the summer, they directly confronted the university with the grievances of the Black college athletes. But the Black Student Union was planning a more drastic action, for the issue of the racist treatment of the athletes was symptomatic of a larger problem. On October 14 twelve students took over North Hall. Among their seven demands was a call for a "college of Black Studies."[86] That call quickly morphed into the short-lived Malcolm X College, and the Department of Black Studies and the Center for Black Studies.

And to struggles over the autonomy of these spaces.

According to historian Karen Miller, the meaning of autonomy was perhaps the predominant concern of the activist-creators of Black Studies across the state and nation.[87] At UCSB in particular, the vision of an all-encompassing Center which housed the "Black Studies curriculum and major, all support programs, and research and public service functions" was never fully realized.[88] Both Department and Center faced considerable challenges to their autonomy and mission. In 1975, after rumors that it was to be defunded and possibly dissolved entirely, another North Hall occupation ensued. The Center was reconstituted as a place where faculty development would be foregrounded in order to address the issue that there were simply not enough scholars available to carry out its research mission.[89]

Though the Center was in some disrepair, there was some hesitation with regard to hiring Cedric. A member of the committee, Black Studies scholar Gerard Pigeon, knew that he was the right fit. He had glowing recommendations and a reputation for radicalism. Both were looked at with suspicion. Yet Pigeon prevailed on them to hire Cedric, reasoning with them that there must be some truth to the letters, given the reputations of the scholars that had written them. A paragraph announcing the move was printed in *Jet*.[90]

In the winter of 1979, Cedric began work at the Center. A new class of dissertation fellows followed in the fall of 1979, and included Brenda Gayle Plummer and Travis Tatum, the latter whom Cedric had worked with at Michigan. By then, Cedric had established what Plummer described as a space that "helped close the distance between the university and the surrounding community." As the administration sought, like most, to make "black studies a poster child for budgetary retrenchment," the Center for Black Studies, under Cedric, received a renewed vitality for emancipatory Black thought in connection and conversation with Black residents of Santa

Barbara and Goleta.[91] Reviewing this legacy, Cedric recalled that this work, and the student revolt which made it possible, "deepened the academy in a way that it would not organically move. The academy continued to produce racist texts. But now there was a resistance that was in your face."[92]

Plummer has also noted how Cedric's radical scholarship reached beyond the academy in one other way: radical publishing.[93] Beginning in 1978, he had begun to write in the London periodical *Race and Class*, a publication of the Institute of Race Relations. In early February 1980, the editor, A. Sivanandan, and director, Colin Prescod, were among the participants at a Center for Black Studies conference considering "Black Movements in the Western World." Two sessions focused on Black life in Great Britain in a conference that featured updates on social movements in France, Canada, and the United States. Sivanandan and Prescod were joined by an array of thinkers, including the university's chancellor, Robert Huttenback, as well as Manning Marable and former Communist Party organizer Harry Haywood, in a conference that featured academics but was necessarily broader.[94] In fact, this was what the Institute of Race Relations and the Center for Black Studies shared – a belief "in radical scholarship with communitarian objectives"[95] and that, as Sivanandan asserted, "the people we were writing for were the people we were fighting for." Later in the year, Cedric joined the Editorial Committee of *Race and Class*, which was composed of "scholar activists and radical thinkers" that believed "the function of knowledge was to liberate, that we should think in order to do, not think in order to think."[96] In the summer, the Robinsons embarked upon a return trip to Brighton to attend a conference on "Race, Class, and the State," where Cedric spoke alongside Prescod, Sivanandan, and others. They would return to the country for a longer stay the following year.

None was immune

The beginning of the decade saw the publication of Cedric's first book, *The Terms of Order*, by the State University of New York Press. His dissertation with a new title, it contained an acknowledgment to Charles and Margot Drekmeier and his friends from England, Dominic Sankey and family, as well as colleagues from Binghamton, Terence and Gloria Hopkins and Immanuel and Bea Wallerstein. And of course there was Elizabeth.[97] But the work was dedicated to Winston Whiteside, who had passed in 1979 in Georgia. This "grandson of slaves" had made a return to the South before joining the ancestors. Cedric remembered him as his "first teacher."[98]

As far as the text was concerned, it was not widely reviewed or heralded. For years, it was impossible to find. So later generations did not have much of an opportunity to engage it if they even knew that it existed. As critical as it was to Cedric's approach to political theory, and to thinking western civilization, it was destined to acquire another life and a renewed appreciation years down the line.

For the 1981–2 term, Cedric received a postdoctoral fellowship from the Ford Foundation, which he used to return to England. The Robinsons found accommodations in Radwinter, a small village south of Cambridge University, where Cedric pored over the archives and continued writing *Black Marxism*. As one of the first to go abroad with this fellowship, many viewed him and his work with suspicion. He later recalled that there was a "depth of fear that established the ceiling of work with respect to the left at the time."[99] Though relatively isolated in Radwinter, the Robinsons would foster connections with a coterie of thinkers in London that also allowed them to hone their thinking about the nature of history, race, and capitalism.

In a text which sought to map "the historical and intellectual contours of Marxism and Black radicalism, two programs of revolutionary change," the English archive and historical and literary tradition was an optimal space to think their relation.[100] If western civilization was capitalism's setting and thus the occasion for the emergence of Marxism, then these "historical contours" needed to be excavated and understood. So too the colonial archives and the records left by radicals that also traversed the metropole. In his search, Cedric found that the national projects through which capital was stabilized were permeated with racialist discourse and that differentiation marked the emergence of the working class – a set of considerations he eventually labeled "racial capitalism."

These were concerns that intersected with world-systems thinking, even as its practitioners failed to fully follow through with their implications. Yet Binghamton was certainly a place where Cedric thought through the meaning of this process of racialization. He co-taught a course in Afro-American Studies, titled "The Concept of Race in Western Culture," with Audrey Smedley, Benjamin Bowser, and Akbar Muhammad. It sought to trace the "transformation of racial categories reflected in western science, literature and political thought," beginning in "late feudal Europe." The course was concerned with "how race materially ordered western culture and consciousness from the arena of everyday life to science and philosophy."[101]

In his section, Cedric critiqued the liberal adage that race's social constructionism required a dismissal of race's "realness." In another critique of scientism, he made clear that rational thought contained within it residues of myth and metaphysics. Science was not the only way of knowing. And race's "empirical unverifiability" did not prevent it from constituting a "primordial coding of the world." Race mattered. These were the roots of Cedric's exploration of racial capitalism. It was no doubt grounded in his study of European thinking traditions – namely the question of consciousness as it emerged in western societies. But as the syllabus to the Binghamton course indicated, Black thinkers obviously were well-equipped to describe the lived experiences of raced life. Cedric utilized fiction – the work of Chester Himes and Ishmael Reed in particular – to illuminate this phenomenon.[102]

As many have pointed out, however, there were simultaneous conceptions of these relations by activists in England that also used the phrase "racial capitalism." This has led to historical debates that sometimes focus on who used the term first.[103] While perhaps it is important to ask such questions in academic corners where "firsts" matter, it is unlikely that Cedric would have given much energy to them. Or to the necessity of linking his name to the term's "invention." In the midst of academic trends come empty citations, some of which filter into critical discourse among organizers.[104] And, in the end, meaning often gets lost. The question that should animate these discussions is what different conceptions and usages of racial capitalism say about the nature of the war we are fighting. In other words, it is not simply a question for the historical archive. It is about ideology. Cedric's work was more than a phrase, but in that phrase, not unlike others who deployed it, he sought to reveal one way that the world-system evolved, one way that Black life was interdicted by modernity. The roots of that methodology are in Black thinking traditions that ranged beyond mere adaptations of western social science or philosophy. Of the many places in the African diaspora to find them, there was London.

By the latter half of the 1960s, Black Power had arrived in a Great Britain embroiled in a struggle over questions of race, immigration, anticolonialism, and self-determination. Visits by Malcolm X and Stokely Carmichael further spawned the development of several vehicles for Black Power.[105] But a transnational organizing tradition among Africans from the continent, the West Indies, as well as the United States had long existed in the metropole.[106] In some cases, there were figures that bridged both moments. Along with C. L. R. James who remained active in these circles, even as he was still living in DC, Cedric connected with towering figures like Peter Blackman, the poet from Barbados. The Robinsons also made connections with their contemporaries. There were Black radicals, like the Guyanese educator Gus John, who were part of this activist generation that asserted Black cultural autonomy as a force against racist immigration policy, police brutality, and the white nationalist sentiment that first emerged under the sign of Powellism and became part of the intellectual architecture of Thatcherism.[107] In fact, the differences between the overt racism of Enoch Powell and the structural racisms of Margaret Thatcher's political and economic orientation paralleled similar shifts in the United States. As Black scholars inspired by anticolonial struggles created organizations in the United States to confront the 1970s, so did Black radicals in Britain.[108]

By the time the Robinsons arrived in 1981, the Black Power movement had retained critical bases from which to think, organize, and act. Reading practices were not only necessary for breaking the yoke of the colonized mind, they were directly connected to radical organizing and institution building. The study group was buoyed by Black radical libraries, the development of radical bookshops and publishing houses, and eventually by alternative educational formations. Appearing on the reading lists were the generative works of Malcolm X, George Jackson, and Angela Davis and also the works of Karl Marx, V. I. Lenin, and G. W. F. Hegel.

Questions of the meaning of race and class abounded.[109]

But it was the racial violence at the hands of both citizens and police – their form of managing immigration and immigrant behavior – that created the conditions for a conception of "political Blackness" that stimulated radical British thought during this period. Organizations like the Black Panther Movement, the Race Today Collective, the Organisation of Women of Asian and African Descent, and the Racial Adjustment Action Society, among many others, advanced the idea that Blackness constituted a position and posture against the racist foundations of British political order. It was the necessary outside that did not desire entrance inside as much as it desired the destruction of that order. It was a conception of Blackness that encompassed all who were denied entrance, regardless of ethnicity or region. South Asians, for instance, were "Black" under this political canopy.[110] It was A. Sivanandan, a Sri Lankan librarian at the Institute of Race Relations and an important participant in Black Power organizing in London, who became the Robinsons' entrée into this milieu.

Sivanandan had been part of a revolt that reimagined the Institute of Race Relations, which was born out of the logic of white paternalism. Emergent in the early years of African independence, it was founded to perpetuate a neo-colonial conception of race relations that sought to make Africa safe for resource extraction. Domestically, then, it had to take a more cautious route, variously supporting liberal immigration politics. But it was no radical space. Its support of immigration reform existed within the limits of the race relations industry. Sivanandan, as well as a group of African scholars and white radicals, began to push against these corporate-centered conceptions of race relations. In embracing the movement, they lost the financial backing that had supported the Institute. But it was a necessary break. From that point on, the Institute was part of the fight to make political Blackness a critical affront to the growing neoliberal consensus in London – a consensus that was as anti-Black as it was anti-working class.[111]

Among its contributions to this thinking was *Race and Class*, a space Cedric would embrace to develop his thinking on racial capitalism. Under Sivanandan's editorship, the journal was reimagined as an organ devoted to "black and Third World Liberation."[112] Rather than the liberal racial frame, it began a new life as a resource for comprehending "the connection between oppression and exploitation, production and distribution."[113] One of the two articles that Cedric published here in 1979 was a piece that shared the title of Part I of *Black Marxism*, "The Emergence and Limitations of European Radicalism."

At the outset, Cedric addresses a major perennial in radical thought: the idea that racism was an epiphenomenon of capitalism: "The historical development of world capitalism was influenced in a most fundamental way by the particularistic forces of racism and nationalism. This could only be true if the social, psychological and cultural origins of racism and nationalism both anticipated capitalism in time and formed a piece with those events which contributed directly to its organization of production and change."[114]

By this declaration, Cedric was clearing space to understand racism beyond the historical particulars of capitalist development at the same time he was critiquing the idea that the world-system was somehow devoid or untouched by the racisms and nationalisms that characterized western life. World-systems theorists had not only argued that capitalism began as a coherent process but was a rational break from feudal society. But this process "never achieved the coherence of structure and organisation which had been the promise of capitalism as an objective system." The inherent limitation of Marxism was that it relied on a "presumption of a determinant economic rationality" that failed to comprehend that capitalism was a projection of the "social, cultural, political, and ideological complexes of European feudalisms."[115] Rather than its negation, capitalism simply served as a system that extended these feudalistic tendencies into the modern world.

From here Cedric proceeds to demonstrate this thesis through a historical journey from the formation of the concept of Europe out of the ashes of the Roman Empire, the development of Christendom, and eventually the Absolutist state. It was this medieval period and the pre-modern era that mattered to understanding Europe as a project. Relying on secondary historical works, largely those of Henri Pirenne and Fernand Braudel, Cedric argues that it was indeed differentiation between laborers, between soldiers in the armies of conquest, between Christians and non-Christians, that set the stage for national identities within the newly created states, and thus indeed for "racialism." This project of weaponizing identity and of the exaggeration of human difference became the central feature of capitalism's development, and thus of the modern world. The celebrated division of labor relied on human difference, groups of people who came from "particular cultural and ethnic groups," who came from different regions, belonged to different families, and not merely those who performed different jobs. Capitalism would only continue this trajectory. Cedric stated it plainly: "The tendency of European civilization through capitalism was thus not to homogenize but to differentiate – to exaggerate regional, subcultural and dialectical differences into "racial ones."[116] As capital expanded, so too did these assumptions of difference, which were mapped onto new populations – often, through religious, cultural, and philosophical differentiations. But these would all become racial. For racial differentiation was necessitated as "capitalist domination abroad" required "new mystifications."[117] But, as Cedric demonstrated, this should not be confused as racism's origin story: "racialism and its permutations persisted, rooted not in a particular era but in the civilization itself . . . the effects of racialism were bound to appear in the social expression of every strata of every European society no matter the structures upon which they were formed. None was immune."[118]

In the entire article, Cedric never used the term "racial capitalism." However, when it appeared four years later in *Black Marxism*, its title was changed to "Racial Capitalism: The Nonobjective Character of Capitalist Development." Whether or not it was a borrowing or appropriation of the term from others he may have encountered while in England, the irony is that the basis of the ideas collected under the term did not require the term itself in order to be understood. The decision to include it, then, is a curious one. And perhaps it was simply adopted as shorthand for conceiving of not simply the relationship between capitalism and racism, but for how the two are inherently conjoined, and were necessarily so, as he explained in the introduction to *Black Marxism*.[119] Most importantly, however, whether as a term of convenience or as grand philosophical and conceptual intervention, Cedric demonstrated that for Africans "racial capitalism" constituted "an unacceptable standard of human conduct."[120] And it is from *this* meaning that we might understand the nature of Black people's entanglement with it.

Between 1978 and the 1983 appearance of *Black Marxism*, Cedric would write five other articles in *Race and Class*. Some rehearsed the arguments that would appear in book form, while others were concerned with different subject matters, including the urgency of ongoing rebellions. The Robinsons arrived in England soon after the Brixton uprising. Black youth, fed up with the policing of the communities, responded in kind. It had occurred mere months after the killings of nine children in the New Cross Massacre. This spawned a great deal of radical commentary about the nature of the youth rebellion and its relationship to revolutionary change.[121] To demonstrate the diasporic network as well as the global vulnerability of Black children, Cedric invited Toni Cade Bambara to the Institute of Race Relations to speak on the Atlanta child murders that were happening at the same time. Racial capitalism was global in scope. And so was resistance. Cedric, writing two years later in a short-lived radical journal *Emergency*, argued that the current unrest in Britain was being propagated by descendants of African peoples whose resistance emanated from "similar, if not identical cultural, historical, and social bases."[122] They were a link in the long chain of Black radicalism. There was something beyond the reach of racial capitalism. It was necessary that this legacy be known.

5

The Making of the Black Radical Tradition

The revolutions of the seventies were met with force. In 1983, the year that saw the publication of *Black Marxism*, the world it sought to contextualize was itself undergoing deep transformation, an evolution which has proven consequential for our times. One historian has described it as a "world at the brink."[1] Indeed, Cedric would write that "everywhere one cares or turns to look, the signs of a collapsing world are evident."[2] And though he was speaking to the strength of the resistance movements in precipitating that shift, another sign of collapse was the desperation of white nationalist projects of reassertion, of global military misadventures which supported neocolonial plunder. Its domestic form was the creation of a neoliberal order, the remaking of the state as a conduit for the activities of the market. Year Two of Reaganism had wreaked devastation on Black communities, both domestically and globally. And that racial violence was accompanied by economic depression. Their world was collapsing. In more ways than one. Revolutionary activity produced another possibility.

Mosquitoes

As activists celebrated the independence of Zimbabwe, the African struggle against the "anticolonial" settler colonial regime that had just broken from Great Britain, the Black Power movement in the United States reeled from external attack and inner contradictions. Its reimagination as a form of electoral politics – which had never achieved a consensus – had, at best, achieved uneven results. Though electoral representation was more important than not, by the early eighties those looking for evidence of its impact and potential would also bear witness to the kinds of political maneuvering that could only be seen as a betrayal. Black elected officials could enact racial violence too. As disappointing as these episodes were, openly white supremacist political regimes continued to provide the most direct example of the harms made possible by the modern world-system. The apartheid government of South Africa flexed its muscles through the continued repression of the liberation struggle, even extending its military reach to neighboring countries. The carnage it left in its wake was broadcast on television screens. It was a time that revealed the impotence of "politics as usual."[3]

After their return to Santa Barbara, the Robinsons continued community-based political work which addressed these and other issues. When they arrived in the late seventies, Cedric joined a group known as the Black Action Committee, which focused on inequity in housing, education, and healthcare in the Black community, which in the eighties routinely reached unemployment figures in the double digits. As one of several spokespersons for the group, Cedric focused on racism within the city's mental health services, often appearing on local television to present their views.[4] He was also a founding member of the Santa Barbara Coalition Against School Fees, a member of the George Washington Carver Social Club, a board member of the local American Civil Liberties Union, and a member of the Santa Barbarans Against Apartheid. In the spring of 1979, he was invited by assemblywoman Teresa P. Hughes to appear before the California Assembly in support of legislation which would make advertisements for the sale of Krugerrands carry information about the United States' arms embargo of South Africa's government.[5] Southern Africa remained important to Cedric's conception of Black liberation. And though addressing the state directly in the halls of power could be meaningful, perhaps no arena was more critical to the Robinsons' activism than political communication geared directly to the people.

It is now a commonplace to assert that the United States media offer a narrow and often misleading picture of global events. Its beholdenness to the Washington consensus and corporate interests is now broadly realized. But this was not so in 1980 when Cedric founded the *Third World News Review* alongside Corey Dubin, a UCSB student journalist and eventual news director, and in association with Peter Shapiro, a local activist. Utilizing a slot on the campus and community's KCSB radio station, they reported on global news stories that were either being ignored or distorted by the national press, a hegemon that had achieved an easy consensus among the public by simply limiting what could be known. So the radio program was one way to address the problem of ignorance that led ordinary Americans to accept that the corporate media's enemies were also theirs, that the people the state marked as abhorrent truly deserved the annihilation the military meted out. In explaining the necessity of their work, Cedric asserted that "the more people know about international needs and desires, the less likely they will be manipulated into convenient hostilities."[6]

In the early years of the *Third World News Review*, the "hot zones" of the Cold War such as southern Africa, the Caribbean and Latin America, and the Middle East achieved wide coverage. Composed entirely of volunteers, many with little to no media experience, the program's hosts used foreign newspapers found in UCSB's library to highlight stories from international perspectives that were not previously vetted by White House or Pentagon officials. Those fluent in non-English languages offered valuable translations from press clippings from around the world. Elizabeth, who would eventually take a job at the radio station, remembers that the early impulse stemmed from coverage of the Iran hostage crisis. The Robinsons' Iranian contacts shared direct experiences that greatly differed from the way that the situation was being depicted every night on *Nightline*.[7] Shapiro's interest in southern Africa also inspired the creation of the program. His earlier show, *South African Perspectives*, which was also broadcast on KCSB, served as a counterweight to the "official" narratives coming from Pretoria.[8]

The events surrounding the United States, military presence in Lebanon, and the invasion of Grenada three years later were clear instances where this kind of media activism would prove necessary. Lebanon was a nation rife with tensions between the country's Christian minority and Muslim majority. In an event exploring the conflict, Elizabeth noted that this majority, which had provided the resistance to the French colonial project, was now disenfranchised and poor.[9] These contradictions led to a protracted civil war in 1975, with several interventions from foreign powers. In 1982, Israel invaded the country, ostensibly to attack the Palestinian Liberation Organization. Subsequent fighting hastened the

PLO's withdrawal, leading to a vacuum that was filled by radical and sectarian militias. When American troops were brought in to preserve the peace, this invasion was rightly viewed with hostility. The bombing of the military barracks of the American and French peacekeepers by sectarian forces on October 23, 1983 brought the issue directly to American television sets. Many viewed Reagan's deployment of troops as reckless. But it was the logic of colonial imposition that created the recklessness.[10]

In Grenada, the New Jewel Movement, led by Maurice Bishop, had represented the vibrancy of Black radical organizing and its possibilities in the achievement of state power. According to Cedric, the Grenada of the New Jewel Movement's dreams necessitated a withdrawal from the world-system and from British and American economic interests, and the creation of an economy for its people.[11] In 1979, after a successful revolt against the reactionary regime of Eric Gairy, they began their work. Though the People's Revolutionary Government of Grenada exhibited van-guardist tendencies that disturbed many radicals of Cedric's persuasion, a Black socialist state in the Caribbean was too much for Washington.[12] Fearing an alliance with Cuba and the example that this experiment presented to other countries in the region, defense department officials war-gamed an invasion scenario in 1981. Two years later, utilizing an opportunity of internal fracture and a power struggle that led to Bishop's execution, Reagan authorized an invasion of several thousand troops under the pretext of rescuing American medical students. They arrived two days after the bombing in Lebanon. Dubbed Operation Urgent Fury, the killings of ordinary Grenadians defending their homes was celebrated by the American press. And condemned internationally.[13]

Cedric and others in Black and radical communities condemned it too. Three days after the invasion, he published an editorial in UCSB's *Daily Nexus* that placed the invasion within a long history of US aggression in the region dating to the Monroe Doctrine. But it was also contextualized by a Reagan administration that continued to operate "unchecked." This invasion was not its first. It had been preceded by similar actions in El Salvador, Nicaragua, the Sudan, Chad, and Libya. Cedric highlighted the ominous pattern to demonstrate that as a "media event" the true costs in human lives of the invasion would be wished away. For there were "men and women who have convinced themselves that the deaths of hundreds of thousands and the gambling with millions are necessary concomitants for the world they intend to have." A true accounting of events was required to "discipline" this administration lest the "fractures" created become "chasms."[14] Two weeks later, in an interview with the Santa Barbara *News and Review*, Cedric offered more extensive commentary on the background of the Grenadian revolution, the ways in which the media were manipulated by the Reagan administration in their coverage, and the cautious next steps that were sure to be taken in the invasion's aftermath. His view that the invasion was explicitly "racist" and should be taken up by Democratic presidential hopefuls was heeded most consistently and acerbically by Jesse Jackson. Perhaps most problematic to Cedric was the fact that Ronald Reagan's administration was an "insult to learning, to intelligence, to historical consciousness."[15] In order to resist the violence of American empire, an alternative media was required. And it was more necessary now than ever.

After speaking at a rally – Elizabeth on Lebanon and Cedric on Grenada – the Robinsons were approached about expanding to public access television. Though radio was an important medium, the television version of *Third World News Review* quickly became a critical source of information for Santa Barbarans "hungry for critical media." Cedric and Elizabeth, as well as others who appeared on the show, were often recognized in the streets. They were, as Elizabeth remembered, hailed "from skip loaders, parking attendants would ask about the show, people would stop us on the street, almost all of them wanting to know more – and a few wanting us to go away!" She characterized their work in media as a "mosquito on an elephant's behind," but it was also a reminder that "resistance starts with tiny bites that nourish imagination and audacity."[16] It almost does not have to be said that the work of critical and alternative media has since expanded. There are more mosquitoes now.

Unhappy legacies

By the time Cedric arrived in Radwinter, several of the elements of *Black Marxism* were at stages of near completion. Before leaving, he told G. Pascal Zachary, then writing for the *News and Review*, that his agenda while in England was to research "the development of Marxism in English-speaking Africa and the Caribbean between the two world wars."[17] In a 1977 proposal for the work, Cedric envisioned that the text would cover the development of critiques of race, class, and nationalism as they converged in the life, work, and organizing of W. E. B. Du Bois, C. L. R. James, Eric Williams, and Oliver Cromwell Cox. Over six chapters, the major moments of twentieth-century western Marxism – the Russian Revolution and the development of the Communist International – were to be understood alongside the theoretical and historical development of "the forms and structures through which an emergent Afro-American culture mediated the conditions of slavery." The "Black Marxists" were those who attempted to understand Black movements as an instance of "revolutionary peoplehood."[18]

Five years and several publications later, the basic thrust of the text remained. It was still to be an exploration of the way "blacks, and others in similar circumstances, construct not merely techniques of survival, but techniques of change, of transforming their societies and their experiences."[19] But, in its final form, Cedric decided to organize those elements differently.

As we have seen, the title from the 1979 *Race and Class* article, "The Emergence and Limitations of European Radicalism," became the title of Part I of *Black Marxism*. And after exploring racial capitalism as a significant part of the way western civilization itself must be conceived, Cedric added a case study of class and racial consciousness in England. Quoting E. P. Thompson's *The Making of the English Working Class* on the link between class consciousness and experience, the second chapter of the text understood class consciousness and the related experiences of "expropriation, impoverishment, [and] alienation" as "living categories." Among those categories which remained alive in the English working class was "racialism."[20]

Its roots lay partially in England's history of conquest and colonization. Much like in his treatment of the oppression of the Scottish in his article on George Shepperson, Cedric took seriously the importance of Anglo-Saxon domination in the British Isles as critical to the shaping of social and political consciousness. This time the focus was on Ireland. During their first stay, the Robinsons had developed an "appreciation for the Irish experience" through conversations with Dominic Sankey, whose Irish mother, Veronica, visited and was eventually interviewed by Cedric. In a later recollection, he noted that she was "doubly cursed in the eyes of the English" for she was not only Irish, she had married a Nigerian man while living in the then British colony. Living a life which rejected much of the proper carriage expected of

British women, she chose an African revolutionary she met in 1948 in her travels to be Dominic's godfather. His name was Kwame Nkrumah.[21] For Cedric, the Irish were a people whose relations to the modern projects of white world supremacy could offer important insights.[22]

Though it had begun in many respects with the Norman invasion of the eleventh century, the colonization of Ireland was crystallized with its "plantation" phase in the sixteenth century. The subjugation of the Irish produced a dialectic of resistance and repression. In the nineteenth century, the resulting migrations into London by Irish workers further exacerbated the tensions between the colonizer and colonized. And when there were moments of working-class unity, these were often fractured by the nationalism of the native English working class. Those identified as English were a people whose identity and sense of themselves were consciously linked to the nation's elites rather than to their fellow laborers.[23]

The expectation was that capitalism would create a universal proletariat, but it instead exacerbated national differences. That the English working class was heterogeneous and that rebellions took on a "national" character was of course not lost on Karl Marx and Friedrich Engels. Cedric showed that some of their writing had recognized its import. But the issue was that questions of national identity, the ways in which it constituted a "'haunting' of radical European thought, and its Eurocentrism" did not neatly map on to the scientism of historical materialism that for Marx and Marxists purported to explain history. There was a gulf between the experience of working-class nationalism and the theoretical assumption of a universal revolutionary class as historical inevitability. But this can be gleaned from their work as well. Cedric believed that, "Like Marx, Engels understood that their attempt to construct a total system of 'the materialist conception of history' bore the historical imprint of their historical moment."

This meant their work, itself the critique of "bourgeois society" and industrial capitalism, would someday – when the material forces of society had progressed beyond their stage of development in the nineteenth century – be subject to criticism (negation). That which was ideological ("partial consciousness") in their study of history would be transcended by a *necessarily* higher form of social thought corresponding to its historical moment.[24]

Here one sees the imprint of Hegelian thinking in Marx's and Engels' thought. Just as Hegel's thought had sought a kind of regulation of a world in flux, historical materialism was the scientific attempt to wring order out of the complexities of modern society. However, it was still a question of whether the conditions of industrial capitalism could produce universal truths, particularly when it came to the nature of revolutionary struggle against that system. National difference also implied that there were prerational and prescientific forms of thinking that emanated from a people's culture, which enabled the revolutionary traditions of a people. Though Marxists would come to categorize such thinking as false or partial consciousness, Cedric argued that such consciousness was indeed responsible for revolutions of "extraordinary historical achievement where failure was 'objectively' immanent."[25] People faced the various incursions of the capitalist world-system on their own terms. This was an issue, whether a problem of theory or practice, that would become a perennial concern for Marxists throughout the twentieth century.

In the third chapter, Cedric traced at least part of how it came to be addressed. It is a chapter that is rarely engaged. Yet it is essential to the argument and contribution of *Black Marxism*. "Socialist Theory and Nationalism" begins with the premise, taken up more forcefully in *An Anthropology of*

Marxism, that a legend of socialism's emergence has replaced a broader history of those older moral and ethical systems that were arrayed against private property and power. With the advent of modernity came a "scientific" and largely petit bourgeois variant of socialist thought that was consonant with Marxist thought and the historical trajectories it constructed for itself.[26] That tradition, Cedric argued, began with the era of the French Revolution and the Conspiracy of the Equals. And it injected both a bourgeois and nationalist strain into the meaning and unfolding of revolutionary class struggle.

Using a quick case study of the Italian War of 1859, Cedric showed the ambiguity of Marx and Engels' thought with regard to nationalism. At certain points, nationalism was seen as the necessary agent of organizing the state, which of course provided the condition for the emergence of the bourgeoisie and thus the revolutionary agent – the proletariat. But nationalism was also counterrevolutionary when it prevented the rise of an international proletariat. This contradiction would bedevil many Marxist thinkers. And when the Bolshevik revolution succeeded, it became a question for Russian theorists to resolve. V. I. Lenin's and Joseph Stalin's famous statements about the national question were critical interventions in that discourse.[27]

Nevertheless, national identity persisted as a way to both organize socialist revolution and to conceive of the revolutionary subject. It was a consequence of a political-economic order, which produced the nation as its emblem. But, as Cedric repeatedly reminds us (and what Marx and Engels also realized), the constitutive materials of national identity also preceded the economic. Engels had lamented – in a quote that is shared twice in Part I of the text and numerous times across Cedric's other writings and lecture notes – that "Marx and I are partly to blame for the fact that the younger people sometimes lay more stress on the economic side than is due to it."[28]

The overemphasis on rationality and scientific method imperiled later theorists of historical materialism and their ability to understand the meaning of the conscious activity of the proletariat as well as the peasantry, the folk revolutionaries who required no vanguard. In this instance, Cedric was continuing an analysis of the imposition of rationality through the figure of the leader – the project taken up in *The Terms of Order*. Though that text rarely engaged Marxist thought specifically, it might be usefully read alongside *Black Marxism*. For leadership, like the socialist legend concocted by Marxian historiography, also appropriated, misused, and in some cases ignored the very "moral and architectonic traditions" that had produced the ethical systems of the ancient world and early Christianity.[29] The Enlightenment rationality of the French Revolution and the mechanization of the Industrial Revolution became the new grounds from which to create a socialist tradition. So racialism necessarily penetrated it. It was "racial ordering" that had made possible that historical moment – a modern world generated upon the beliefs in rationalism and science that Cedric characterizes as "the unhappy legacies" of western civilization.[30] A true socialist movement would have to reckon with "ideational systems indigenous to those peoples exploited by the world market" and not simply with their objective condition.[31]

For those "objective" processes unfolding in European society were world historical, but they were not *the* world. The theories of evolution and change they generated were critical, but they would never be complete. In this first part of *Black Marxism*, Cedric intended to show that Europe's very formation was racial. It was a formation that insinuated itself into the economic and political, but also the intellectual and ideational. That formation, he argued, if we are not careful, could occlude that there were other ways of being. It was these other ways which would end up in a critical confrontation with the European legacy of rationalism, a legacy that manifested in the nation-state's concomitant: colonialism.

We will be Black

Conceptions of modernity rendered Blackness as lack, as nothingness. But there was a something beyond the time of capitalist exploitation, a something Cedric would name the "Black Radical tradition." It is in Part II where that tradition is elaborated and extended. It is here where its history becomes the basis for theorizing one form in which revolutions that opposed capitalist exploitation were realized. But that tradition remained concealed, hidden from view in western conceptions of time, of meaning. A companion to the political and economic features of racial capitalism, the denial of any coherent intellectual tradition among the African (and the Indigenous for that matter) pervaded all western philosophical systems. Such ideas were "inspired or at least influenced by the ideological requirement that modern Western thought obliterate the African." But, as Vincent Harding once wrote, "there was a river." And that river was Black struggle, a tradition of resistance.[32]

> The makings of an essentially African response, strewn across the physical and temporal terrain of societies conceived in western civilization, have been too infrequently distinguished. Only over time has the setting for these events been integrated into the tradition. The social cauldron of Black Radicalism is western society. Western society, however, has been its location and its objective condition but not – except in a most perverse fashion – its specific inspiration. Black Radicalism is

a negation of western civilization but not in the direct sense of a simple dialectical delegation. It is certain that the evolving tradition of Black Radicalism owes its peculiar moment to the historical interdiction of African life by European agents. This experience, though, was merely the condition for Black Radicalism – its immediate reason and object for being – but not the foundation for its nature or character.[33]

In offering that "black radicalism, consequently, cannot be understood within the particular context of its genesis," Cedric quotes Walter Rodney's *History of the Upper Guinea Coast* where he stated that "the essential oneness of African culture" served as a "shield which frustrated the efforts of Europeans to dehumanize" the African.[34]

Cedric's idea of a "specifically African response to an oppression emergent" from European social and economic order has been reduced to an endorsement of essentialism.[35] Yet what he is after is not a simple idea of African sameness across time and space. He was instead opening the door for people to reject the Hegelian notion that Africa and Africans constituted "no historical part of the World."[36] The prevailing philosophies of histories it inspired were inadequate, not only for framing histories of that part of the world that experienced slavery and Black resistance but for understanding histories of *the world*. What was "essential" in Cedric's argument is that enslaved Africans resisted rather than became empty vessels of European conquest. The oneness that Rodney evokes was in African struggles to *be one* against European order. To be one for another. African cultural traditions prepared them for *that* struggle; they were the basis for not only the manifestation of struggles for resistance, but for their ethical and moral content. These obviously took on different forms and different improvisations because the Black Radical tradition was constituted by the many ways of being one. And as an intellectual project, revealing the nature of Black radicalism could be seen as less a correction of Hegel than a rejection of the very ideational systems that produced Hegelian philosophies of history.

That this was not obvious to American social thinkers in particular was by design. They could not afford for it to be. Cedric explains how Hegel's ideas suffused American thought and the stakes involved before walking through how Africa was "transmuted" in the life of the western mind. When we think of this process as occurring over a thousand years, we realize that Hegel was relatively late to the party.[37] For it was in the very formation of Europe and its engagement with Islam that we begin to see a momentous shift. In tracing that change, Cedric takes us through the ancient period where Africans engaged Greco-Roman culture, the medieval period where we see the emergence of African Muslims in various parts of the eventually European world, and then from here to the development of Portugal. A nation that Cedric described as less a nation and more "a metaphor," Portugal was a "deceptive categorical referent" signifying the "mixture of political and economic forces" that were instrumental in transforming "African labor into capital."[38]

All of this was a preview and context for the "Columbian exchange" that created the New World.[39] Cedric focuses on Christopher Columbus to truly illuminate the link between the history of capitalism – in the Italian merchants, the finance capitalists of the era – and the Age of Exploration that marked the beginning of African slavery in the western hemisphere. The competing rationales and rivalries of Portuguese and Spanish monarchies, driven sometimes by religious zeal and at others by greed, met with the financial markets of the Italian city-states, and almost naturally transitioned to the use of enslaved Africans in the New World – they were both "infidels" and a ready-made supply of cheap labor.[40] Their enslavement was already being practiced in the Azores, Madeira, and Cape Verde, among other destinations off the coast of Africa and Europe. Here, Cedric directly links to the work of Oliver Cox and his critical studies of early capitalism, where he had argued that Venetian traders had "first capitalistically organized commerce in human beings."[41] And if that was true, an African presence in the form of unfree labor was there at the very beginning of the capitalist world-system. Cox was among the Black radicals who understood the world-system from his position as an "outsider" to the dominant histories and legends of western historiography.[42] Writing on the contributions of Cox's trilogy on capitalism seven years later, Cedric argued that his "subterranean" history of the development of the West simultaneously adopted the premises of the "myth of Venice" and demonstrated that the early capitalist formation it set in motion was permeated by racial order.[43]

Then there was the role played by Great Britain, the latecomer to the western orgy of plunder. Its lateness had no bearing on the virulence through which it practiced the violence of the trade. Its impact was devastating. As a historian, Eric Williams was one of its most perceptive witnesses. In his *Capitalism and Slavery*, he demonstrated the relationships between merchant capitalism and the development of British industrial society. But such a connection was then and continues to be too much for disciplinary history. In a 1987 article for *History Workshop Journal*, Cedric maintained that "Williams struck a vital nerve at the ideological core of western historiography."[44] Walking through the contexts of the largely puerile academic attacks on *Capitalism and Slavery*'s basic thesis, he argued that bourgeois historians required "an acceptable discursive reality for a world-system in which the relationship between the western metropoles and non-western peoples is one of continuing and deepening exploitation."[45] That this exploitation is rooted in the historical theft of enslaved labor is more an ideological question than a numbers game. Yet the numbers are there and striking. So much so that many have even viewed British involvement as synonymous with the trade itself. But their participation was indeed only a part of a world-system.[46]

As that system penetrated the western hemisphere, it produced a philosophical discourse and a political-economic project that led ultimately to African slavery and modern capitalism. But, as indicated above, it was the setting of another sort of exchange and encounter – "a consequence entirely unintended and unanticipated."[47] Cedric asserted that it was not simply as chattel that the African entered this space. These "cargoes of laborers also contained African cultures, critical mixes and admixtures of language and thought, of cosmology and metaphysics, of habits, beliefs, and morality. These were the actual terms of their humanity." As was his wont, Cedric quoted from Amilcar Cabral yet again to emphasize that these terms were also "the seed of opposition." He continued, arguing that the transfer of Africans to the plantations of the Caribbean and Americas "meant also the transfer of African ontological and cosmological systems; African presumptions of the organization and significance of social structure; African codes embodying historical consciousness and social experience; and African ideological and behavioral constructions for the resolution of the inevitable conflict between the actual and the normative."[48] It would not be enough to state that Africans resisted. And it would not be enough to declare that they were in fact humans. Specifying that such work had already been accomplished in the field of history by Black thinkers like John W. Blassingame and Leslie Howard Owens, Cedric argued that the more "authentic question" was "just what *sort* of people they were . . . and could be."[49]

This was the point of departure of the critical sixth

chapter, "A Historical Archaeology of Black Radicalism." It is a rejoinder to the world-systems theorists who had not fully revealed the terms of the consciousness of the Black laboring classes throughout the history of capitalism. It is a reaching back to the elements of Black social consciousness that were explicitly denied within "the political," and denied as even a possibility in political theory. It is a theorization of and thinking with Black struggle that more solidly connected Cedric's familial and communal groundings to the organizing and activism of his earlier life. The making of the Black Radical tradition was new language for seeing oneself, for realizing ourselves. And it did not require European interpreters. It made manifest a practice Ngugi wa Thiong'o later termed "re-membering."[50]

So Cedric's is not the project of a historian. Where most historians pursued knowledge of the past to scaffold national myths of progress, to place the "erased" within national frames, Cedric's work was archaeological. If it addressed erasure, it was also about what Nahum Dimitri Chandler means by "desedimentation": "A tracking of the problem of the Negro for thought exposes then the fault lines within the layers of sedimentations that have gradually gathered as the very historicity of modern thought."[51] Those fault lines, of course, become for Cedric the mythologies structuring the idea of Europe, the idea of nation. Black life was buried so that a mythos of Black inferiority, "the Negro," could be imposed. This construct "suggested no situatedness in time, that is history, or space, that is ethno- or politico-geography ... no civilization, no cultures, no religion, no history, no place, and finally no humanity that might command consideration."[52] *Black Marxism* then can be understood, as Elizabeth has described, as a project of "uncovering the erased" – an "archaeological task" that simultaneously recovered ancestral names while desedimenting the terms under which the Negro was substituted for human.[53] It "set loose new soil," preparing the way for "new thinking."[54]

It was the making of the Black Radical tradition as intellectual task. It restored the Africans to their time and space. And from these terms the meaning of their resistance to western time and space could be gleaned. It began in the sixteenth century with Nueva España and the resistance of Black communities of fugitives in San Lorenzo de los Negros. From there, Cedric traced the phenomenon of *marronage* across the Spanish settler colonies as well as those of Brazil, with a focus on the formation of Palmares. These *palenques* and *quilombos*, as these communities were called, were originary articulations of Black radicalism.[55] Cedric would later assert that in his research in the archives, this encounter was consistent. Although the derisive term for "runaway," *cimarrones*, came from the Spanish, the principle, or what Cedric calls "the first impulse" of Africans, was the same whether they were enslaved in Spanish, Portuguese, Dutch, and later French and British colonies.[56]

So he followed the maroons. To Jamaica. To Suriname. To British North America. And to Saint Domingue – a place which by the turn of the nineteenth century confirmed that *marronage* would now be more than disengagement and retreat. The entire colony would have to be liberated, consecrated as maroon space. In his 1980 talk which rehearsed many of the themes of these chapters at the "Race, Class, and State" conference in Brighton (later published in *Race and Class* as "Coming to Terms: The Dialectics of Third World Liberation"), Cedric had argued that the nineteenth century was "the century of the modern world's adolescence," and thus an important time period in which to understand the spontaneity of Black revolution.[57] With the increased rationalization of the modern world-system, its extension and expansion, the enslaved moved toward a "more direct confrontation with European domination."[58] Yet these were revolutions inspired by the maroon imperative to "recreate their African homelands." Such were the African impulses that helped create the "republic" of Haiti.[59] Revolutions in other parts of the New World would follow – South Carolina, Bahia, Barbados, and the 1831 rebellion in Jamaica. They were inspired by the desire to be free, strengthened by a sense of order, a charismatic expectation that African life was worthy of being protected and honored.

All of these risings were connected to the shifting economic situation on the ground that would eventually lead to the erosion of slavery. Black self-activity created new republics, hastened abolition and emancipation but, above all, it forced the world to take notice that African enslavement would not be a permanent form of exploitative capitalism. Cedric argued that "whatever the forms primitive accumulation assumed, its social harvest would also include acts of resistance, rebellion, and, ultimately, revolution."[60] But the end of the nineteenth century "marked the beginnings of a profound reorganization of the capitalist world system. In Europe, Africa, Asia, and the Americas, through the deepening penetrations of monopoly capitalism and the impositions of hegemonic colonialisms, slaves were displaced as a source of cheap labor power by peasants and migrant laborers."[61] As this colonial shift took hold of the continent of Africa itself, the Black Radical tradition as both *marronage* and outright revolt would find itself in opposition to the afterlives of slavery. The historical archaeology closes where Cedric often began – in Africa, where the achievement of resistance based "on the African identities of its peoples" served as a native critique of the development of imperialism.[62]

In an important chapter, which closes Part II, Cedric offered a reflection of the *meaning* of that resistance, what he described as its "nature." Surprisingly to many observers,

Black resistance did not produce the response they deemed appropriate. There was an "absence of mass violence." But for Cedric, the Black Radical tradition was not animated by the ideal of vengeance or retaliation. Resistance was not simply an attack on an external subject but was generated by an internal desire: "The renunciation of actual being for historical being; the preservation of the ontological totality granted by a metaphysical system that had never allowed for property in either the physical, philosophical, temporal, legal, social, or psychic senses."[63] The "social formations of capitalist slavery or the relations of production of colonialism" did not define the whole historical experience of Black people. Though it could never totally ignore the material reality, the Black Radical tradition granted supremacy to the metaphysical. African people saw the world in broader terms than what could be seen, gathered through the sense of eyesight. And this kind of seeing is what informed "revolutionary self-activity." So when it came to questions of liberation, African people chose to "make history in their own terms": "They lived on their terms, they died on their terms, they obtained their freedom on their terms. Thus it was with *obeah*men and *obeah*women, and *papaloi*. These were the terms that these African peasants and farmers brought with them to their captivity. They were also the only terms in which their freedom could be acquired."[64]

This was the nature of the Black Radical tradition. Its making was in the long struggle to achieve liberation against the earliest instantiations of capitalist development. The "obligation to preserve the collective being, the ontological totality" was its aim.[65] To live again is its promise.

Though many leftists confuse the metaphysical as inherently anti-materialistic, it is crucial to remember that Cedric's emphasis and life's work never reduced the material conditions of life to the dustbin.[66] Whether it was his own

life's circumstances or the lives of the children he met outside Mexico City, the workers in Tshabalala, the people of
Ife, or his people in West Oakland, these realities constantly
confronted him. They showed up in real ways. But that also
allowed him to see them as whole people, with histories *and*
legends – people who realized life within a spiritual universe.
His thinking with activists on the London scene, then, is
also important here. In the previously mentioned *Emergency*
article which excerpted parts of chapter 6 of *Black Marxism*,
Cedric closed by speaking to the relationship between the
Black Radical tradition and current struggles to transform
material reality:

> At the core, in the metropolitan societies, we must repli-
> cate the social forces which are being assembled by Black
> peoples elsewhere. Indeed, this is a minimum political ini-
> tiative. Every conscious effort must be made to construct a
> Black liberation movement which marshals the maximum
> of the human resource contained in our communities. This
> means a cultural movement which transcends mere politi-
> cal objectives. We will be Black not because we are not
> white, but because of our history and the achievements of
> our struggle. Our ideologues and intellectuals must follow
> us into this new universe of work and thought. They must
> be disciplined in new ways so that they may strengthen our
> articulation in the political struggle against racist States and
> the systemic discriminations we oppose in our jobs, in hous-
> ing our communities, and in educating our children. We
> must forge our organizations into political steel with the
> capacities for breaching national boundaries and forming
> alliances with international organizations and multinational
> volunteer agencies alike. We must not fail. We cannot con-
> cede. We must succeed for ourselves and for all those others
> who are threatened.[67]

Truer genius

Because of its title, many assume *Black Marxism* is a book about Black people who were Marxists. Indeed, in early outlines for the volume, there was ample space given to the history of the Black left and the travails of organizing in the era of Bolshevik revolution and subsequent rise of European fascism.[68] But in its final iteration, these questions were reserved for the last section of the text, "Black Radicalism and Marxist Theory." It is a section that could easily have been a stand-alone book. Yet it is important to understand the treatment of Black theorists of Marxist thought alongside the historical archaeology of the Black Radical tradition. For Cedric, the two were not synonymous.

The objective of Part III was to explain how largely bourgeois Black intellectuals came to confront or identify the Black Radical tradition in the twentieth century. The one-hundred year increments that marked centuries were arbitrary signifiers of meaning, but the post-slavery world produced a class, an intelligentsia, that would come to confront the evolution of racial capitalism that was occasioned by colonialism and the industrial order. In making sense of that world, some members of this Black petit bourgeoisie became "renegades" who broke from their expected role in that order. Their stories often included an embrace of western radicalism.

Because their models of engaging with radical ideas have been attractive to subsequent members of this class, these earlier exemplars have achieved a kind of exalted status in radical circles today. These assumptions have guided how they are read and understood in Cedric's work. But twenty years after he had made this point clearly in the foreword to the text, Robin D. G. Kelley found himself again insisting that the point of Cedric's engagement was not to generate "a list" of Black radicals.[69] As many continue to focus on who was excluded from this section, it is necessary to assert that Cedric intended to explore the particular ways in which this "Black Radical intelligentsia" discovered the deeper registers of Black radicalism "all around them," rather than "enshrine" them for inclusion in some sort of Black radical hall of fame.[70]

The trio of thinkers that became the basis of this part of the book consisted of W. E. B. Du Bois, C. L. R. James, and Richard Wright. While earlier plans had included Oliver Cox and Eric Williams, the exemplar that best illustrated the kind of critique Cedric wanted to highlight was Amilcar Cabral. But the reason there is no chapter on Cabral was because he had intended a separate volume which specifically focused on continental Africa, the subject of his research fellowship.[71]

Given that women like Dona Beatriz appeared prominently in Cedric's teaching at this juncture, it is likely that she and other Black radical women – at work on the continent as both examples of everyday resistance and creators of radical theory – would have made an appearance in this volume.[72] The most ardent critique of Part III has been around their absence. Indeed, if one were to read the work as if it were *the* text on Black radicalism, it is easy to see how one might come to the conclusion that there were "no Black radical women."[73] Not only was Cedric's trio composed of men, there was little in the way of citation that indicated that this intelligentsia included women.

Yet the idea that this enunciation of the Black Radical tradition was "masculinist" must take into consideration that Cedric's account of the tradition incorporated the presence of Black women in the stories of on-the-ground resistance. Addressing this question years later, H. L. T. Quan, after interviewing Cedric, argued that the ways in which women animated Black radicalism was through their constitution of "Black communities" rather than through narratives of "individual achievement." The latter, of course, would appear once the Black Radical tradition was foregrounded: "women are not only merely the architects but also constitute the architecture itself of that radical tradition."[74] Yet it is provocative to speculate, as Carole Boyce Davies has, how the text might have been transformed with a chapter on Black women radical intellectuals like Claudia Jones.[75] Given the communities they belonged to during their stays in England, it is difficult to imagine that he never once confronted her work. But, like Jones, his emphasis was always on the masses of the unnamed, the force through which they created spaces for freedom.

An analysis of gendered oppressions does show up in later texts. As Quan writes, Cedric saw *Black Marxism* as having no ending, no final say.[76] In both *Black Movements in America* and *An Anthropology of Marxism*, he extends his thinking to these domains. And in an interview in 2013, Cedric imagined how *Black Marxism* might have been transformed by such an analysis:

> Another area that I'm currently fascinated with is the intersection of gender and Black Studies. I think I would've written some things differently in *Black Marxism* if I had been more aware. Jennifer Morgan's *Laboring Women* is a brilliant intervention . . . to encounter plantations in Barbados that are all female and to begin to transfer our sense of the fundamental economy of slave production and how African and Black women were involved in it . . . I allude to them in my description of the nanny towns in Jamaica, but there's so much more to discuss.[77]

Part III was premised on the idea that the role of the renegade intelligentsia – both men and women – was not to lead but to comprehend, to theorize, to think through the ongoing radical struggles. Throughout his oeuvre, Cedric would argue that revolutions were spontaneous. They did not require a vanguard or an elite for direction. In fact, it was the intellectuals who trailed behind. In "Coming to Terms," he put it succinctly:

> organisation and ideas come out not from the leadership but from the masses. Organisation and idea. Now, this is essentially the position of people like [C. L. R.] James and [Wilhelm] Reich, who argued that it is inappropriate for an elite to emerge with a sense of what organisations are required, what structures are required and then begin to influence or to impose this notion on a following, on a collectivity.[78]

They were not the leaders. But they did have unique skills. Cedric writes that: "Among the vitalizing tools of the radical intelligentsia, of course the most crucial was words. Words were their means of placement and signification, the implements for discovery and revelation to come to an understanding and appreciation of the Black Radical tradition."[79] Again, they did not create that tradition. They could not. And they *alone* could not fully constitute it. Still, the "formation of the intelligentsia" was unexpected and met with repression. In addressing themselves to the worlds of oppression, of which their harassment and vilification was concomitant, they would reveal that it was within the cultures of resistance – where "the struggle was more than words, but life itself" – where the "truer genius" resided. Any genius that they were to possess as a consequence was "derivative."[80]

Choose wisely

At the 1963 March on Washington, Roy Wilkins, the leader of the National Association for the Advancement of Colored People (NAACP), informed those gathered that W. E. B. Du Bois had made his transition. And then damned him with faint praise: "Regardless of the fact that in his later years Dr Du Bois chose another path, it is incontrovertible that at the dawn of the twentieth century his was the voice that was calling to you to gather here today in this cause."[81] If Cedric had heard them, he likely would not have been surprised that Wilkins chose these words. As a former student leader in the NAACP, he had clashed with its national headquarters. More importantly, Wilkins's sentiments represented the beginning of a general disavowal of Du Bois's work which would take place over the ensuing years. Thankfully, Martin Luther King, as well as others active in the Black freedom struggle in the sixties and early seventies, refused to participate in that silencing. So too did members of the Communist Party USA. But it would take another generation before Du Bois's ideas would become acceptable within the academy. And then not fully so and "with caution and trepidation." But by that time *Black Marxism* had long been out of print.[82]

While at Binghamton, Cedric had begun to think about Du Bois beyond the perfunctory evocations of *The Souls of Black Folk*. He turned to works like *Black Reconstruction in America*, Du Bois's 1935 historical text, which had appeared in Black radical reading lists dating back to the early sixties, but which Cedric believed was rarely actually read.[83] The result was a long essay written in 1975 entitled "Marxist Theory and the Black Savage: Du Bois's Critique in *Black Reconstruction*." Presented the next year at the New York Critical Issues in Afro-American Studies Conference, it was one of the earliest drafts of any of the material that would become part of *Black Marxism*. Over the course of sixty manuscript pages, Cedric develops the argument that would be later refined as its ninth chapter, "Historiography and the Black Radical Tradition." Some of his handling of the historical context of Black radical critics of the myth of the Negro did not make the cut. Neither did the full discussion on questions of Marxist conceptualizations of the peasantry and a section on the reception of the text. But the basic thrust of the argument was fully formed in 1975. Though he struggled to find a publisher for the article in this form, a shortened version, comprised of the sections on Du Bois's reading of the links between slavery and American political economy, did find a ready audience in a 1977 issue of *The Black Scholar*.[84]

The concern of the chapter was a question that had somewhat quietly been present in Cedric's thinking throughout the 1970s: the nature of Black radical historiography. Placing him within a context where Black history became the simple assertion of humanity against "the national myth" of the Negro as part of a middle-class politics of respectability, he showed how Du Bois rejected elite prerogatives concerning representation.[85] Struggles within and external to the movements to which he belonged forced him to conclude that history could not be a project of race vindication, it had to be premised on "the relations of things."[86] Cedric described Du Boisian radical historiography as a "theory of history, which by its emphasis on mass action was both a critique of the ideologies of American socialist movements and a revision of Marx's theory of revolution and class struggle."[87] It was not to be an academic project. And in a moment where the Great Depression had forced a younger crop of Black radical intellectuals to emphasize class over racialism, Du Bois would show how in order to fully reckon with the history of class struggle in the United States, the history of Black self-activity that emerged in the wake of the United States Civil War and era of Reconstruction needed to be understood. It was a journey that took place in the midst of what Cedric called a "fearsome maelstrom."[88]

Among the major insights gleaned from Du Bois's 729-page tome was the centrality of slavery to the development of capitalism and how that phenomenon affected labor struggles in the United States, the relationship of the slavocracy to political power, and how that shifted with the emergence of a Black political elite during Reconstruction. In so doing, Du Bois applied Marxist insights about Black labor and historical materialism while refusing the orthodoxy that emerged in the context of early twentieth-century organized Marxism. Cedric walked through the evolution of that tradition – through the impact of Bolshevism on American communism to the organizing of Black radicals within the African Blood Brotherhood and finally to Black radicals who had organized within the Communist International – to reveal Du Bois's contribution: the meaning of class struggle in an American context could not proceed along the basis of orthodox Marxist-Leninism. Of the orthodoxies necessary to understanding not just American but global class struggle, Cedric writes that:

> Du Bois would insist on the world-historical significance of American slavery in the emergence of modern capitalism and imperialism. In this, he went no further than Marx, but this is merely where he began. Next, he would demonstrate, historically, the revolutionary force of slave and peasant laborers – this is in proposition to a reactionary industrial working class. Finally, with Lenin in mind, Du Bois would question the presumed roles of a vanguard and the masses in the development of revolutionary consciousness and effective revolutionary action.[89]

Black Reconstruction announced the global meaning of American slavery in the modern world-system. It revealed the competing goals of American labor in black and white – the latter of which was animated by what Du Bois called the American Assumption.[90] And the former by the "coming of the Lord," a consciousness that emerged from "whimsy and parable, veiled wish and wisdom" where "right and wrong, vengeance and love . . . sweet Beauty and Truth" created the General Strike.[91] These elements of consciousness, rooted in the historical and social conditions of African life, are what produced the all-important Black movement that changed the course of the Civil War. For Cedric, "revolution had caused the formation of revolutionary consciousness and had not been caused by it. The revolution was spontaneous." In writing (and righting) the history of the Black worker, Du Bois had discovered for himself "the hidden specter of Black revolutionists."[92] In a conclusion which only appeared in this final version of this treatment of Du Bois, Cedric argued that this hidden specter was "an antilogic to racism, slavery, and capitalism" that was initiated from a revolutionary consciousness that was "remote" from the expectations of a "proletarian consciousness" that had defined "Marx's theory of revolution."[93]

In the closing sections of the chapter on Du Bois, Cedric detailed the distinctions between peasant-based struggles of the Russian Revolution and those of the United States South. It was a question that had concerned him since the early 1970s. In a series of letters to Cedric, C. L. R. James reflected on Lenin's views of the peasantry and revolution.[94] James was an appropriate interlocutor. It was after reading Leon Trotsky's *History of the Russian Revolution* that he was drawn into the orbit of western radicalism, becoming one of the most creative thinkers in the Black engagement with Marxist theory. So Cedric's chapter on James was framed around two of the critical texts to come from that engagement: *The Black Jacobins* and *Notes on Dialectics*.

Cedric proceeded by documenting the contexts surrounding James's emergence in post-emancipation Trinidad. The colony, buoyed by the continued exploitation of labor and the importation of migrant labors from other parts of the British Empire, was also home to a coteric of "self-made" Trinidadians. This middle-class community defined itself against the cultural traditions of the people. As Anglophiles, they were oriented toward English culture but they also began to struggle toward self-government. This was the class to which James belonged. But as Cedric would write, the "Black Victorian" became a "Black Jacobin."[95]

The sport of cricket inculcated a classed and racialized system. Through that system, James found himself embroiled in the politics of the sport. And in the early 1930s he moved to England to write on Learie Constantine, one of the sport's stars.[96] While there, he would encounter English radicalism, and it immediately thrust him into an understanding of colonial contexts of life in Trinidad, of working-class struggles there, and led him to a confrontation with his own middle-class upbringing. Among the questions facing a class of Black radicals in Britain – which included the father of the Robinsons' friend, Nigerian-born Edward Sankey – was the freedom and flexibility to practice an "anti-imperialist" politics from the metropole. For Ras Makonnen and the intelligentsia for which he played a critical role, London was a draw because it was only there where he could actually develop radical platforms, such as his publishing ventures. Such an enterprise in the colonial outposts would have been immediately destroyed. So from this center of action, the fight for Black liberation back home could be more effectively organized.[97]

Living in Nelson, Lancashire, James would experience

that action differently. But when the fascist rise of Italy and its aggression toward Ethiopia became a cause célèbre for Africans around the world (which contrasted starkly with the indifference of the radical movements of Europe and their priorities), James joined the Pan-Africanist struggle. Organizing alongside his childhood friend George Padmore, Amy Ashwood Garvey, and others, James volunteered to fight to defend Africa. It was this shift that contextualizes the development of what Cedric called his "theory of the Black Jacobin."[98]

The Black Jacobins was a history of the Haitian Revolution, but it was also an attempt for James to locate a revolutionary "example to study."[99] For what was needed was a historical example of proletarian struggle that addressed racial exploitation as it dealt with the question of colonial imposition as consequential to class struggle. He would famously write that "the race question is subsidiary to the class question," but to "neglect the racial factor as merely incidental [w]as an error only less grave than to make it fundamental."[100] In the *bossales* of St Domingue, he found a proletariat that was deeply significant, if not world-historical, but was nevertheless not the traditional Marxian proletariat. Perhaps it should have been.

And though much of the story focused on that question through the figure of Toussaint L'Ouverture, Cedric showed that James's work also revealed something else about the revolution. The mass action which Toussaint could not "create" was inspired by African spirituality: "Voodoo was the medium of the conspiracy."[101] It was that sensibility which inspired the belief that victory was possible. Cruelty was not its aim: "The cruelties of property and privilege are always more ferocious than the revenges of poverty and oppression. For the one aims at perpetuating resented injustice, the other is merely a momentary passion soon appeased."[102] In his application of Marxist theory to the Haitian Revolution, Cedric read an implicit meaning of James's historical work: Toussaint was not the source nor the inspiration of the revolution; no "leader" could be. And as the revolution unfolded, it would be Toussaint's inability to represent their wishes and dreams of liberation that led to his demise. Cedric remarked that, in Toussaint, James saw himself. It would cause him to question for his own time the role of the intelligentsia and affirm that the "revolutionary masses must preserve to themselves the direction of the revolutionary movement."[103]

In a 1971 talk at the Institute of the Black World, James spoke to this question, stating that if he were to write it again, *The Black Jacobins* would encompass the many Toussaints, the "two thousand leaders" General Leclerc feared would follow him after Toussaint was sent to die in the French mountains.[104] Speaking before the group of Black Studies scholars, James remarked: "Now, if I were writing this book today, having begun with more concrete detail about the mass of the population, by the time I reach here that would be no footnote, it would be a part of the work itself."[105] Echoing Toussaint's own final warning that he was only the trunk, that the revolution had deeper roots, James declared: "That is the book I would write. There are two thousand leaders to be taken away. If I were writing this book again, I would have something to say about those two thousand leaders. I have mentioned a few here and there, but I didn't do it with that in mind."[106] James, through his witnessing of the insurgent movements of the fifties and sixties, had come to understand that Black radicalism required a different conception of revolutionary leadership.

Cedric understood James's *Notes on Dialectics* as an attempt to come to terms with other aspects of the Marxist tradition. It was a work that was spawned by the debates of Trotskyists in the United States over the question of the labor movement, the state, and revolutionary struggle.[107] But its "grammar" was Hegel's dialectic.[108] And it traced the history of the class struggle to the English and French Revolutions. Cedric argued that the work, though limited to European theaters of struggle, ultimately freed James to argue that ongoing revolutionary struggles within organized Marxism could no longer be beholden to the professional revolutionists: "The proletariat will decide."[109] Such a conclusion of course had obvious implications for the struggles taking place in the postwar world in which it was written, as well as in the neoliberal world in which Cedric was writing. And our world, too.

Finally, there was Richard Wright. As with Du Bois, Cedric had written a series of earlier treatments of Wright, including a conference talk at the African Studies Association – a place where one rarely if ever encountered him.[110] Earlier forms of the chapter that would become "Richard Wright and the Critique of Class Theory" first appeared in a 1978 article in *Race and Class*. "The Emergent Marxism of Richard Wright's Ideology" issued from the premise that Black artists and writers had been the ones to break free from the liberal orthodoxy that had held hegemonic status in postwar social science. In a period where radical social scientists had been muted, it was the writers who "as social analysts *and* propagandists" became the "most important spokesmen of the Black intelligentsia":

> Richard Wright, Ralph Ellison, Margaret Walker, Chester Himes, Ann Petry, William Gardner Smith and James Baldwin, to name the more prominent. It is they who brought Black consciousness of racism and capitalism to the fore. In their work are declarations of the terms upon which liberation is to be achieved; the nature of American society, and the critical sensibilities of survival. We turn to them to

rediscover the dreams, frustrations, and most importantly the social history of the post-War period.[111]

The novel was a way of knowing.[112] Cedric cautioned the reader to avoid the ruse of seeing it *only* as a literary phenomenon. Richard Wright's work was more significant than how it had been understood by those critics who subordinated it to questions of the alienation of a writer. It had the advantage of producing a social history that was more effective than social commentary or social science. His background, both as a child born into the peasantry of Mississippi and as a cadre within the Communist Party, had provided him with perceptive insight.

In this initial foray, Cedric examines the achievements of Wright's *Native Son*. These were to his mind an intervention into the vexing questions of the nature of the proletariat, of the "necessity for understanding the working classes on their own terms." The Black masses in Mississippi, Arkansas, and in Chicago first needed to "reproduce themselves spiritually and culturally" if they were to "fulfill the historical role that Marxian theory assigned them."[113] This question of consciousness was not a "mechanistic reflex." And it did not emerge in the rigid terms then available to the social scientist. Working-class Black folk were capacious. Wright and the other writers were able to represent the "range of contradictions which have made up Black consciousness" because it existed in a realm that Du Bois had once called "something Incalculable."[114] Bigger Thomas was nothing if not evidence of that range, of that which was "Incalculable."

In the fall of 1978, Cedric returned to Ann Arbor to give a presentation on Wright that would become the second evolution of the book chapter, a piece that was eventually published in *Race and Class* in 1980.[115] In a series of offhand comments during the lecture, Cedric again insisted on thinking beyond the conventions of literary criticism, asserting that we "understand that we're dealing with a real political situation when we're talking about Richard Wright ... publishing in this country has never been an innocent venture." Wright's self-imposed exile was routinely monitored by the forces of the American state, which intended to vilify and repress those elements of the expatriate community that criticized US domestic and foreign policy. Wright's career as a radical writer, then, can be understood within these Cold War contexts. His revival, as Cedric stated in this lecture, was simply a feature of the contradictions of American capitalism. The movements he predicted in his work created an "irresistible market" for their republication in the 1960s. What was left to do was to think with them.[116]

In its final form, the chapter that appeared in *Black Marxism* proceeds from a discussion of "Blueprint for Negro Writing," the 1937 essay that Wright wrote for *New Challenge*. It was an essay that, Cedric claimed, possessed ideas that had gotten him "disciplined" by the party.[117] For one of its ultimate claims was that there was indeed a perspective that connected the struggle of his people to an objective of the Black writer to "create values by which his race was to struggle, live, and die."[118] That perspective, those values, often lay beyond "what his experience of western radicalism and activism could encompass." Though he had written that the earlier party's vision of the unity of Black and White workers in the United States was a hopeful one, he would spend the remainder of his life thinking the nature of how these processes impacted life in the Third World.[119] In his introduction to the republication of *White Man, Listen*, Cedric would later write that the complex of writings and concerns that would characterize this period of his life produced a critique of the postwar era that implicated "an alternative historical agency, an alternative signification of liberation, an alternative reconstruction of modern history, an alternative epistemology of human desire."[120]

Wright would leave the party soon after the publication of *Native Son*, but he never abandoned Marxist social theory. One of the contradictions that had always concerned Cedric was the party's successes and failures to organize Black Southerners, a failure related to its sense of party discipline.[121] So Wright's abandonment of the party may have been due more to internal party politics than to the Marxist ideology it represented. With reference to Wright, Cedric asserted:

> Marxism was (and remains) a superior grammar for synthesizing the degradation of labor with the growing destabilization of capitalist production and accelerating technological development; the increasing resort to state coercion mediated by bureaucratic rationalism; and the strangulation of whole regions (most of them formerly colonies) through pricing mechanisms, market manipulation, monopolization of advanced technology, the international organization of production, international banking, military assistance, and the stultifying dependencies of monocultural economics.[122]

Wright found this grammar useful. But organizing the Black proletariat also required other recognitions. As Wright asserted in "Blueprint for Negro Writing," "Marxism is but the starting point. No theory of life can take the place of life."[123] The recreation of Black life, the reproduction of those values which animated it, would have to proceed from other bases. For Cedric, "Wright came to terms with western thought and life through Black nationalism."[124]

Through his reading of *The Outsider*, Cedric traces the applications of this formation of nationalist consciousness.

If Wright believed that it was "a nationalism whose reason for being lies in the simple fact of self-possession and in the consciousness of the interdependence of people in modern society,"[125] the novel explored those questions against a backdrop of a critique of "the two ideological and philosophic traditions at the heart of modern western culture:" Christianity and Marxism.[126] By constructing a story through his protagonist Cross Damon's pursuit of liberation, Wright exposed the limitations of these western traditions in the pursuit of working-class unity thought to be the key to undoing the capitalist and imperialist world. In many ways, the work allegorizes Wright's own experience. Cedric concludes his analysis with these words: "From his experience in the American Communist Party, and from his reading of Marx, Wright had come to the conclusion that no people's liberation is the result of their abject surrender of critical judgment. Certainly it was not the prerogative of Black intellectuals to surrender the cultural heritage of their people: the emergent revolutionary consciousness of Black nationalism."[127]

Near the beginning of the chapter, Cedric cited Harold Cruse's dismissal of Wright's radical legacy and his doubtful connection to that revolutionary consciousness, ideologically or personally. At the talk in Michigan, Cruse can be heard interrupting Cedric's presentation several times, asking for clarity or correcting what he presumed to be a historical mistake. After all, Cruse had had the privilege of being there for some of the history that converged with Wright's radicalism. In one of their exchanges, the two discussed Marx's ideas about the appearances of classes and their negation. Citing *The Communist Manifesto* and *The Eighteenth Brumaire of Louis Bonaparte*, Cedric reviewed the idea that feudalism was negated by the appearance of the bourgeoisie and the assumed appearance of a class (the proletariat) that would serve as the negation of capitalism. As much of *Black Marxism* indicated, the nature of that revolutionary class was more a mystery than it was a logical progression of science and rational thought (which Cedric saw as a conceit).[128] For Wright, however, there was a latent hope that the "cunning of Reason"[129] would produce revolutionary national liberation movements of Black people, who, as the negation of capitalism, might construct a "universal consciousness."[130] As he wrote in *The Outsider*, the hope was that one day "they will be centers of knowing."[131]

This is where *Black Marxism* ended, but it was "an ending." H. L. T. Quan called it a "non-ending ending."[132] Years later, Cedric would famously assert that "it was never my intent to exhaust the subject."[133] In lieu of any kind of resolution, Cedric offered a sense of the stakes involved in reorienting how we perceive radical thought. As a tradition that had "not been conscious of itself as a tradition," it had the advantages of no sacred texts or leaders who had been exalted over the masses, no dogmatic theory to discipline movement. But the lack of awareness of that tradition had also had a disadvantage: "the fractioning of African people."

The world created by racial capitalism was and always remains in its final, violent clash. The clock of the modern world was and is still ticking down. Cedric believed that our lives were at stake. It is still true. But what was also true was that African peoples could play a role in forestalling disaster: "Physically and ideologically, and for rather unique historical reasons, African peoples bridge the decline of one world order and the eruption (we may surmise) of another. It is a frightful and uncertain space of being. If we are to survive, we must take nothing that is dead and choose wisely from among the dying."[134]

A Marxist ideology imbued with a "racialist order that

contaminates its analytic" could not be a total theory of liberation. The Black Radical tradition may not either. But as a people's cultural tradition, its elements suffused Black responses to oppressions across time and space, and for Cedric it provided Black liberation struggles with their own sense of "authority."[135] It was not up to "one people to be the solution or the problem." But a tradition formed in consequence of and in opposition to the very crystallization of the modern world was one "part of the solution." And in what was an important theme of all of his work, Cedric's non-ending proclaimed, "for now we must be as one."[136]

Published by Zed Press, a London-based independent publishing house founded by Roger Van Zwanenberg just six years earlier, *Black Marxism* has had an interesting ride as a text. Though it has been said that the reception of the book was not great, there were several reviews published in small radical journals in London and the Third World, including one by a comrade, Paul Gilroy. His colleagues at *Race and Class* commissioned an early review authored by Errol Lawrence.[137] In the United States, critical reception would take longer. Reviews in Du Bois's *Phylon* and the radical *Monthly Review* were penned by V. P. Franklin in 1986 and Cornel West in 1988, respectively.[138] They were not uncritical, but these reviews mostly spoke only to the ambition of the project and the avenues of inquiry it opened.

But for Cedric's former Binghamton colleague John McClendon, the text's impact and "penetration . . . cannot be measured" based only upon "book reviews in scholarly journals." He points to how *Black Marxism* cleared a space to engage radical thought that was attractive to Black Marxists and non-Marxists alike.[139] By the early 1990s, the book was hard to find. For those like Fred Moten in younger generations, the book "circulated underground, as a recurrent seismic event on the edge or over the edge of the university."[140] During that period, Cedric and Elizabeth attempted to get Zed Press to republish the text, largely so that students could have copies. But due to the press's financial predicament, those plans fell through.[141] By the end of the decade, plans resurfaced to get the book republished. Through the efforts of Robin D. G. Kelley, one of Cedric's advisees, the 2000 edition, published by University of North Carolina Press, has given *Black Marxism* a second life. It has come with costs. Among many, there is an almost comical uncritical endorsement and celebration of the text often sight-unseen. Sadly, the same is true of many critics who summarily reject it by cherry-picking those portions of the text that impugn their orthodoxies. Honest readings are rare. Yet when they do come, whatever limitations the book possesses become generative rather than restrictive. The point has always been to enlarge our horizons, to think differently. The most recent 2021 edition promises to continue that lesson.[142]

As he completed *Black Marxism*, Cedric was working on two additional projects that would have become his next books. The aforementioned manuscript on Black radicals in the English-speaking world, culminating in a treatment of Amilcar Cabral, was to follow along a similar trajectory as *Black Marxism*. Looking at the continent of Africa as the core of the tradition would have taken Cedric back to his earliest scholarly impulses, dating to his time in southern Africa. It was never completed, but we do have some indication of what he would have said in a book-length treatment of African resistance and Cabral. In 1981, Cedric published "Amilcar Cabral and the Dialectic of Imperialism" in the *Indian Political Science Review*. There, he reviewed the political history of national liberation struggle in the former Portuguese colonies, highlighting Cabral's understanding of liberation as "the complete destruction of foreign domination."[143] When those forms of domination issued from the sensibilities of his own class, Cabral's theory of revolution envisaged *its* destruction as well. The full "integration" of the petit bourgeoisie with the peasantry in a collective pursuit of cultural restoration and political autonomy constituted the Cabralism that so influenced revolutionary ideology in the seventies and eighties.[144]

The other planned book was a treatment of fascism. From the US national archives, Cedric had assiduously collected documents exploring the historical evolution of fascism in the 1920s and 1930s. In 1983, he published an article which argued that Italian fascism had been largely supported by significant elements of American industry among immigrant populations. It was, however, similarly opposed by the Black masses, who, having witnessed the occupation of Haiti and the incursion upon Liberia by the Firestone Company, were thus enraged at the Italian invasion of Ethiopia in 1935. Two years later, he reprised these ideas for *Race and Class* pointing to a Black Radical tradition among the African masses around the world which saw in fascism an occasion for resistance. He asserted that it was these Black masses, far more than the elite, who understood the racial foundations inhered in the logic of fascism.[145] In a surviving chapter of *The Black Response to Fascism*, Cedric traces the intra-European development of racism, much like in the first chapter of *Black Marxism*, arguing that "since the preponderance of western scholarship intercepts the genealogy of racism in the West with the 'appearances' of the Jews and Africans in late medieval European history, we are asked to presume that the earlier intra-European tribal predations had no cultural or ideological consequences."[146] The historical roots of fascism were those consequences. And a "Black response" – the response of those who would become "the preternatural sign of difference" – issued from a "privileged position from which to determine through their encounters with fascism whether it was emblematic, modular, or anomalous to the West."[147] Though the book was never published, Cedric spoke at the African Studies Association on the subject and asserted the conclusions of those in that position: "the West was pathological and fascism [was] an expression of that nature."[148]

In 1988, he was again encountering it directly. At the end of November, Cedric was part of a medical delegation led by Alice McGrath to Nicaragua. It was a country in the midst of a revolution that was strenuously opposed by the West. The United States government under Ronald Reagan had illegally financed its opposition with proceeds from weapons and drugs sales. Both Cedric and Elizabeth went (separately) to observe firsthand and offer solidarity with their struggle. In a letter to Paul Oquist, a scholar and government minister that he met in Managua, Cedric warned that the public scandal around Iran-Contra had only changed the tactics of United States policy. The opposition to the revolution had not lessened. He then offered that part of addressing the media bias around Nicaragua was to utilize universities as spaces where conferences and research might be conducted. He offered resources to support the cause from his position as the recently appointed chair of political science at UCSB.[149]

Whether it was Nicaragua, South Africa, Lebanon, or El Salvador, the concerns to which Cedric and Elizabeth addressed themselves were not wholly academic. Whether in taking trips to Central America, broadcasting alternative perspectives of the news, or organizing and attending political rallies, the last decades of the twentieth century gave scholars committed to liberation very little occasion to rest on their laurels. In 1982, after a bit of a struggle, Cedric was awarded tenure. He managed to keep up a research agenda as well as continue in his administrative role in the Center for Black Studies, while Elizabeth continued to edit for

Figure 5.1 Cedric Robinson in Nicaragua, 1988
Image courtesy of Elizabeth Robinson

Africa World Press. As he became chair of political science, she took a job managing KCSB radio. Their lives transitioned alongside global change. The demise of the Soviet Union made American imperialism the only game in town. The university was a critical site to observe the meaning of these and other changes. It was the site of racial and cultural crises that were in the end related to Reaganism but also to the larger valences of white supremacy of which it was constituted. What to do with and in the university of this era became yet another issue for the Robinsons to address.

6

Culture and War

As a space which helped produce the conflagrations of the closing years of the Cold War, the academy was a site of intense opposition. The ensuing "culture wars" featured pitched battles over the nature and purpose of education. Conservatives and racists of all stripes condemned the "loss" of the university amid student and radical attempts to make space for the full humanity of everyone. But when the students of this generation continued the struggles of their parents, they continued what was at heart a militant demand not simply for representation but for a reimagined university. Theirs was an opposition that acknowledged the real consequences of the imposition of an idea like "western civilization." For Black folk, and others who had always borne the brunt of this regime, the struggle over culture was also the recognition of an ongoing war.[1]

They knew that he was authentic

Part of a wave of student action in the wake of the consti-
tutional changes that took place within the South African
government, students in California, beginning at Berkeley,
led enormous protests in the spring of 1985 in an effort to
withdraw the US$1.7 billion UC had invested in the apart-
heid state.[2] At UCSB that spring, a rally turned into an
occupation. Renaming the university after Nelson Mandela,
students held classes in occupied Cheadle Hall. In one of
the first sessions, Cedric reminded the occupying students of
the "ideological, economic and racial parallels between the
United States of America and South Africa. . . . Between the
prison populations, Black life in cities and Bantustans,"
and the "American leaders that extended comfort and aid"
to the racist regime; there was more than a simple resem-
blance between the two USAs.[3] As students in California
and all across the country were carted off to jail, the moral
and political sentiment began to turn against apartheid, forc-
ing the university to divest a year later. That same year, a
national movement, led by women like Sylvia Hill and other
veteran Pan-Africanists in organizations such as TransAfrica,
was able to push the United States government to enact sanc-
tions on South Africa.[4] Through it all, Cedric and Elizabeth
were present in these struggles alongside students as well as
the broader Santa Barbara community.

As incoming chair of political science, Cedric was excited
to help the department grow in new directions.[5] As he settled
into the new position in the summer of 1987, he noticed that
the outgoing chair had appointed a lecturer without the con-
sent of the other faculty members. But there was more at
stake than a procedural irregularity. The appointed instructor was a thirty-year veteran of the Central Intelligence

Agency named George Chritton. The discovery would lead to a year-long struggle to get the CIA "off-campus."

That year was also the first for new chancellor Barbara Uehling, a veteran administrator who had been the first woman to head a land-grant university. In her last days as a fellow at the American Council of Education, she was approached by Washington operatives about the CIA's new Officer-in-Residence program. After bringing it to then political science chair Dean Mann, who immediately supported the idea, UCSB was primed to join the University of Texas-Austin, Georgetown, and Harvard, as one of the four universities piloting the program. But when Cedric became chair it foiled their plans. He first alerted the press by sending them a letter from the CIA that was addressed to Mann. Then in October, the Academic Senate got involved in addressing the procedural question. Motivated by broader concerns, student activists occupied Uehling's office the following month.[6]

There were many faculty members who supported Chritton on the grounds of academic freedom. But others, like many in the anthropology department who knew about the legacy of the CIA around the world (as they came from a discipline which had often been complicit), were vehemently opposed to his presence on campus. This program was, among many things, a cynical attempt to restore the agency's image after a series of embarrassing scandals.[7] But there was also another part of the resistance to this appointment that largely escaped press attention. The CIA had long targeted UCSB. Cedric's Black Studies colleague Gerard Pigeon remembered that its presence was noticeable in language programs going back two decades. From there, it would soon grow, with CIA operatives across the disciplines, including history and sociology. There had even been a dean that was a former Mossad agent. By bringing attention to Chritton,

Cedric also brought attention to the phenomenon of intelligence agencies functioning clandestinely in the university.[8] If the Officer-in-Residence program was grounded in good faith and openness to academic debate, he asserted that this flew in the face of the very purpose of an intelligence agency, "which operates under secrecy." Cedric acknowledged that this was an issue they had been "dealing with [. . .] for a very, very long time."[9] After a series of meetings, the political science department agreed to downgrade the appointment to a fellowship. The result of that vote was that Chritton would be available for events but would not teach any classes. And, importantly, he could not recruit.[10] At the end of a year which saw Cedric and others develop events that explored government and intelligence operations, the department voted not to renew Chritton for another term.[11] But it was not the end of the war of which the Chritton affair was one battle.

The movement to expose the CIA came in the midst of a campaign to enact an ethnic and gender studies requirement. Dating back several years, it was intensified in the spring of 1987 when a group called United Cultural Front launched a major protest. They saw the requirement as the first step in ending racism and sexism on campus and beyond, a responsibility that the university must accept given its role in creating those conditions. On February 19, the group picketed a Regents meeting held on campus. The university attempted to wait the students out, stalling with the explanation that it needed to first secure a new chancellor.[12] As the fall semester rolled around, a group called Concerned Students Against Racism began to raise the issue again, alongside the university's unwillingness to significantly address its failure to recruit Black students and faculty. One of its leaders, Helen Quan, who would become close to the Robinsons, told the *Daily Nexus* that their purpose was to make racism an "issue" so they could no longer "sweep it away."[13] Along with his

Black Studies colleague Douglas Daniels, Cedric provided direct support to the activists in the form of advice but also in proposing the requirement before the Academic Senate.[14] But as schools across the UC system joined the campaign, the UCSB administration again delayed.

There were other faculty supporters, like Gerard Pigeon, who tried to push the initiative through the various levels of approval. But the resistance at that level was considerable. Even leftist faculty members were uncomfortable with the idea of the requirement, which only seemed to resonate with faculty of color. To force the issue, students developed a protest movement, which began with a disruption of an Academic Senate meeting in November 1988.[15] When it was revealed that the faculty of the College of Letters and Science voted against the proposal the following January, students responded with a twelve-day hunger strike against "institutional racism." In a letter to the campus community, the Students Concerned About a Quality Education asserted that "the struggle to implement an Ethnic Studies requirement" was part of a larger effort aimed at "confronting the issues of institutional racism, sexism and student disempowerment." Over the course of this long battle, many had "sacrificed their grades, jobs, relationships, social lives and peace of mind."[16] The strike was its logical evolution.

A little over a week into the strike, Pigeon and the Robinsons joined the strikers for three days, building a tent under a placard reading "Faculty Club."[17] As other faculty, including the aforementioned leftists, condemned the hunger strike as too dangerous, Cedric and others chose to practice solidarity. Though it was the student action which was decisive, Pigeon remembers how important Cedric was to their struggle: "the students loved him for that, they respected him for that. They knew that he was authentic. No promise that he said he wouldn't keep."[18] Although it did not meet all of their demands, that summer a one-course requirement in ethnic studies was implemented.[19]

Before constituting themselves as a formal organization designed to address questions of affirmative action and faculty recruitment and retention, minoritized faculty also organized vigils in support of the striking students.[20] Throughout the next year, the Minority Faculty and Staff Association worked to ensure that promises to diversify UC campuses made by system-wide president David Gardner were met.[21] Elizabeth joined Charles McKinney from the admissions office in proposing summer programs targeted toward potential Black students.[22] As director of the Center for Black Studies, Cedric had traveled as part of a delegation to Jackson State University in 1985 with hopes of creating a formal partnership with that institution aimed at, among other things, increasing the Black faculty. After the tumult of the ensuing four years leading to the hunger strike, there was talk again of reenergizing that and similar programs.[23] But issues of faculty diversity remained throughout the early 1990s. And they were much larger than simply adding more professors of darker hue. While the department of Black Studies was able to recruit historian and activist Gerald Horne to its chairmanship, there were also unsuccessful attempts to recruit Manning Marable, June Jordan, and Angela Davis to campus.[24] Perhaps more vexing, the Center's postdoctoral fellowship program, designed to be a pipeline, had failed to produce many new UCSB faculty.[25]

Info-tech wars

As these skirmishes took place on campus, the Robinsons maintained their focus on the outside world. The *Third World News Review* kept Santa Barbarans informed of events in El Salvador, Nicaragua, Panama, and eventually Somalia. And when President George H. W. Bush invaded Iraq, the Robinsons continued to expose the ways in which the press manipulated the public in service to the presidency and the corporate interests that stood to gain. Throughout the early nineties, Cedric taught courses on mass media and politics and wrote several articles which continued to make connections between the shifting media environment that conspired to narrow the breadth of knowledge, particularly when it came to American misadventures abroad. What he had observed in the early eighties was only worsening.

In his contribution to *Questioning the Media*, Cedric argued that as a result of the decline of the adversarial press in the latter half of the twentieth century, the coverage "during the US war against Iraq" and other military invasions was "dismal."[26] The media uncritically supported the official line, as every "new US military intervention abroad" was treated "as though it had no precedents." Their performance conspired to "blind us with authoritative-sounding statements . . . or the superhuman technical brilliance of the US military's weaponry."[27] Here and in a 1991 *Critical Times* article, Cedric began to document that the news was itself a "business" more than it was a source of sound information from which to support democratic dialogue.[28] Fully addressing the implications of Desert Storm required other streams. So the Robinsons attended and organized antiwar teach-ins and rallies to help reframe the meaning of the invasion to a public whose critical lens was corrupted through a media beholden to the "interests of corporate capital."[29]

It was also from these contexts that Cedric read the meaning of the "pavement lynching" of Rodney King.[30] In a biting analysis of this moment for Robert Gooding-Williams's *Reading Rodney King/Reading Urban Uprising*, he made clear the connections between King's brutalization and the "info-tech war" in the Persian Gulf. He demonstrated how those logics of "white-American might" were also implicated in the "defamation of Anita Hill."[31] The Reagan years had yielded the "debauchery of an unfettered capitalism and political and bureaucratic corruption" which obliterated any sense of a social contract engendered by declining the New Deal order.[32] So the beating of King was a "reverberation" of this "disintegration," the continued desire to eliminate the presumed deviants. Race was one of its signals, the increasing numbers of racialized people in prisons its logical outcome. But Cedric argued that it all supported a historic transfer of wealth, produced by foreign and domestic policy shifts.[33] Such an economic imposition would also produce its own contradictions:

> The social deprivations which are the concomitants to these hemorrhaging transfers of wealth constitute the circumstances which have historically spawned revolutionary movements. Presently, however, largely through the efforts of the western intelligence community and military agencies, the preferred antitoxin is tyranny: fascist military dictators like Saddam Hussein, Ferdinand Marcos, Anastasio Somoza, and Sese Soko Mobuto.[34]

When their tyrannical allies could not be controlled, military interventions were required. And when the reactions to the verdict of the brutalizers of Rodney King could not be controlled, the police were required. The violence of American empire occasioned negations.

Toward fascism?

In his essay on King, Cedric closed by arguing that the "bizarre phantasmagoria" of the culture wars, like "political correctness" and "reverse discrimination," should be placed alongside the "real aspirations of women, workers, the poor, and peoples of color."[35] Political correctness had emerged, he had earlier argued, as a way to conceal the contradictions inherent in the foreign and domestic wars taking place. In his comments at a panel on the phenomenon, he proposed to think of multiculturalism in more radical terms: "liberation and democratization."[36] Orienting the rupture of American knowledge with the campus struggles of the sixties and seventies, Black Studies and other formations could be transformative if we would only remain focused on the question of liberation and resist becoming distracted by "attempts to change the subject – like the deceit of political correctness – or meaningless designations like 'multiculturalism.'"[37] In a series of conference presentations through the late eighties and early nineties, he extended these ideas as the vagaries of late capitalism began to take hold.

In 1989, the Center for Black Studies – under the new directorship of Elliot Butler-Evans – sponsored a three-day conference called "Speaking the Subject: Poststructuralism, Postmodernism, and Black Theoretical Practice," which featured papers from Cedric, Stuart Hall, Paul Gilroy, Kobena Mercer, Sylvia Wynter, Joyce A. Joyce, and Clyde Taylor, among others.[38] In his comments, Cedric began from the premise that the new signification of "African American" to describe the descendants of Africans enslaved in the United States was less a matter of de-essentializing Blackness than "an expression of Black bourgeois political ambition." He placed the phenomenon within the context of Jesse Jackson's recent campaign, which he argued was an attempt to address "the excesses of capitalist exploitation, class privilege, and racial insurgency rather than the structural transformations foregrounded by American imperial decline, militarism, deindustrialization, and the decay of the global economy."[39]

But by centering the "least of these," Jackson's campaign discussed domestic and foreign policy in a way that intruded on the global plans for exploitation and production that the Reagan years had extended through war – economic and militaristic.[40] The corporate media's response "recodified the campaign in racial terms," forestalling any potential to create a Black politics that "extended the discursive meaning of the essential black so that it encompassed class, gender, ethnic, and sexual exploitation/oppression and the domination of the Third World."[41] "African American," Cedric cautioned, could substitute this kind of politics for an "ethnic politics" – he even used the phrase, "politics of representation" – which could become less about who we really are and what others can make us to be. And the lesson to be drawn from the elite's corruption of racial and representational politics was unquestionably what "we can be made to be."[42]

Three years later, in the wake of the urban uprisings and the election of Bill Clinton, Cedric's UCSB colleagues, Christopher Newfield and Avery Gordon, convened a conference entitled "Translating Cultures: The Future of Multiculturalism?" In his conference paper, Cedric sought to clarify some meanings and possible radical uses of multiculturalism by focusing first on the "specular imaginings from the western interior." It suggested what could be seen from the vantage point of those "materially positioned in western society," but who "imagine and realize a joint and mutually ratified peripheralization within the West."[43] Their view of the West reveals it as a construction in ways that pierced the anti-multiculturalist conceit that the West was a "transcendent universal culture."[44] Those neoconservative elites arrayed against multiculturalism, Cedric argued, were akin to those who persecuted medieval heretical ideas like Manichaeism. As an oppositional discourse, a radical form of multiculturalism had the potential to organize "an

ethics between the desperate particularity of the Same and
the anguished universality of the Other."[45] But a materialist
framing that only concerned "one condition of our being"
could not substitute for that oppositional discourse and the
resistances it emerged from.[46]

In a 1994 essay in David Theo Goldberg's *Multiculturalism:
A Critical Reader*, Cedric continued to uncover the genealogy of this oppositional discourse. In doing so, he showed
that there was also a racist multiculturalism that was older
than the current iterations which imagined themselves as
anti-racist. The very evolution of western civilization was
preceded by discourses that relied "on a construction of con-
tamination" as it developed the political and social orders that
were "intended to conceal the prerogatives of power, conceal the humanity of the Other, conceal the awful policing
devices of subordination."[47] With the advent of the modern
world and the later development of the social sciences, these
racist multiculturalisms were dominant within centers of
knowledge: the museum and the university. But as indicated
in Cedric's evocation of the perspectives of Ota Benga and
Geronimo at the 1904 World's Fair – those marginal but
necessary to the construction of those centers – there were
those who created an oppositional discourse from the jump.
From the Black anthropological thinking of Martin Delany
and George Washington Williams in the nineteenth century to the more recognizable Caroline Bond Day and Zora
Neale Hurston, the roots of a Black Studies critique of western cultural discourse were available. And could be extended.
For the race science which occasioned that critique is always
ready to re-emerge in new guises.[48]

Indeed, Black Studies spaces were the location for subsequent musings on the various crises of the early nineties. In
1994, Cedric returned to Stanford University and accepted
an invitation to participate in a conference hosted by the

African and African American Studies department entitled, "The Two Reservations: Western Thought, The
Color Line, and the *Crisis of the Negro Intellectual Revisited.*"
Playing a major role in the proceedings was a group of students that had formed Institute NHI in the wake of the 1992
rebellions. NHI stood for "No Humans Involved," slang
utilized by the Los Angeles Police Department to signify
the presence or "criminal" activities of Black folk. Thinking
alongside Stanford professor Sylvia Wynter, this group
sought to develop a knowledge for the twenty-first century
which addressed the questions at the heart of a society which
had designated certain people "NHI."[49] The symposium
was an opportunity to think beyond the narrow confines of
multiculturalism and to understand Black and Latinx life
in the "reservation" of the inner city and its connections to
the meaning of life on the more well-known reservations of
the Native Americans. Joining Wynter were scholars like
Joyce King, Patricia Fox, Clyde Taylor, Paget Henry, and
Robert Hill. But the conference was keynoted by Harold
Cruse whose work was a guide, and the questions it raised
a framing, for how to understand the crisis. This was a collection of scholars who understood the depth of the political
and economic roots of capitalist oppression, but who also
understood that Black Studies must provide a "native radical
theory of social transformation" rather than mimic the radicalisms that emerged at other times and places.[50]

Cedric's contribution to that theorizing was a talk he
titled, "Toward Fascism? Race, the Two Reservations, and
the Materiality of Theory." Revisiting the roles of intellectual leadership and Marxist theory, he evoked Frantz Fanon
to remind us that "the Black bourgeoisie" was a "pathological
class, psychologically and politically ill-formed." The hopes
of revolution – as recently demonstrated in the rebellions
– resided in the people of the ghettos, in these "sites of

resistance." He continued, "the homeless have developed a knowledge of how to survive and help others survive; they are an enormous resource. I say that we cannot invent this stuff from some university, we can only help it along." And one way was to show that "racial capitalism finds its natural end in fascism." This was the danger of the nineties. It was perhaps for the historians to remind our communities that "We who are Black have to be the first target [of fascism] . . . given that we have interfered before."[51] This was the connection between race and the two reservations. In an earlier draft, Cedric wrote:

> Racial Capitalism . . . is a system of production and exploitation whose natural development propels the social categories of class and achieves its epistemological justifications in the creeds of individualism and logical positivism. Modern capitalism, however, assumed its historical character within the race epistemes consequent to slave economies among Europeans (and much later, instituted by Europeans). Race orderings (which in the nineteenth century race sciences extended to females) ruptured the calculi of capitalism, suborning class, liberalism, and scientific discourse. And I believe that the persistence of race wars all over Europe confirms the antiquity of these epistemes.[52]

Which is to say, again, fascism, or its prerequisites, have always been there. And remain. Whatever the culture wars produced, the moment often concealed the deeper wars being fought. For all of the hand-wringing over affirmative action and political correctness which had immense consequences, particularly in California, Cedric argued that the "real world of political correctness" was "a stratified and militarized universe dominated by an imperial state and its publicists, [which] sponsors killings in the tens of thousands and masquerades as a social contract."[53]

A vision of the future

In the midst of this whirlwind, Cedric managed to publish two books. They were both connected to his pedagogy. In his lectures, Cedric would prepare extensive notes for each session. It was a practice that dated back to at least his time in Michigan, if not earlier. These notes were often several single-spaced typed pages, demonstrating his range and command of the subject. So much so that many of those notes were revised and became elements of his later texts.

Published by Routledge in 1997, *Black Movements in America* reflected Cedric's desire to develop a text for under-graduate study. In 1993, Cedric became the new chair of the Department of Black Studies, after having left the same position in political science three years earlier. Among the courses that would use this new book was Black Studies I.[54] This was the foundational course which he often taught, as did Otis Madison, a lecturer and former fellow in the Center for Black Studies who would eventually become a popular figure in the department and one of Cedric's best friends. Cedric believed that these courses should be taught by the most popular and knowledgeable instructors in order to build the discipline. Madison fitted that bill. And texts like *Black Movements in America* were important tools to meet that goal.[55]

It was not his first foray into writing exclusively on the Black American experience. Twenty years earlier, he had written an article for the *World Encyclopedia of Black Peoples* which examined the social conditions of Black people in the United States against the backdrop of Black life in the larger Americas.[56] And there was also an excellent review essay written in 1982 that rehearsed many of the themes in *Black Movements in America*. In that essay, Cedric engaged the work of his colleague Douglas Daniels's *Pioneer Urbanites*, along with *Exodusters*, a study written by Nell Irvin Painter, a friend from his undergraduate years, unpacking the political and ideological motivations of Black migration.[57] Even as he was working on *Black Movements in America*, Cedric and his students were developing community calendars which showcased the history of Black Santa Barbara.[58] But as with all of his works, it did not read the Black experience through a teleology of American progress. Instead, it privileged Black mass action with a particular emphasis on the quest for self-determination among "ordinary" Black folk and the role of revolutionary women in the development of an alternative political culture which defined the history of African America.[59]

In less than two hundred pages, Cedric traced the history of this political culture from the colonial period to the civil rights era. At every turn, it argued, Black political action was geared toward assuring a measure of autonomy against a political order that erected a "rule of law as the warrant for the justness of [America's] claims and practices in breaking free from the British." But for enslaved Africans, that "rule of law was an injustice, a mercurial and violent companion to their humiliations, a form of physical abuse, a force for the destruction of their families, and an omnipresent cruelty to their loved ones."[60] Positioned against that rule was the tradition of Black American *marronage* and revolt. Positioned against that rule was a tradition of abolition and emigration among the "free Blacks" of the North, which was connected naturally to the general strike and fighting against the Confederacy during the Civil War. In several talks on David Walker and Black Studies in 1997, Cedric had suggested that his vision was animated by a Black Christian ethic that did not fit the "moral and existential universe" of politics.[61] It was an ethic that he – as an intellectual connected to the eventual tradition of Black Studies – shared with the masses, who in turn clandestinely circulated his works throughout the South.[62]

There were, however, other approaches that emanated from some elite Black abolitionists who shared Walker's social location. Many of them would come to see freedom differently than the fulfillment of Walker's charismatic invocation of the "grace of the Eternal"[63]: "within this galaxy of liberalism, regardless of variant, a special affection for republican values predominated, grounded on a presumption that leadership was reserved for an elite defined by nature and excellence." In the struggles to make America work for them, the elite created a tradition of protest. But Cedric argued that it was an "illusion and self-serving conceit that such values and interests represented Blacks en masse." The history of Black movements showed that "the social values" of the Black masses who were "largely agrarian people generated a political culture that distinguished between the inferior world of the political and the transcendent universe of moral goods."[64]

At the very moment that Black citizenship was secured constitutionally, it was reversed through a range of legal and political maneuvers, during an era that Rayford Logan had called "the nadir."[65] So this new rule of law would have to be rejected too. Its negation lived through Ida B. Wells and her anti-lynching campaign and through Ella Baker and Septima Poinsette Clark and the organizing tradition which opposed Jim Crow. In a moment of intense violence and vulnerability, the focus remained care of and for each other.

> For a particular stratum of Blacks and a select few, Republicanism retained its hold on the imagination, but for the masses it lost power. For the former, America was an unfulfilled promise; for the latter, America held little special significance. It was merely one more land of troubles. With

this understanding, the mass of Blacks bent to the task of rescuing family, community, and their race.[66]

In the end, this was a lens which would prove to be a more useful way to understand the history of our movement through America. The dialectic of the rule of law and Black self-activity demonstrated finally that "the power of the movement came from the masses, from a century or two of their ancestors, under acute distress, elaborating a vision of the future and how it might be attained."[67] The text would be widely reviewed and well received, and in a certain respect might be the logical introduction of Cedric's work to new readers.[68]

In the midst of the publication of *Black Movements in America*, Cedric was involved in proposals to develop a PhD program in Black Studies. Temple University had been the first to develop a doctoral program under the leadership of Molefi Asante in 1988. They were followed by the University of Massachusetts-Amherst in 1995. Each had its strengths. And at UCSB the proposed program was to focus on critical cultural studies of the African diaspora and a US-centered approach focused on social policy. The program's strength was a collection of scholars who studied both the Anglophone and Francophone Caribbean and African societies as much as it focused on North America.[69] Yet it was never approved, much to the loss of the Black Studies movement in California and beyond. But around that time Cedric gave a short talk which clarified his view of the role of Black Studies in a moment in the mid-nineties that was experiencing the birth pangs of a so-called new world order:

It is a time to recall Du Bois and James. They provided a formidable mission for Black Studies: radical critique and truth. Black Studies is not merely a site in the universities

of America for alternative research and scholarship; it is a
home for scholars and students who are dedicated to the
critical knowledge which will eventuate in democratic societies. I invite you to join us in this task. It is not enough to
use the university to prepare for a career, you must also prepare yourself for a life of decency, a life of moral authority, a
life which will provide your children and grandchildren with
a life of meaning.[70]

And in terms of the nature of those "democratic societies," Cedric was clear that the western models that were
then being imposed on the world through military aggression were not what he had in mind. In a 1995 paper in the
National Political Science Review, the organ of the National
Conference of Black Political Scientists, he had argued that
perhaps one reason for the persistence of Plato's *Republic* in
American political thought was that it justified the construction of a "counterfeit democratic discourse."[71] It was the
Republic – which Cedric had regularly taught in his Classical
Political Theory course – that was the conceptual foundation for an antidemocratic American society, where racial
orders established the mechanisms for rule.[72] It was but a
slight revision of Plato's natural order of the nobles. "If he
had not existed," Cedric argued, "he would have had to be
invented."[73]

Returning to England for a conference commemorating
the fiftieth anniversary of the Fifth Pan-African Congress,
Cedric offered similar thoughts. This time, however, he
focused on "political pan-Africanism." The political, and the
modern form it took, "the nation-state," was "an undeserving
venue" of African liberation and it produced the contradictions facing independent African nations, led by a bourgeois
elite.[74] These leaders had "hybridized freedom with material
ambition."[75] They had evacuated a tradition of cultural Pan-

Africanism – the actual terms of Black resistance – that had preceded the reduction of liberation struggles to the form of the political. And even some of that tradition's most important chroniclers, like W. E. B. Du Bois, were often seduced by these ideals.[76]

Returning to concerns first voiced in *The Terms of Order*, Cedric imagined a society that privileged the abolition of private property, was grounded in the community over individuals, and was not reliant on the state or the leader as the horizon for a Pan-African future.[77] Proposing the development of a Pan-African commonwealth, he declared that we "must seek to fulfill Sekou Toure's recognition that 'Since revolutionary pan-Africanism basically refers to an Africa of Peoples, it is in its interest to uphold the primacy of peoples as against States.'"[78]

Nowhere was this more imperative than in South Africa. It had just defeated apartheid and represented the great potential of a new beginning, not just for its citizens but for all who had participated in the struggle to end it. For a volume on the United States and South Africa that unfortunately never appeared, Cedric developed an essay entitled "The Utopian Break: South Africa as Other." It was a critique of the Alan Paton novel and eventual film, *Cry, the Beloved Country*, which Cedric used to contextualize the passing of liberal notions of empire – the white man's burden – to the "race wars" that would dominate the Cold War era.[79] Though western liberals attempt to "other" the racial extremism of South Africa, societies like the United States also "orbited around ideological contingencies" which required similar forms of racist exploitation and the repression of Black radicalism.[80]

Unfortunately, those contingencies would not evaporate in the post-apartheid state. In 1999, Cedric visited South Africa to participate in a conference at the University of the Witwatersrand on the Truth and Reconciliation Commission.

The othering that would bedevil understandings of the connections between South Africa and the United States would persist when it came to the meaning of truth and reconciliation. It was a process that was more political performance than an accounting of the actual terms of apartheid. In such a process, the quotidian nature of the racial regime would be excluded. The inner workings of racial capitalism would be conflated with the excesses of its brutality. And neither truth nor justice would issue from such a reckoning, not simply because of the provision of amnesty granted to participants but because truth and justice belonged to "different knowledge universes." Cedric wrote:

> Truth is inexhaustible, like irrational numbers, always expanding, moving, searching. Justice is fixed, always seeking to surrender the complex to the simplicity; the obscure to visibility; multiple possibilities to singular exactness. Justice seeks to tame the indeterminate, to subjugate difference to sameness. The rituals and procedures of justice are designed to give the appearances of justness by exacting revenge or manufacturing the fiction that something that has already happened can be rescinded or reversed. Justice, then, is either an intentional lie or a kindness. It routinely sacrifices truth, whether by fair or foul means. Justice, as Thrasymachus told Socrates, is whatever the powerful say it is.[81]

The "truth" of racial capitalism was a Du Boisian truth, a Mari Evans truth – a "truth that the new South African state could not afford."[82] It is a truth that the political can only contain or suppress.

Cedric's next book would appear two years later. The graduate seminar lectures collected under the cover *An Anthropology of Marxism* were explorations of the prehistory of Marxism and its relationship to the larger universe of

European socialism. The text had begun as lecture notes in a series of courses that he taught on Marxism beginning in the seventies. In those notes, we see again his deft reading of the significance and evolution of Marxist thought. There is a clear demonstration of the philosophical nuances of Marx's theory of revolution, but perhaps most importantly the lectures captured the context driving much of this theory.[83]

In her preface to the volume, Avery Gordon wrote that in undertaking that deeper context, Cedric would come to emphasize the "divine agents" of history, not as some messianic ideal, but as a way to demonstrate the power of an agency that could "measure our freedom less by what subordinates us and more by what we are capable of divining."[84] He had chosen anthropology as a vehicle for this investigation, given its role in comprehending "cultures and civilizations and the mundane social practices and fabulist and technical habits which sustain them" – though it was rare that it turned its gaze toward Europe.[85] Perhaps this was a case of Cedric signifying on the complicated histories of anthropological discourse.

After explicating the specific national traditions of the "Marxian taxonomy,"[86] Cedric found in the earlier peasant revolts and heretical traditions of Europe more than just "proto-forms" of socialism.[87] Among these folk, questions of materialism were addressed through different logics than what would come down to Marx, influenced as his era was with the Enlightenment. For the working classes of the medieval period, "Consciousness of class and the struggle against a ruling class, for instance, assumed an anti-clerical as well as a secular form, and distilled from millenarian prophecy apocalyptic and then revolutionary expectations."[88] And among the most prominent carriers of resistance were European women, whose very bodies in some cases were seen as temptations to do evil. Here, Cedric engaged scholars like Caroline Walker

Bynum to postulate that gender difference produced critiques of material power and exploitation that preceded the movements that would come in the twentieth century. The elite reaction to heretical and millenarian thinking, of course, was repression and appropriation. As the Catholic Church became the center of organized capital, it variously renounced and banished those expressions of poverty that would mark the revolutionary movements of the era.[89]

Throughout the remainder of the text, Cedric returns Marxism to its context, first philosophically to the German idealist tradition: Immanuel Kant and G. W. F. Hegel. And then from a medieval conception of socialism to a nineteenth-century reality of a world defined through economistic thinking. It was here where Marx would pick up on this tradition. It is here where those earlier elements would be de-emphasized.

> Marxism absorbed the conceits of bourgeois historical consciousness: a formal (mathematical), rationalist epistemology costumed in a teleological historicity which, in turn, gave primacy to commerce. Objectivity and necessity (the dialectical development of successive organizations of production) displaced tradition and the vagaries of creativity, imposing on historical movement the logic of the dialectic (the relations of production). And in bestowing the bourgeois narrative of class upon the proletariat, Marx and Engels inserted the working class into their own more familiar historical system.[90]

As he had earlier introduced in *Black Marxism*, Cedric systematically showed how Marxist theoreticians – through the authority of scientism – posited a theory of revolution that largely dismissed, caricatured, or de-emphasized previous discourses of socialism in favor of an image of the proletariat (and of the peasantry) that was more familiar to bourgeois sensibilities. And yet, *despite* these contradictions, "non-western revolutionists" have creatively appropriated its elements.[91] For Cedric, this was possible only because the "socialist impulse" was larger than any one tradition of theoretical explanation, even in the context of Europe. The "warrant" for such an assertion was what he described as "the persistence of the human spirit." He concludes with the assertion that as "the past and our present demonstrate, domination and oppression inspire that spirit in ways we may never fully understand." And that in the grand scheme of things, it is "immaterial" where that spirit is located.[92]

Though it was intended for the classroom, many publishers passed on the manuscript when Cedric sent it out in 1991. So he continued to utilize it as a course reader for the next decade before he came to an agreement with Ashgate, a small publishing house which was recommended to him by Abebe Zegeye, a friend and colleague at UCSB.[93] There were few reviews of the text and it would soon be out of print and almost impossible to find,[94] a fate not unlike *The Terms of Order*, the other book central to Cedric's intellectual project that was sadly ignored. Elizabeth speculates that this shared fate was probably because the word "Black" did not appear in their titles.[95] Nevertheless, the reappearance of both volumes in more recent years may yet spawn new interest in this aspect of Cedric's work.

The closed text has been ruptured

One of the things that Margot Dashiell remembered about Cedric was how he would often get an urge for them to sneak away and go see a foreign film.[96] This affinity for cinema was long-standing. There was something about its power to influence mass consciousness that attracted him to film as both an object of study and of fascination. Because *Black Marxism* has overdetermined in many respects how people come to understand Cedric's ideas as a scholar, it has overshadowed the fact that the meaning of film *always* loomed large in his work. We should probably abandon such assignations, but if we were to label any work as his magnum opus, Cedric's final book-length work, *Forgeries of Memory and Meaning: Blacks and the Regimes of Race in American Theater and Film before World War II*, published in 2007, fits the bill as much as any other. It crystallized almost four decades of scholarship and a lifelong interest in a text that went far beyond the narrow confines of film criticism.

While at the University of Michigan, Cedric, along with Travis Tatum (then a graduate student and member of the Black Matters Committee), had created the Black Film Society. In its founding document, the group's stated purpose was to uncover "the context and consequence of the projection of Black people through the film media." In the winter of 1972, they decided to come together to screen films, host discussions, and invite lecturers to assess the question of Black representations in film and whether or not they might be taken as "serious statements on at least a portion of the reality of the experience of Black people." Films were vital for what they revealed about the perceptions and interpretations of Black life and its "political, social, and economic evolution within Black America." More importantly, the group argued that "it then becomes our duty to at least determine for ourselves, if no one else, the truth or falsity of Black representation in the mass media, in general."[97]

That semester, the group hosted screenings of *Body and Soul*, *Green Pastures*, *Cotton Comes to Harlem*, and *Dutchman*, among others. Along with Cedric, faculty members like Harold Cruse and William Ellis participated in the discussions with graduate and undergraduate students. Tatum was involved with a proposal to extend the work, which would have enlarged their budget and helped development of, among other vehicles, a journal of Black film.[98] But with the changes to come at Michigan, this dream never materialized.

Yet, for Cedric, the questions raised continued to resonate. After he arrived at Binghamton, he grew close to Tom Denyer, one of his colleagues in the sociology department. Together they penned a critique of American film criticism, using as a case study the hoopla surrounding the production and reception of *All the President's Men*. It was too much for film studies journals to consider for publication. Because it impugned their very practice, they all declined it. And it has remained unpublished.

"Liberal Fantasies and the Politics of American Movies" meticulously situated the evolution of American film criticism within the ideological parameters of liberal ideals such as individualism and realism. The development of a "native criticism" – that dispensed with the earlier forms of critique, which often looked beyond the United States – was a product of the 1930s. It grew up alongside the industry itself. This meant that radical criticism had to be dismissed in favor of a form that was "grounded in positivism; that is, the truth of any film attempting a social statement could only be evaluated by reference to incorrigible facts."[99]

They then turned to *All the President's Men* to reveal that what constituted these unimpeachable facts was a realism that masked its own liberal fantasies. For a film which focused on Watergate, it reproduced the very persona – individualistic ambition – it supposedly repudiated in its depiction of the "bad president."[100] But what their essay showed most forcefully is that American film and its focus on realism could not afford to advance larger realisms.

Among the repressed historical memories are: the Cold War, Vietnam, domestic rebellions, Nixon's political history, the constellation of actors and forces required to overthrow his regime, the surveillance harassments of the left; and at another level, the possibility of understanding later but related events ... the film does not even suggest the historical dimensions of the crisis.[101]

But this is what made liberalism important to American film-makers. And it was connected to their quest to eliminate radical elements from native criticism: "What distinguishes liberals and rightists is style and often timing; what distinguishes liberals and leftists is a fundamentally different conception of political practice and social order."[102] Hollywood had a responsibility, and it was not to radical traditions. From an industry beholden to the "logics of monopoly capitalism," we cannot be expected to learn very much about Watergate, or about American and global politics.[103]

Nor can we expect honest depictions of its domestic enemies. But in the twentieth century, when minstrelsy was discredited as a dominant form, there were other kinds of portrayals that took its place. Hollywood became more subtle. In a series of articles composed throughout the years, Cedric focused on this shift. The caricature of Black women in films was central to his thinking. In an article for *Elimu*, the newsletter for UCSB's Department of Black Studies, he showed that this practice was rooted in a "strict discipline" that consistently read "young Black women as maids, prostitutes, or entertainers." It was, of course, never an honest treatment of the many Black women that occupied these positions. The intent was to evacuate the sexual agency of Black women's lives, to re-commodify it or otherwise eliminate it. And we find the subtle continuities of this strict discipline in later films like *Ghost* and *Sister Act*.[104] In the case of the Blaxploitation period, the objective was to remake it entirely under a ruse that simultaneously connected it to the iconography of liberation, but without the substance. For *Race and Class*, Cedric wrote that the reimaginings of radical Black women as neighborhood vigilantes replaced community struggles for liberation with inter-communal revenge fantasies (while erasing entirely the presence of agencies of repression of those struggles). The sexualization of Black women in these films framed this "exaggerated unreality": "that body is transformed into that of the destroyer, a fascination with that violence overtakes and converges with sexual voyeurism. The pleasure of the flesh convenes with the excitement of revenge so that they might double for a notion of social justice."[105]

These were conceits that had even implicated filmmakers from the Black middle class. Too often, Cedric wrote in 1974, they "reflected a consciousness of the mass of Blacks almost indistinguishable from [D. W.] Griffith's."[106] They were too alienated from them to do otherwise. Even in films that sought a radical break, there was a decidedly elite or middle-class rendering of the cultures of the folk more intimate with traditions of resistance, material and spiritual, of the not-so-long-ago past.[107] Cedric imagined a Black film that could recognize this, but what he also saw was an industry that refused the possibility. In a prescient analysis of *Indiana Jones*, a film series that trades in both the colonial trope of savagery of the Other and assumptions about foreign enemies of the Cold War, he made the point that the racism and sexism of Hollywood was no mistake. Nor was its ability to reflect, as *Indiana Jones* had, the presumptions of America's foreign policy elite. Filmmakers provided a "cinematic canvas" from the very real "political and moral culture" which had remade the world through the project of western colonialism.[108] It even implicated our fantasies.

These were the considerations that Cedric had in mind when he began the work that would become *Forgeries of*

Memory and Meaning in the early nineties. When the book finally appeared in 2007, published by the University of North Carolina Press, it became probably the most reviewed of all his works. In addition to extending the robust scholarship of such film critics and scholars as Donald Bogle, Thomas Cripps, Gladstone Yearwood, Ed Guerrero, Anna Everett, and others, Cedric added an element of analysis that connected the entertainment industry to its critical role in the preservation of capitalism and American empire, while also taking stock of Black filmmaking as response to these conditions. Where more recent discussions have taken on questions of diversity in Hollywood, Cedric's concern remained the intersections of Black material reality and the complicity of the entertainment complex. Hollywood was another domain of racial capitalism. That this method and thinking, so crucial to all of his scholarship and activism, would be applied to a text considering film is more a logical than a surprising turn in his scholarship.

Yet it did raise newer questions. Among these, the most crucial may have been his concept of the racial regime. It was an idea that extended the notion of racial capitalism. But where the latter explained the origins of the system, the racial regime spoke to its dynamism.

> Racial regimes are constructed social systems in which race is proposed as a justification for the relations of power. While necessarily articulated with accruals of power, the covering conceit of a racial regime is a makeshift patchwork masquerading as memory and the immutable . . . Employing mythic discourses, racial regimes are commonly masqueraded as natural orderings, inevitable creations of collective anxieties prompted by threatening encounters with difference. Yet they are contrivances, designed and delegated by interested cultural and social powers with the wherewithal

sufficient to commission their imaginings, manufacture, and maintenance.[109]

The concept of the regime was capacious enough to encompass not merely formal economic systems but the cultural systems that were created by and supported political economies. But because they were fictions, racial regimes were subject to revision. Moreover, "moving pictures appear at that juncture when a new racial regime was being stitched together." This was a book that would trace the construction of whiteness and the maintenance of that racial regime through the modes of theater and film, showing how the fiction of race supported the ambitions of "finance capital, the dominant center of American commerce in the late nineteenth and early twentieth centuries."[110] But it was the resistance of Black filmmakers and the development of Black film that provided Cedric with a connection between Black cultural work and the larger tradition of Black radicalism. The "admissible and possible knowledges" it cultivated produced negations of the racial regime that in turn required those in power to practice "regime maintenance."[111]

Forgeries of Memory and Meaning begins in England, the site of Cedric's most significant engagements with western thought. He returns to the Elizabethan period to examine the constructions of the Negro that animated English society. Through an analysis of Shakespearean theater, he traces the differences between performances that occurred within the context of Britain's participation in the slave trade in the seventeenth and eighteenth centuries and earlier moments. Performances and receptions of *Othello*, for example, were something of a Rorschach test that enables us to understand the emergence and intensity of anti-Blackness within racial regimes that would become necessary to the "capitalist bourgeoisie" of the 1600s.[112] By the time this reached D. W. Griffith – the creator of the infamous *The Birth of a Nation* – race science and museum culture had intervened to create the Negro archetype of the nineteenth century, the cultural object that was reified through minstrelsy and popular culture.[113] *The Birth of a Nation* (1915) was film and it was spectacle. As a historical film, it reframed the era of Reconstruction as an assault against white Christian nationalism. As a cultural spectacle, it was the nation's first blockbuster. So, with Griffith, the racial regime had found a cultural register. Blackness would harden into the modes so familiar to us – toms, coons, bucks, mulattoes, and mammies.[114] And it happened against the backdrop of the changes of the year 1915, a backdrop of racial violence and imperialism.[115]

All of this required a rejoinder. Especially from the Black middle class. Where Cedric had earlier criticized their adoption of the same characters, he extended his critique to include those who resisted within these same materials. In the world of Black Blackface minstrelsy, with important figures like Bert Williams and George and Aida Overton Walker, there developed a theater of resistance. Black colleges developed acting troupes alongside Black professional ones to advance a Negro theater. Its record was not unblemished. But it offered a response. And without that response the possibilities of a Black cinema would have been limited. Cedric argues that "a Black independent film movement, drawing on the talent encased in the melodramatic genre of Black dramatic theater" would be involved in attempts "to counter Black representations in the dominant movie picture industry."[116]

As the industry settled into a powerful example of the connections between corporate and federal power, the Black middle class tried its hand at film. Cedric examined their creation of the mulatto genre as a response to "fabulist national narrative" announced in films like *The Birth of a*

Nation.[117] They were a class that was targeted by a Jim Crow regime intent on stamping out Black middle-class ambition. And in a 2003 article with an undergraduate student, Luz Maria Cabral, Cedric even explored this phenomenon in the Mexican cinema of the same era.[118] Alongside the attempts to rehabilitate the mulatto were those films which were labeled "race films." An extension of the labels "race men" and "race women," these were films one would assume were aimed at the harmful images of Black folks in the industry through direct political commentary. But, for the most part, they were simple melodramas: "few directly addressed the issues around which political struggles were being waged during the first half of the twentieth century: peonage, sharecropping, lynching, segregation, inferior public education, the sexual exploitation of Black women, and child labor."[119] Though several Black film companies were created, these were not radical interventions.

That "oppositional cinema" would come with the more militant approach of an Oscar Micheaux. Of his films, Cedric chose as an exemplar the 1926 picture, *Within Our Gates*. In both form ("the historical and technical provenance of jazz"[120]) and content (the abandonment of the traditional melodrama and the embrace of the "social drama"[121]), this film did more than simply counter the assumptions of Black inferiority then dominant in the industry. Rather than simply flip the script, it offered an otherwise explanation for the conditions and experiences of the Black community: "Because the closed text has been ruptured, we now apprehend that the principal forces acting on our rare characters are not love, or romance, or jealousy, or even coincidence. Their lives are actually hedged in by a racial conspiracy enforced by spontaneous acts of violence."[122] This is what marked it as a Black film.

But a Black cinema had to compete with the golden era of

film in America. With the sound film came a more organized assault against America's enemies, domestic and global. The western, and its demonization of the Indigenous and/ or Mexican figure, was an extension of the jungle genre and its demonization of the colonized. They were joined by the plantation genre, a kind of film that turned the South from a site of racial violence into the celebration of genteel culture and the blissful ignorance of song and dance. The racial regime had adjusted. And with it the market attempted to eliminate the possibilities for producing the kinds of film that Micheaux had produced. Though he has heirs (Cedric pointed to Julie Dash's *Daughters of the Dust*[123]), the racial regime of Hollywood has managed to keep them at bay. Black film exists only in the underground,[124] its creation a subversive act. Whiteness as the grounds for the reproduction of the American film industry has survived the contemporary cries for Black visibility and diversity. It even lives on through Black directors. Cedric's work shows that this is endemic.

Conclusion: I Am You

The classroom had always been a site of Cedric's radicalism. The practice of teaching – which in the university had been doubly charged with reproducing disciplinary avatars and the academic markets through which they came – was the creation of a space that was enlarged into something greater. The classroom, office hour sessions, events, and eventually Cedric and Elizabeth's home became locales for cultivating family, for inculcating beauty, for reproducing an ethics of love and care. There may be no greater embodiment of radicalism. And, for Cedric, it manifested in numerous ways. He was not concerned with reproducing himself or with developing scholars in his image. The tradition was more important.

Family was about relationships. It was also about a responsibility to each other, a reciprocal practice of ensuring that in the end we would all be alright. When recruiting students to the University of Michigan, as part of the legacy of the Black Action Movement protests, Cedric would speak to the families of the candidates. Darryl C. Thomas remembers that it was a conversation that Cedric had with his mother that convinced her he would be taken care of. He was not simply joining an intellectual community.

But that ethics *did* produce thinking. Cedric utilized communal spaces to encourage reading and thinking: Friday nights at the Robinson home, Saturday mornings in seminars he led, late nights in the libraries, jaunts to Borders bookstore. The struggle to know was a collective one. The Black Matters Committee to which Cedric and the graduate students belonged became book hunters, acquiring new texts and spreading them among the members of the group, "breaking copyright laws" in the process.[1] Knowledge had to be all our possession.

That openness was transported with the Robinsons to the State University of New York. One of Cedric's students, Bruce Cosby, remembers that he was an "unusual" professor. He dressed differently – always in a dashiki. He was the only professor Cosby had ever seen in the library. When books like *Black Marxism* finally appeared, Cosby was deeply familiar with the style and range, remembering that such ideas were forged in the classroom first. It was an experience that was also defined by rigor and a seriousness that was not felt or seen as punitive or disciplinary. The rigor was *part* of his generosity and support for students. For he had been through what they were experiencing not just as students but as Black folk in the world.[2]

Soon after his arrival in Santa Barbara to direct the Center for Black Studies, graduate student Joanne Madison remembered that Cedric had cultivated a "welcoming" environment. He did away with the normal hierarchies that constituted academia, particularly as it had to do with disciplinary training. He saw his students as equals, and "it made me see myself in a different way, because he saw me like that."[3] Her partner, Otis Madison, a doctoral student in political science, had wanted to work with Cedric while he was still teaching at Michigan. Over the next three decades, however, they became colleagues and close friends, with Madison taking a position as lecturer within Black Studies. They shared a love for Black people, for a kind of intellectual camaraderie that ran up against the norms of respectability, and for teaching, with both of them winning Teacher of the Year awards at UCSB. So when there was an attempt to remove Madison from his position as lecturer, a position that at UCSB, like other institutions, was inherently precarious, Cedric and others protested and stepped in to reverse that decision.[4]

Ensuring that graduate students fulfilled their potential is something that all professors believe in. But for nonwhite students it was always more complicated than studying, passing comps, and writing a dissertation. For many of them, there were few thinkers who could provide direction in resolving some of the questions that they brought to the academy. In many ways, these conditions have not changed.

In 1984, Cedric began a relationship with Robin D. G. Kelley, then a young graduate student in history at UCLA. Though they did not share the same disciplinary domain, Kelley believed that Cedric's work came "closest to the type of analysis" he was interested in doing. As Kelley famously relates in the foreword to the 2000 edition of *Black Marxism*, it was an encounter with his writings that initially drew him to Cedric. But early in their relationship Cedric was warning Kelley to balance his passion for radical change with the practice of producing sound scholarship. A glimpse of that was provided in a letter Cedric sent to Kelley after reviewing chapters of his dissertation, which eventually became the important book, *Hammer and Hoe*. Kelley was then an organizer working in a Maoist Marxist-Leninist organization that often did battle over the question of Marxist theory and pursuing the correct "line." Much of these debates was embedded in those early drafts, where Kelley had criticized the Communist Party USA's racism in an editorial voice. Knowing that the roads toward the dissertation for Black students were often fraught, Cedric wrote: "Scholarship is not dispassionate, but it is deliberate and systematic in the way it reconstructs an event. Try not to indict for racism when the materials will allow you to 'discover' it."[5] For Cedric, it was critical that younger scholars avoid the landmines, without sacrificing or kowtowing to power. If we do our work well, the question of truth and the validity of our judgments will be well taken care of.

Yet it was more than just a warning about one's career prospects. It was about how to recount our struggle. After all, *Hammer and Hoe* was about Black folk. Kelley remembers:

> All that language about line struggles and correct analysis are based on the litmus tests of 1789 [the French Revolution] and 1917 [the Russian Revolution]. Cedric in a subtle way was saying stop that. Pay attention to Tallapoosa County, Elmore County, Birmingham, Bessemer, in the 1930s and before ... That was as important as showing rather than editorializing, because once I moved away from the latter, I could *see* what was happening on their terms rather than the ones I imposed."[6]

In the latter half of the eighties and nineties, another generation of students would come to experience the spaces cultivated by Cedric and Elizabeth. An enduring relationship with Helen Quan, affectionately known as HQ, began in the wake of on-campus struggles as well as protests against apartheid and the military aggressions of the Reagan era and after. Along with Elizabeth, HQ was a part of women's organizations which protested American imperialism. And she also studied with Cedric as an undergraduate and graduate student. Though she initially sought to complete her dissertation on Amilcar Cabral – a topic which Cedric no doubt found critical – HQ's pivot to studying questions of Brazilian development and Japanese capital found in him an equally enthusiastic advisor.[7]

One story that HQ tells illuminates the relationship Cedric had with students. Soon after they had first met, HQ enrolled in a senior-level political theory course, though she was only a sophomore. In that course, Cedric taught about the nature of democracy and the state, demonstrating the differences between the power of the people and its corruption in forms of state power that only gestured to the ability of people to rule. The group of students taking the seminar decided one night near the end of the semester that they would demonstrate *their* power by submitting their take-home final exam as a collective product. But as they got cold feet, someone in the group suggested that HQ call Cedric to see if it would be okay. After listening to her explain their plan, Cedric's response was simply: "So why are you calling me?"[8]

This modeling of community was intimately connected to Cedric's ability to be the embodiment of the values that he wrote about. A graduate student who came to Santa Barbara in the 1990s, Tiffany Willoughby-Herard noted that it was this aspect of Cedric's life that made Black Studies authentic. She remembered that Cedric and Elizabeth's door was always unlocked, which is also a metaphor for the kind of approach they developed toward younger scholars. Willoughby-Herard would be one of the many graduate students that would take this as one of the prevailing lessons from Cedric's life and example. Being open meant listening to the creative ways students applied and extended our ideas.

Not disciplining them. Because that "doesn't get us free." Studies of Black life are far too vibrant to be constricted in such a way.[9]

This extended to younger colleagues like Avery Gordon, Fred Moten, Abebe Zegeye, and Clyde Woods. When they got to UCSB, Cedric's office door was always open. And in similar ways, Cedric became someone that could be a sounding board, an intellectual companion, someone equally committed to the disruption of the university as normal. For Moten, Cedric's work introduced him to a kind of Black Studies that was different from his earlier encounters. He described his work as an entire curriculum that had to be mastered, and that mastering is seemingly never completed. But more than that, Black Studies was about how we should be: "if Black Studies is a critique of western civilization, you challenge the metaphysical foundations of the goddamn civilization. And that actually manifested itself at the level of your own ethical comportment in the world."[10]

That manifested on many levels for Gordon, but it was perhaps most present in the way Cedric demonstrated the importance of breaking free from disciplinary constrictions, in the way he affirmed that she was already practicing this, and how necessary it was. Gordon arrived at UCSB in the midst of the Gulf War and found in the Robinsons colleagues who shared her political sensibilities. Their relationship would deepen as she worked with Elizabeth on the radio show *No Alibis*, a show that extended the work of *Third World News Review*, and with Cedric as they shared classroom spaces and notes on working projects. For their radical colleagues, the Robinsons' home became the true space of collegiality. The university remained inhospitable to their presence.[11]

It is always necessary to honor the living. In 2003, former students of Cedric contacted HQ about commemorating the thirtieth anniversary of the publication of *Black Marxism* with a conference. But if it is important to honor the living, then Cedric reminded us all that it was the Black Radical tradition itself that must be honored. Uncomfortable with attempts to name the conference after him, Cedric encouraged the organizers of "Black Radical Thought" to center the tradition. Those organizers – his students Tiffany Willoughby-Herard, H. L. T. Quan, Marisela Marquez, Françoise Cromer, Crystal Griffith, and Ilya Ahmadizadeh – took from this idea that the point of the conference was to do something different. Instead of paper presentations, they encouraged dialogue. Instead of only panels, they encouraged workshops. Participating were many of Cedric's former students and colleagues including Mary Agnes Lewis, Joel Samoff, Rovan Locke, Ruth Wilson Gilmore, alongside many of the others already mentioned. Though they talked about Cedric's work and its meaning and impact, they also looked to the current situation and imagined a future. In 2005, many of the papers were published in a special edition of *Race and Class*, entitled "Cedric J. Robinson and the Philosophy of Black Resistance."[12]

This continued in the years after the conference. Cedric continued to teach in the Black Studies department as a professor emeritus, encountering several students like Greg Burris, Jordan Camp, Christina Heatherton, Damien Sojoyner, Jonathan D. Gomez, and others who would be shaped by his pedagogy. Years later in a volume of essays, *The Future of Black Radicalism*, which largely comprises these voices, Erica Edwards used the label "Cedric People" to describe the folk who had been taught, mentored, or otherwise affected by his presence, by its "touch."[13] She had been one of them, though she was not a student or colleague at UCSB. So it is not a closed circle. For what animates this touching is the reality that we all share its first principles,

Figure 7.1 Cedric Robinson at the Radical Thought Conference, 2004

Image courtesy of Elizabeth Robinson

and we share them in common. At that level, work is accessible in a way that goes beyond its words, its language, its conceptual interventions. It is ontologically total.

At the Radical Thought conference, Cedric convened a session with many of the students of the younger generation and reminded them that they had all come to him "fully intact."[14] Like Black people and others who were forcibly brought here and told that they possessed nothing, they too must reject that assumption. The real meaning of thinking together in Black Studies, and in the tradition of which it is an extension, is that we must search for the love and beauty that makes us, that knows us, that will keep us. It is something Cedric People recalled most consistently about the nature of the Black Radical tradition, the nature of Cedric's life and work.[15]

After being introduced by Gerard Pigeon, who walked through his courageous efforts to preserve Black Studies not just as a space at UCSB but as an idea writ large, Cedric appeared overcome with emotion. He then looked out to these students and intoned, "I am you." And after a long pause, he continued, "So I find it very difficult to take credit for your being me."[16]

The appropriation of Cedric Robinson

Some narratives have it that the time of the Movement for Black Lives began in the wake of the police killing of Michael Brown in Ferguson. But it is more honest to say that it continued. It is a movement that is a part of the response to the ongoing violence produced by racial capitalism.[17] As the resistance in Ferguson and then around the world moved toward an inflection point, Ruth Wilson Gilmore, Christina Heatherton, and Jordan Camp brought Cedric and Elizabeth to New York City to attend a conference entitled "Confronting Racial Capitalism." Scholars and organizers spoke to that ongoing violence, looked to the past, and connected these ideas to the international scene. Gilmore, a longtime comrade of Cedric, is one of the most prominent prison abolitionists and an ardent theorist of racial capitalism. And in that moment of upheaval in 2014, she remembered: "he hit me – not with his hand but rather most firmly with his look and tone. 'I've been trying to tell you,' he said. 'It's consciousness, not experience.'"[18]

Cedric, who had directly engaged with the police and confronted police brutality going back five decades, saw in that moment that it was consciousness that mattered. It was one of his final reminders to those engaged in the work of organizing today. In the archives of the *Third World News Review* and *No Alibis* lie even more reminders of the need to forge connections between people struggling for better worlds in the shadows of media silences and the intensity of state violence. In their article, "The Killing in Ferguson," the

Robinsons made connections between the media coverage of Michael Brown's killing, Operation Protective Edge in Gaza, and the Iraq War. It was not merely the link between the militarism of the police response and the usage of similar weaponry, practices that crossed national boundaries. As media events, these were also attacks on our consciousness. State violence in the form of policing and poverty are for certain media forces reducible to "conflict." And when images of those moments are supported by official rationalizations from journalists, we might accept the idea that we are deserving of this harm. We might accept the right of states and property to defend themselves against the right of people to live and to survive.[19]

Yet underneath all of this other things are happening. Other possibilities are being realized. Our people possess a consciousness that can be tapped into, relied upon, to generate the world we want. Cedric's work, and our work, is about both the elements of consciousness that are occluded, denied, and otherwise ignored, and how they are also the tools for creating the conditions for freedom. We must remain aware of where that work is happening, beyond national boundaries, in places where we least expect it. Police brutality is the violent extension of an entire world we have to struggle to end. Success is not guaranteed, as Elizabeth has always reminded us.[20] But we must find the beauty in struggling.

Cedric James Robinson passed away a year and a half later on June 5, 2016. Seven years earlier, his mother, Clara, had passed. He was also preceded in death by many critical family members like his aunts Wilma and Lillian, early influences on his thinking. When one reads the dedication pages of his books, the names of those family members are there. And so too are the names of Cedric's descendants. As much as he was writing for us, he was writing for Najda Ife Robinson, and her son Jacob. His desire was that their consciousness also not be subject to the vicissitudes of the racial regime. They were his students too.

In the wake of his transition, we have been witness to the kind of appropriation he had once noticed with regard to Frantz Fanon. In the early nineties, Cedric had written that Fanon's "death has inspired claims and counter-claims to his legacy. Some detractors, indeed, in the name of dogma or even less attractive causes, have sought substantially to diminish his political history and contribution." And: "Though I am certain, there is much to challenge in Fanon's work, it is an ungracious conceit to employ him as merely a background device."[21] A full accounting of a similar practice with regard to Cedric's work since his passing would require a separate project. Yet we must remember that the larger environment of academia and publishing actually encourages this appropriation. The rewards of attaching oneself to radical figures, as if they were a spectral presence in Black Studies, seemingly have no end. It is the logical order of things in a commodified market environment where simple citation is valued over deep study. So much of Cedric's Black life is lost in the demands of such a political economy of academic citation. What he wrote in the preface to *Black Marxism* is also true of the inspiration animating his work: it cannot be "traduced by convenient abstractions or dogma."[22] And since Black Studies is no less subject to these conditions, it is an "ungracious conceit" to cite Cedric and ignore his critique of academic contexts for knowledge production, or "to employ him as merely a background device" for considerations of Black radicalism that misread or fail to fully engage his thinking. For there is still much to extend in that work. Nothing was complete.

To end this appropriation, we must end the insistence that individual scholars constitute the beginning or end of any idea. We all belong to communities of meaning. And for Cedric's community, there was an ethic of resistance that was more important than what passed in the academy or in the worlds of organizing as "the right answer." That ethic is often lost in these moments of revival, and his work cannot be decoupled from that thrust. The consciousness that animates that work, a consciousness that is clearly grounded in Black thinking traditions, cannot be abstracted from those contexts and still truly be his (and ours). That consciousness is what this book has attempted to describe.

As Avery Gordon relates, though Cedric was against all orthodoxies, we are *also* in a dangerous moment where we risk making his thought orthodox – or, worse, simply excusing his thought from consideration in service to another orthodoxy.[23] None of this liberates us. We have to remember that it was never about him as a scholar. And it is not about any of us unless it is about all of us together. It is the consciousness that matters.

So we do not need to create new stars, for as difficult as it is to live against it, it is the star system itself that must be abolished. Speaking of the "seduction" of the star system at the 1994 Stanford gathering, Cedric offered that we might "reinvite" them back down "from the stage."[24] We might then destroy that stage. And if we listen closely, Cedric was pointing us in this direction. For his was a life that modeled how that would look. The forms of debate to which we are subjected in the academy and the larger political culture will likely not get us where we want to go. We might instead produce better forms of being together, even in disagreement, through engaging in struggle where the grounds of that community are love and care. Where how to get free is foregrounded by a deep respect for who we are as human beings and what we bring to that humanity, where it is "more than words or ideas but life itself."[25] Much like in his reading of Fanon, we too can return Cedric to his context: a Black life of struggle, a Black life lived in opposition to oppressions, a Black life lived in and grounded by radical love for all of humanity. And what we will find there is an intellectual project, but also a consciousness of how to be in the world that was motivated not by an attention economy, or by any party line, but by a freedom dream.

In another moment where there was great disagreement and debate on the particularities of class struggle and organizing, a moment which often degenerated into sharp polemics and missives, Cedric encouraged us to remain focused on what ultimately mattered, to think beyond a kind of polemicizing. He asked us to consider each other, "that we not dismiss each other as perverse or diseased or whatever we might be tempted to do, but move on to the work." May his words and spirit speak to us. For it is still true that "we have no time for polemics . . . to presume that the enemy is the person who doesn't obtain the same interpretation that we do. That every thought is precious, that every debate is reckoning with the end of the world, I think is a mistake."[26]

Notes

CRP: Cedric Robinson Private Papers, under the care of Elizabeth Robinson, Santa Barbara, CA.
GHP: Gerald Horne Papers, Sc MG 559, Manuscripts, Archives and Rare Books Division, Schomburg Center for Research in Black Culture, The New York Public Library.

Introduction: Cedric's Time

1 This conversation about the Bakongo is based on the work of Tata Kimbwandende Kia Bunseki Fu-Kiau, the Congolese intellectual who has contributed vastly to our understanding of Bakongo worldviews and their application to contemporary problems. See his *African Cosmology of the Bantu-Kongo: Tying the Spiritual Knot: Principles of Life and Living* (Athelia Henrietta Press, 2001), 35–8, for a discussion of the *tuzingu* and many of these other principles. For an anthropological perspective, see Wyatt MacGaffey, *Religion and Society in Central Africa: The BaKongo of Lower Zaire* (University of Chicago Press, 1986).

2 Jacob Carruthers, *Mdw Ntr: Divine Speech: A Historiographical Reflection of African Deep Thought from the Time of the Pharaohs to the Present* (Karnak House, 1995), 50–2.

3 Cedric Robinson, *Black Marxism: The Making of the Black Radical Tradition* (University of North Carolina Press, 2000), xxx.

4 John K. Thornton, *Africa and Africans in the Making of the Atlantic World* (Cambridge University Press, 1992); Linda M. Heywood and John K. Thornton, *Central Africans, Atlantic Creoles, and the Foundations of the Americas, 1585–1660* (Cambridge University Press, 2007); Michael Gomez, *Exchanging Our Country Marks:*

The Transformation of African Identities in the Colonial and Antebellum South (University of North Carolina Press, 1998); and Robert Farris Thompson, *Flash of the Spirit: African and Afro-American Art and Philosophy* (Vintage, 1983), 103–58. Cedric found the Bakongo conception useful for understanding questions of the state. See Cedric Robinson, *The Terms of Order: Political Science and the Myth of Leadership* (University of North Carolina Press, 2016), 225n40.

5 Carruthers, *Mdw Ntr*, 65–87.

6 On the Black radicals discussed in *Black Marxism*, Robinson would write, "But always we must keep in mind that their brilliance was also derivative. The truer genius was in the midst of the people of whom they wrote." *Black Marxism*, 184.

7 Erica Edwards, "Foreword," in Robinson, *The Terms of Order*, ix.

8 Damien M. Sojoyner, "Dissonance in Time: (Un)masking and (Re)Mapping of Blackness," in Gaye Theresa Johnson and Alex Lubin (eds), *Futures of Black Radicalism* (Verso Books, 2017), 60.

9 Robinson, *Black Marxism*, 177.

10 Michel-Rolph Trouillot, *Silencing the Past: Power and the Production of History* (Beacon Press, 1995), 82.

11 Sylvia Wynter, "Unsettling the Coloniality of Being/Power/Truth/Freedom: Towards the Human, After Man, Its Overrepresentation – An Argument," *CR: The New Centennial Review* 3 (2003): 257–337; and Sylvia Wynter, "A Black Studies Manifesto," *Forum N. H. I.: Knowledge for the 21st Century* 1(1) (1994): 3–11.

12 Hans Ruin, "Time as Ek-stasis and Trace of the Other," in Hans Ruin and Andrus Ers (eds), *Rethinking Time: Essays on History, Memory and Representation* (Soderton, 2011), 54–5. See also Reinhart Koselleck, *Futures Past: On the Semantics of Historical Time* (MIT Press, 1985).

13 Johannes Fabian, *Time and the Other: How Anthropology Makes its Object* (Columbia University Press, 1983), 2–6.

14 Fabian, *Time and the Other*, 6–21.

15 Robinson, *The Terms of Order*, 6.

16 A. Sivanandan and Hazel Waters, "Introduction," Special Issue, "Cedric Robinson and the Philosophy of Black Resistance," *Race and Class* 47 (October 2005): iii.

17 Chuck Morse, "Capitalism, Marxism, and the Black Radical

Tradition: An Interview with Cedric Robinson," *Perspectives on Anarchist Theory* (Spring 1999): 8.

18 Robinson, *The Terms of Order*, 215. On notions of "improvement," see Stefano Harney and Fred Moten, "Improvement and Preservation; Or, Usufruct and Use," in Johnson and Lubin (eds), *Futures of Black Radicalism*, 83–91.

19 On Black Study, see Stefano Harney and Fred Moten, *The Undercommons: Fugitive Planning and Black Study* (Minor Compositions, 2013) and Ashon Crawley, *Blackpentecostal Breath: The Aesthetics of Possibility* (Fordham University Press, 2016), 237. The methodological implications for that mode of critique and the possibilities inherent in that intellectual work are connected to the work of Cedric Robinson as well. See Joshua Myers, "The Scholarship of Cedric J. Robinson: Methodological Implications for Africana Studies," *Journal of Pan African Studies* 5 (June 2012): 46–82; Greg Carr, "What Black Studies is Not: Moving from Crisis to Liberation in Africana Intellectual Work," *Socialism and Democracy* 25 (March 2011): 178–91; Fred Moten, *Black and Blur* (Duke University Press, 2017), 1–27; and my *Of Black Study* (Pluto, forthcoming).

20 Sojoyner, "Dissonance in Time," 65–7.

21 Robinson, *Black Marxism*, 71.

22 My thinking here aligns with Imani Perry, "Black Studies in the Tradition, for the Future," 67th Charles Eaton Burch Lecture, Howard University, March 19, 2019.

23 Robinson, *Black Marxism*, 170.

24 Ibid., 168–71.

25 Wendy Brown, *Undoing the Demos: Neoliberalism's Stealth Revolution* (Zone Books, 2015).

26 Edwards, "Foreword," xv.

27 Cedric Robinson, *Forgeries of Memory and Meaning: Blacks and the Regime of Race in American Theater and Film before World War II* (University of North Carolina Press, 2007), xiii–xiv.

28 Christina Sharpe, *In the Wake: On Blackness and Being* (Duke University Press, 2016), 13.

29 Cedric J. Robinson, "What Is to Be Done? The Future of Critical Ethnic Studies," plenary session, Critical Ethnic Studies Conference, Chicago, September 21, 2013, https://www.you tube.com/watch?v=tKnf100jCFI.

Chapter 1 All Around Him

1 In his biography accompanying a 1999 interview with Chuck Morse, Robinson placed Whiteside's name, alongside C. L. R. James and the sociologist Terence Hopkins, as his "individuals or thinkers who had had the greatest influence upon his work." Chuck Morse, "Capitalism, Marxism, and the Black Radical Tradition: An Interview with Cedric Robinson," *Perspectives on Anarchist Theory* (Spring 1999): 6.

2 See, in particular, Greg Carr, "Toward an Intellectual History of Africana Studies: Genealogy and Normative Theory," in Nathaniel Norment (ed.), *The African American Studies Reader* (Carolina Academic Press, 2006), 438–52.

3 See Kate Cote Gillin, *Shrill Hurrahs: Women, Gender, and Racial Violence in South Carolina, 1865–1900* (University of South Carolina Press, 2013); Danielle McGuire, *At the Dark End of the Street: Black Women, Rape, and Resistance: A New History of the Civil Rights Movement from Rosa Parks to the Rise of Black Power* (Vintage, 2010).

4 Cedric Robinson, *Black Movements in America* (Routledge, 1997), 116.

5 Robin D. G. Kelley, "Cedric J. Robinson: The Making of a Black Radical Intellectual," *Counterpunch*, June 17, 2016, https://www.counterpunch.org/2016/06/17/cedric-j-robinson-the-making-of-a-black-radical-intellectual/

6 Cedric Robinson, *Black Marxism: The Making of the Black Radical Tradition* (University of North Carolina Press, 2000), 170.

7 Robinson, *Black Movements in America*, 153.

8 Robinson, *Black Marxism*, xxx.

9 This section is based on the family research conducted by Robin D. G. Kelley in Robin D. G. Kelley, "Winston Whiteside and the Politics of the Possible," in Gaye Theresa Johnson and Alex Lubin (eds), *Futures of Black Radicalism* (Verso, 2017), 255–62.

10 Heather Andrea Williams, *Help Me to Find My People: The African American Search for Family Lost in Slavery* (University of North Carolina Press, 2012).

11 Michael W. Fitzgerald, *Urban Emancipation: Popular Politics in Reconstruction Mobile, 1860–1890* (Louisiana University Press, 2002), 24.

12 Ibid., 152.
13 See ibid., 168–9, 233–8.
14 Ibid., 61.
15 Robert H. Woodrum, "'The Past Has Taught Us a Lesson': The International Longshoremen's Association and Black Workers in Mobile, 1903–1913," *Alabama Review* (April 2012): 113.
16 Woodrum, "The Past," 7–11; Christopher MacGregor Scribner, "Progress versus Tradition in Mobile, 1900–1920," in Michael Thomason (ed.), *Mobile: A New History of Alabama's First City* (University of Alabama Press, 2001), 166–8.
17 Woodrum, "The Past."
18 Scribner, "Progress versus Tradition." See also David E. Alsobrook, "Alabama's Port City: Mobile during the Progressive Era, 1896–1917" (PhD Diss., Auburn University, 1983), 152–91.
19 Delores Nason McBroome, *Parallel Communities: African Americans in California's East Bay, 1850–1963* (Garland, 1993), 55–90. See also Lawrence P. Crouchett, Lonnie G. Bunch III, and Martha Kendall Winnacker, *Visions Toward Tomorrow: The History of the East Bay Afro-American Community, 1852–1977* (Northern California Center for Afro-American History and Life, 1989), 31–3.
20 Crouchett et al., *Visions Toward Tomorrow*, 9–10. For more on the significance of the porters in Oakland, see McBroome, *Parallel Communities*, 65–9.
21 Kelley, "Winston Whiteside," 260.
22 Ibid., 261–2. On the foundations of Oakland's religious community, see McBroome, *Parallel Communities*, 36–8.
23 Margot Dashiell, email communication, December 27, 2019.
24 "Helpful," *San Pedro News-Pilot*, December 19, 1933.
25 Crouchett et al., *Visions Toward Tomorrow*, 35–41.
26 See Robert O. Self, *American Babylon: Race and the Struggle for Postwar Oakland* (Princeton University Press, 2003), 53; and Crouchett et al., *Visions Toward Tomorrow*, 41. Oakland was not unique, as this period saw an increase in Black radical organizing that explicitly critiqued capitalism. See, among others, Robin D. G. Kelley, *Hammer and Hoe: Alabama Communists during the Great Depression* (University of North Carolina Press, 1990); Minkah Makalani, *In the Cause of Freedom: Radical Black Internationalism from Harlem to London, 1917–1939* (University

of North Carolina Press, 2011); and Jonathan Scott Holloway, *Confronting the Veil: Abram Harris, Jr, E. Franklin Frazier, and Ralph Bunche* (University of North Carolina Press, 2002).

27 Kelley, "Winston Whiteside," 261.

28 Donna Murch, *Living for the City: Migration, Education, and the Rise of the Black Panther Party in Oakland, California* (University of North Carolina Press, 2010), 26–7.

29 "25 Busy Years in Unemployment," *Oakland Tribune*, May 16, 1965.

30 Kelley, "Winston Whiteside," 256. The biographical details in the following paragraphs draw from this article, as well as Kelley, "Cedric J. Robinson."

31 Kelley, "Winston Whiteside," 262.

32 Margot Dashiell, email communication, December 27, 2019.

33 Elizabeth Robinson, personal communication, April 12, 2020.

34 Cedric Robinson, "Why Is There Black Radicalism?" Lecture presentation at the University of Wisconsin-Madison, November 6, 2015, Youtube.com.

35 Robinson, *Black Movements in America*, 97.

36 Alain Locke, "The New Negro," in Alain Locke (ed.), *The New Negro* (Albert and Charles Boni, 1925), 6.

37 Crouchett et al., *Visions Toward Tomorrow*, 45.

38 McBroome, *Parallel Communities*, 100–8.

39 "25 Busy Years."

40 Self, *American Babylon*, 46–58; McBroome, *Parallel Communities*, 132–43.

41 Self, *American Babylon*, 45–6.

42 Ibid., 25–34, 58–60.

43 Chris Rhomberg, "White Nativism and Urban Politics: The 1920s Ku Klux Klan in Oakland, California," *Journal of American Ethnic History* 17 (Winter 1998): 39–55.

44 Self, *American Babylon*, 96–100; Murch, *Living for the City*, 38–42.

45 Murch, *Living for the City*, 48–9.

46 Douglas Wachter, email communication, October 30, 2019; Margot Dashiell, personal communication, December 13, 2019; Joe Hibble to Cedric Robinson, November 16, 2010, CRP.

47 Kelley, "Cedric J. Robinson." On tracking in Berkeley, see Berkeley Unified School District, *De Facto Segregation Study*

Committee Report to the Board of Education (Berkeley Unified School District, 1963).

48 Cedric Robinson, "Joshua Fit De Battle . . ." English V Paper, January 8, 1957, CRP.

49 Elizabeth Robinson, personal communication, August 8, 2020.

50 Cedric Robinson, Berkeley High School Transcript, copy in author's possession; *Olla Podrida*, Spring 1958, Berkeley High School, Berkeley Public Library, Central History Room; Dashiell, personal communication.

51 Margot Dashiell, email communication, December 27, 2019.

52 Morse, "Capitalism, Marxism, and the Black Radical Tradition," 6.

Chapter 2 The Town and Gown

1 Peter Hartlaub, "Origins of 'Oaktown': James Copes Says it Started on a T-Shirt," *San Francisco Chronicle*, November 2, 2017.

2 One framing of the foundation of the modern western university is William Clark, *Academic Charisma and the Origins of the Research University* (University of Chicago Press, 2006), and on the United States, see Laurence R. Veysey, *The Emergence of the American* (University of Chicago Press, 1965). On the contexts of the transition to mass higher education, see Martin Trow, "Problems in the Transition from Elite to Mass Higher Education," in Michael Burrage (ed.), *Twentieth-Century Higher Education: Elite to Mass to Universal* (Johns Hopkins University Press, 2010), 88–142; and, on California in particular, see John Aubrey Douglass, *The California Idea and American Higher Education: 1850 to the 1960 Master Plan* (Stanford University Press, 2000), 170–97.

3 Donna Murch, *Living for the City: Migration, Education, and the Rise of the Black Panther Party in Oakland, California* (University of North Carolina Press, 2010), 74–5; Douglass, *The California Idea*, 10.

4 Martin Trow, "The Second Transformation of American Secondary Education," in Michael Burrage (ed.), *Twentieth-Century Higher Education*, 72.

5 Elizabeth Robinson, personal communication, December 22, 2019.

6 Ibid.; Robin D. G. Kelley, "Cedric J. Robinson: The Making of a Black Radical Intellectual," *Counterpunch*, June 17, 2016, https://www.counterpunch.org/2016/06/17/cedric-j-robinson-the-making-of-a-black-radical-intellectual/. The university did not keep data on the racial composition of its students, perhaps because they did not need to. There's a consensus, however, that there were around one hundred Black students until 1966, the first year in which the data was recorded, with 226 students of African descent. See Murch, *Living for the City*, 75.

7 Kelley, "Cedric J. Robinson."

8 Douglass, *The California Idea*, 1–45.

9 Patricia A. Pelfrey, *A Brief History of the University of California* (Center for Studies in Higher Education, 2004), 10.

10 See W. E. B. Du Bois, *Black Reconstruction in America, 1860–1880* (Free Press, 2000), 580–636. On the expansion of the railroad after the war, see Stephen E. Ambrose, *Nothing Like it in the World: The Men Who Built the Transcontinental Railroad* (Simon and Schuster, 2000).

11 On modeling UC after Yale, see Douglass, *The California Idea*, 38–41. In these years, both UC and Stanford were supported by captains of industry who had outsized influence on the direction of these universities. While this was clear to see in the case of Leland Stanford, the railroad magnate's university, which became an early rival to UC, the UC Board of Regents was largely made up of these figures as well and was considered an autonomous branch of the California government. With the emergence of the Gilded Age, higher education in California and elsewhere was increasingly under the control of business interests. On these issues, see Douglass, *The California Idea*, 61–72, 92–103; Pelfrey, *A Brief History*, 14–19; John R. Thelin, *A History of American Higher Education* (Johns Hopkins University Press, 2004), 122–7.

12 The "California Idea" is from John Aubrey Douglass, and it describes the "rise of a cohesive and popular vision of public higher education as an ameliorative and proactive agent of state and local government, which would set the stage for a modern and scientifically advanced society. More specifically, the California Idea is the manifestation of this vision into a system of public colleges and university campuses." *The California Idea*, 82.

13 The experiences of the early generation of Black students are based on Lawrence P. Crouchett, Lonnie G. Bunch, III, and Martha Kendall Winnacker, *Visions Toward Tomorrow: The History of the East Bay Afro-American Community, 1852–1977* (Northern California Center for Afro-American History and Life, 1989), 26–31.

14 Keith Gilyard, *Louise Thompson Patterson: A Life of Struggle for Justice* (Duke University Press, 2017), 38.

15 "Lonely endeavor" is from Crouchett et al., *Visions Toward Tomorrow*, 27.

16 W. J. Rorabaugh, *Berkeley at War: The 1960s* (Oxford University Press, 1989), 6, 48–86; and Clark Kerr, *The Uses of the University* (Harvard University Press, 1963).

17 J. Herman Blake, interview with the author, November 13, 2019.

18 Margot Dashiell, email communication, November 20, 2019.

19 David P. Gardner, *The California Oath Controversy* (University of California Press, 1967); Clark Kerr, *The Gold and the Blue: A Personal Memoir of the University of California, 1949–1967, Volume II: Political Turmoil* (University of California Press, 2003), 27–47.

20 See Fred Haines's account in David Horowitz, *Student* (Ballantine Books, 1962), 70–81. For the Berkeley student perspective, see "Student Invokes the Fifth," *Daily Californian*, May 13, 1960; "Students Passive during Friday 'Raid,'" *Daily Californian*, May 16, 1960.

21 "Students are 'Dupes' Says HUAC," *Daily Californian*, May 16, 1960; Horowitz, *Student*, 81–105, 130–43; Jo Freeman, *At Berkeley in the '60s: The Education of an Activist* (Indiana University Press, 2004), 39–41, 172.

22 Douglas Wachter, email communication, October 30, 2019.

23 Freeman, *At Berkeley*, 14–22; Mike Miller, "Establishing SLATE on the Berkeley Campus," The SLATE Oral History Project, Oral History Center, Bancroft Library, University of California, Berkeley, 2018.

24 Horowitz, *Student*, 7–22; Kerr, *The Gold and the Blue, Vol. II*, 150–2; Miller, "Establishing SLATE"; Julianne Morris, "SLATE and Student Activism," The SLATE Oral History Project, Oral History Center, Bancroft Library, University of California, Berkeley, 2019.

25 Mike Miller, interview with the author, November 16, 2019.
26 Murch, *Living for the City*, 75–6. See also John Henrik Clarke, "The New Afro-American Nationalism," *Freedomways* 1 (Fall 1961): 55–65; and Harold Cruse, "Revolutionary Nationalism and the Afro-American," *Studies on the Left* 2 (1962): 12–25. On the general tenor of this moment, see Muhammad Ahmad, *We Will Return in the Whirlwind: Black Radical Organizations, 1960–1975* (Charles H. Kerr, 2007), 7–17; Christopher Tinson, *Radical Intellect: Liberator Magazine and Black Activism in the 1960s* (UNC Press, 2017), 13–73; and Peniel Joseph, *Waiting 'til the Midnight Hour: A Narrative History of Black Power in America* (Henry Holt and Co., 2006), 9–53.
27 Margot Dashiell, email communication, November 25, 2019; Margot Dashiell, interview with the author, November 11, 2019.
28 Cedric Robinson, University of California, Berkeley Transcript, copy in author's possession; Nell Irvin Painter, personal communication, November 16, 2019.
29 Blake, interview with the author; Cameron Vanderscoff, "'Look'n M' Face and Hear M' Story,' An Oral History with Professor J. Herman Blake," University of California-Santa Cruz, Digital Library Collections, 2014.
30 Dashiell, interview; Blake, interview.
31 Miller, interview; Miller, "Establishing SLATE."
32 Arthur E. Hippler, *Hunter's Point: A Black Ghetto* (Basic Books, 1974), 165–84.
33 These statements are from a 1972 featured article in the *San Francisco Chronicle* quoted in Paul T. Miller, *The Postwar Struggle for Civil Rights: African Americans in San Francisco, 1945–1975* (Routledge, 2012), 144.
34 Ibid., 144; Dashiell, interview.
35 Cedric Robinson, *Black Movements in America* (Routledge, 1997), 139.
36 Hippler, *Hunter's Point*, 177–82.
37 Dashiell, interview.
38 "Civil Rights Leader Supports Castro's Rule in Cuba," *Daily Californian*, March 16, 1961.
39 Timothy Tyson, *Radio Free Dixie: Robert F. Williams and the Roots of Black Power* (University of North Carolina Press, 1998), 224–32.

40 "Civil Rights Leader," *Daily Californian*.
41 Cedric Robinson, "Letters to the Ice Box," *Daily Californian*, March 21, 1961.
42 "Rally to Test 1915 City Ordinance," *Oakland Tribune*, November 5, 1961; Tyson, *Radio Free Dixie*, 244–86.
43 "Berkeley Pastor – NAACP Pillar – To Speak Today," *Daily Californian*, April 27, 1961; Blake, interview with the author; Vanderscoff, "Look'n M' Face," 62–3. Despite this encounter, students continued to support Nichols' bid for election to the school board, the first African American to hold such a position. Margot Dashiell, personal communication, January 8, 2020; Rorabaugh, *Berkeley at War*, 53.
44 Murch, *Living for the City*, 76; Garrett Felber, "'Those Who Say Don't Know and Those Who Know Don't Say': The Nation of Islam, and the Politics of Black Nationalism, 1930–1975" (PhD Diss., University of Michigan, 2017), 216–17. See his book, *Those Who Don't Say: The Nation of Islam, the Black Freedom Movement, and the Carceral State* (University of North Carolina Press, 2019).
45 Tyson, *Radio Free Dixie*, 149–65, 204–5.
46 Donald Warden, "Letter to the Ice Box," *Daily Californian*, March 1, 1961; Murch, *Living for the City*, 76.
47 On Warden's background, see Murch, *Living for the City*, 77–9, and his autobiographical statements in Khalid Abdullah Tariq Al Mansour, *Black Americans at the Crossroads – Where Do We Go From Here?* (First African Arabian Press, 1981).
48 J. Herman Blake, "Letters to the Ice Box," *Daily Californian*, March 17, 1961.
49 Nell Irvin, "Letters to the Ice Box," *Daily Californian*, March 9, 1961. She would go on to become a noted African-American historian, author of several works that directly intersected with Cedric's own interests. See his review of her work, *Exodusters*, "Class Antagonisms and Black Migrations: A Review Article," *Race and Class* (January 1982): 47–60.
50 Murch, *Living for the City*, 77; Dashiell, interview; Blake, interview.
51 "Black Muslims Deny NAACP Effectiveness," *Daily Californian*, April 17, 1961; Murch, *Living for the City*, 77.
52 Dashiell, interview.

53 "UC Students Will Picket Woolworth's," *Daily Californian*, March 2, 1960; "CORE Pickets Local Stores in Downpour," *Daily Californian*, March 7, 1960; "Racial Equality Goal of Committee," *Daily Californian*, October 13, 1960; "CORE Ends Picket of Lunch Counters," *Daily Californian*, March 6, 1961.

54 Vanderscoff, "Look'n M' Face"; Blake, interview.

55 Blake, interview. On the demonstration, see "Students Stage Demonstration Protest Alleged Discrimination," *Daily Californian*, April 28, 1961. This was in fact part of a larger national NAACP initiative. According to Margot Dashiell's recollections, after this protest, the national leader of the youth division met with her, Cedric, and Blake.

56 Known as the Kerr Directives, these stipulations were vigorously debated among students. See "Regulation on Use of University Facilities," University of California Office of the University President, Permanent Files, 1952–1975, CU-5, Series 8, Box 41, Folder 19, Bancroft Library, University of California, Berkeley; Kerr, *The Gold and the Blue: Vol. II*, 122–57; Freeman, *At Berkeley*, 19–20, 43–6.

57 "Frank Wilkinson, HCUA Opponent, Will Speak on Campus This Noon," *Daily Californian*, March 22, 1961; Freeman, *At Berkeley*, 56; "Muslim Speaker Approval Denied," *Daily Californian*, May 5, 1961.

58 Al Mansour, *Black Americans*, 72–3.

59 See Clayborne Carson (ed.), *Malcolm X: The FBI File* (Carrol and Graf, 1991), 95–100.

60 Adrian A. Kragen, "A Law Professor's Career: Teaching, Private Practice, and Legislative Representative, 1934 to 1989" (Regional Oral History Office, The Bancroft Library, University of California, Berkeley), 171, 173.

61 "'Differential Treatment' Charges Student NAACP," *Daily Californian*, May 8, 1961. Malcolm himself argued that the university's decision was an "excuse," "Malcolm: 'Religion the Excuse to Cancel Black Muslim Talk,'" *Daily Californian*, May 8, 1961.

62 Frances Linsley, *What is This Place? An Informal History of 100 Years of Stiles Hall* (Stiles Hall, 1984), 151.

63 "Black Muslim Advocates Total Separation of Races," *Daily Californian*, May 9, 1961.

64 J. Herman Blake, interview with Denise Gines, January 31, 2007, The HistoryMakers Digital Archive. Session 1, tape 4, story 1, J. Herman Blake describes his social activism in Berkeley, California.

65 Al Mansour, *Black Americans*, 73; Blake, interview with the author.

66 Cedric J. Robinson, "Malcolm Little as Charismatic Leader," *Afro-American Studies* 3 (1972): 81–96.

67 "American Press Distort Truth About Cuba, Students Charge," *Daily Californian*, October 5, 1960; Horowitz, *Student*, 145–7; Van Gosse, *Where the Boys Are: Cuba, Cold War America, and the Making of a New Left* (Verso, 1993).

68 Joseph, *Waiting*, 35–8; Gosse, *Where the Boys Are*, 147–54.

69 Cedric's name appeared as member of the "executive committee" at the bottom of a petition published in the *Stanford Daily*, developed by the Ad Hoc Committee and the Fair Play for Cuba Committee, see "Petition on our Policy Toward Cuba," *Stanford Daily*, April 28, 1961.

70 See, for instance, the *Eleventh Report of the Senate Fact-Finding Subcommittee on Un-American Activities* (Senate of the State of California, 1961), 117–19.

71 "Rally Protests US Aiding Cuba Counter-revolution," *Daily Californian*, April 19, 1961.

72 Kelley, "Cedric J. Robinson"; Elizabeth Robinson, personal communication, December 22, 2019.

73 "Reprimand for Rally Holders Recommended," *Daily Californian*, May 5, 1961.

74 Cedric Robinson, University of California-Berkeley, transcript.

75 Cedric Robinson to Margot Dashiell, May 17, 1961, Margot Dashiell Collection.

76 Margot Dashiell, interview; Cedric Robinson to Margot Dashiell, June 6, 1961.

77 Ibid.

78 Cedric Robinson, "Campus Civil Rights Groups and the Administration," SLATE Summer Conference, July 28–31, 1961, Calisphere, University of California, Berkeley.

79 Michael Myerson and Michael Miller, "One Man's Opinion," *Daily Californian*, June 30, 1961; "Towle Upholds Slate's Loss of UC Privileges," *Daily Californian*, August 11, 1961.

80 Dashiell, interview; Elizabeth Robinson, personal communication, August 21, 2019.

81 Murch, *Living for the City*, 79. On Kwayana, see "Remembering Tchaiko Kwayana," *Guyana Chronicle*, May 16, 2017, guyanachronicle.com

82 Murch, *Living for the City*, 87.

83 Ibid., 83; Dashiell, interview. Gopalan and Harris married and gave birth to Kamala Harris, who wrote about the importance of the study group in shaping her parents: "They talked about apartheid, about African decolonization, about liberation movements in the developing world, and about the history of racism in America." *The Truths We Hold: An American Journey* (Penguin Press, 2019), 9.

84 *Root and Branch* (Winter 1962). It was republished in Al Mansour, *Black Americans*, 44–68.

85 Ibid., 68.

86 Ibid., 53–5; Dashiell, interview.

87 Lee O. Cherry, *Spirits in the Whirlwind: Evolution Towards the African-American Association and Beyond* (Lulu, 2018), 62.

88 Leslie Alexander Lacy, *The Rise and Fall of a Proper Negro* (Macmillan, 1970), 119–20.

89 Ibid., 120–1.

90 Cherry, *Spirits in the Whirlwind*, 108–36; Murch, *Living for the City*, 88–116; Jeffrey O. G. Ogbar, *Black Power: Radical Politics and African American Identity* (Johns Hopkins University Press, 2008), 126–7.

91 Cherry, *Spirits in the Whirlwind*, 73–107; Al Mansour, *Black Americans*, 42; Robert O. Self, *American Babylon: Race and the Struggle for Postwar Oakland* (Princeton University Press, 2003), 222–4; Huey P. Newton, *Revolutionary Suicide* (Penguin, 2006), 60–6; Bobby Seale, *Seize the Time: The Story of the Black Panther Party and Huey P. Newton* (Random House, 1970), 13–34; Joshua Bloom and Waldo Martin, *Black Against Empire: The History and Politics of the Black Panther Party* (University of California Press, 2013), 22–3.

92 Al Mansour, *Black Americans*, 10.

93 Lacy, *The Rise and Fall*, 131.

94 Ibid., 130. On the politics of the Association, Lacy wrote: "Politically and economically they were capitalists. And a capi-

talist without money was a strange breed." See also Newton, *Revolutionary Suicide*, 64–6; and Seale, *Seize the Time*, 21–2.

95 Cedric Robinson, *Black Marxism: The Making of the Black Radical Tradition* (UNC Press, 2000), xxv.

96 Cedric Robinson, "Black Studies," lecture presented at the University of California, Berkeley, February 8, 1986, p. 1, CRP.

97 Murch, *Living for the City*, 80; Dashiell, email communication, December 13, 2019.

98 Murch, *Living for the City*, 89–90. According to Dashiell, Cedric participated in these protests in Oakland. Dashiell, personal communication, December 12, 2019.

99 "Operation Crossroads to be Explained," *Daily Californian*, December 14, 1961.

100 Rev. James H. Robinson, interview with James Mosby, November 1, 1968, Ralph Bunche Oral History Collection, Moorland-Spingarn Research Center, Howard University; John David Cato, "James Herman Robinson: Crossroads Africa and American Idealism, 1958–1972," *American Presbyterians* 68 (Summer 1990): 99–107.

101 James H. Robinson, *Africa at the Crossroads* (Westminster Press, 1962), 59. His critique of previous Pan-African work appears in ibid., 60–1.

102 "The Journal: Account of the Bulawayo Group, Southern Rhodesia," April 1, 1963, CRP (p. 3).

103 Cedric Robinson to Margot Dashiell, July 2, 1963, Margot Dashiell Collection.

104 Ibid.

105 "The Journal," 4–5.

106 Ibid., 8.

107 "City Anger over Crossroads Team's Attitude," *The Chronicle*, July 27, 1962. Cedric sent many of these clippings back home to his grandparents through Margot.

108 Thomas Wentworth Higginson, *Army Life in a Black Regiment* (Dover, 2002), 11–19.

109 Cedric Robinson to Margot Dashiell, July 4, 1962 and July 26, 1962, Margot Dashiell Collection.

110 "The Journal," 24.

111 Ibid., 10, 16.

112 Robinson to Dashiell, July 26, 1962.

113 "The Journal," 23–4.

114 Cedric Robinson to Margot Dashiell, August 15, 1962, Margot Dashiell Collection.

115 Eliakim M. Sibanda, "The Contributions of Joshua Nkomo to the Liberation of Zimbabwe," in Sabelo J. Ndlovu-Gatsheni (ed.), *Joshua Mqabuko Nkomo: Politics, Power, and Memory* (Palgrave Macmillan, 2017), 63; Eliakim M. Sibanda, *The Zimbabwe African People's Union, 1961–87: A Political History of Insurgency in Southern Rhodesia* (Africa World Press, 2005), 88–9.

116 "The Journal," 26–35.

117 Sibanda, "Contributions of Joshua Nkomo," 61.

118 Cedric Robinson, "How Is It in So. Rhodesia?" *Sun-Reporter*, December 8, 1962.

119 Gilyard, *Louise Thompson Patterson*, 185.

120 Margot Dashiell, email communication, November 13, 2019.

121 Gilyard, *Louise Thompson Patterson*; Gerald Horne, *Black Revolutionary: William Patterson and the Globalization of the African American Freedom Struggle* (University of Illinois Press, 2013); Evelyn Louise Crawford and MaryLouise Patterson (eds), *Letters from Langston: From the Harlem Renaissance to the Red Scare and Beyond* (University of California Press, 2016).

122 Horne, *Black Revolutionary*, 194.

123 Cedric Robinson to Nebby Lou Crawford, July 1, 1964, Margot Dashiell Collection.

124 Cedric Robinson to Margot Dashiell, November 30, 1983, Margot Dashiell Collection.

Chapter 3 Authority and Order

1 Robert O. Self, *American Babylon: Race and the Struggle for Postwar Oakland* (Princeton University Press, 2003), 182–91.

2 "Application for Appointment AR 140-100 and AR 601-100," May 13, 1964, Military Service Records, CRP.

3 George C. Herring, *America's Longest War: The United States and Vietnam, 1950–1975* (Temple University Press, 1986); George McT. Kahin, *Intervention: How America Became Involved in Vietnam* (Alfred A. Knopf, 1986); Paul T. Murray, "Blacks and the Draft: A History of Institutional Racism," *Journal of Black Studies* 2 (September 1971): 72.

4 Murray, "Blacks and the Draft," 69–73; George Q. Flynn, *The Draft, 1940–1973* (University Press of Kansas, 1993), 171.

5 Flynn, *The Draft*, 168; James M. Gerhardt, *The Draft and Public Policy: Issues in Military Manpower Procurement, 1945–1970* (Ohio State University Press, 1971), 252–64.

6 "Special Orders, No. 300," December 5, 1963, Fort Ord, California, Military Service Records, CRP.

7 W. S. Nye, *Carbine and Lance: The Story of Old Fort Sill* (University of Oklahoma Press, 1937); Jeffrey F. Burton et al., *Confinement and Ethnicity: An Overview of World War II Japanese American Relocation Sites* (University of Washington Press, 2002), 401.

8 Murray, "Blacks and the Draft," 71.

9 Cedric Robinson, University of California, Berkeley Transcript, CRP. On compulsory ROTC at Berkeley, see David Horowitz, *Student: The Political Activities of the Berkeley Students* (Ballantine, 1962), 22–9.

10 "Application for Appointment."

11 "Request for Tuition Assistance: General Educational Development Program AR 621-5," March 17, 1964, Military Service Records, CRP.

12 Cedric Robinson to Nebby Lou Crawford, n.d., Margot Dashiell Collection, emphasis mine. It is clear that Cedric was in Fort Sill when this letter was sent. And his comments indicate that it must have been sent at some point after the April 1964 protests on Auto Row. On the Auto Row protests, see Paul T. Miller, *The Postwar Struggle for Civil Rights: African Americans in San Francisco, 1945–1975* (Routledge, 2012), 62–87.

13 "25 Busy Years in 'Unemployment,'" *Oakland Tribune*, May 16, 1965.

14 Cedric Robinson to Margot Dashiell, June 1, 1964, Margot Dashiell Collection.

15 Ibid.

16 Robin D. G. Kelley, "Cedric J. Robinson: The Making of a Black Radical," *Counterpunch*, June 17, 2016, https://www.counterpunch.org/2016/06/17/cedric-j-robinson-the-making-of-a-black-radicalintellectual/

17 "Certificate of Clearance and/or Security Determination under EO 10450," October 28, 1964, Military Service Records, CRP;

Memorandum: U.S. Army Artillery and Missile School Office of the Commandment, April 13, 1965, Military Service Records, CRP.

18 Kahin, *Intervention*, 319.

19 Herring, *America's Longest War*, 150; Kahin, *Intervention*, 347–401.

20 Elizabeth Peters Robinson, interview with the author, May 28, 2020.

21 Anthony M. Platt, *The Child Savers: The Invention of Delinquency* (University of Chicago Press, 1969).

22 Kelley, "Cedric J. Robinson."

23 Robinson, interview.

24 See Martha Biondi, *The Black Revolution on Campus* (University of California Press, 2012), 43–78 and Fabio Rojas, *From Black Power to Black Studies: How a Radical Social Movement Became an Academic Discipline* (Johns Hopkins University Press, 2007).

25 John Bunzel, "Black Studies at San Francisco State," *The Public Interest* (Fall 1968): 36.

26 Cedric J. Robinson, "Pluralism and the Power Elite," May 19, 1967, CRP.

27 James Garrett, email communication, October 28, 2019.

28 Cedric Robinson, "Statement of Purpose" and "Master's Thesis: A Research Design," 1967, CRP.

29 On this question, see particularly David Ricci, *The Tragedy of Political Science: Politics Scholarship and Democracy* (Yale University Press, 1984), 70–4; and Raymond Seidelman and Edward Harpham, *Disenchanted Realists: Political Science and the American Crisis, 1884–1984* (State University of New York Press, 1985), 1–11.

30 Sometimes this meant eugenics, other times it could mean a kind of tutelage. Always it meant that "others" lacked something that made them less amenable to governing or being governed. See Jessica Blatt, *Race and the Making of American Political Science* (University of Pennsylvania Press, 2015); and Robert Vitalis, *White World Order, Black Power Politics: The Birth of American International Relations* (Cornell University Press, 2015).

31 Perhaps part of the problem of that legacy was its insistence on the primacy of Herbert Spencer's idea of human evolution.

On the science of political science, see Bernard Crick, *The American Science of Politics: Its Origins and Conditions* (University of California Press, 1959).

32 On this pretense, see Ricci, *Tragedy*, 75–88; Seidelman and Harpham, *Disenchanted*, 101–86; and Crick, *American Science*, 157–209.

33 Kelley, "Cedric J. Robinson."

34 Steven C. Phillips, *Justice and Hope: Past Reflections and Future Visions of the Stanford Black Student Union 1967–1989* (Stanford Black Student Union, 1990), 15–18; "Black Enrollment to Double in the Fall," *Stanford Daily*, May 5, 1968.

35 "BSU Presents Twelve Demands: More Programs, Funds, Control," *Stanford Daily*, February 5, 1969; "Militant Blacks Raid Bookstore; Pitzer's Absence Causes Fury," *Stanford Daily*, February 21, 1969; Phillips, *Justice and Hope*, 18–19, 24–5. See also Richard W. Lyman, *Stanford in Turmoil: Campus Unrest, 1968–1972* (Stanford University Press, 2009), 68–89.

36 As quoted in Gerald A. McWorter and Ronald Bailey, "Black Studies Curriculum Development in the 1980s: Its Patterns and History," in Nathaniel Norment (ed.), *The African American Studies Reader* (Carolina Academic Press, 2006), 737.

37 St Clair Drake, "What Happened to Black Studies?" in Norment (ed.), *African American Studies Reader*, 347.

38 St Clair Drake, "Black Studies and Global Perspectives," *Journal of Negro Education* 53 (Summer 1984): 235.

39 St Clair Drake, "Reflections on Anthropology and the Black Experience," *Anthropology and Education Quarterly* 9 (Summer 1978): 101.

40 Perhaps none more closely than Ogletree. See Charles Ogletree, *All Deliberate Speed: Reflections on the First Half Century of Brown v. Board of Education* (W. W. Norton and Co., 2004), 41–56, 281.

41 Bailey, a student of Drake's, consciously understood his graduate work to be centered in Black Studies. See Ronald William Bailey, "The Slave Trade and the Development of Capitalism in the United States: A Critical Reappraisal of Theory and Method in Afro-American Studies" (PhD Diss., Stanford University, 1980); and St Clair Drake, Ronald Bailey, and Janet Cheatham Saxe, *Teaching Black: An Evaluation of Methods and Resources* (San Mateo County Office of Education, 1972). See also Ronald W.

Bailey, "Black Studies in the Third Millennium: Six Ideas that Can Still (and must) Change the World," *Souls* 2 (2000): 77–90. Thanks to Alan Minor and Fred Moten for reminding me of the Washington and Mackey connections.

42 Cedric J. Robinson to St Clair Drake, June 26, 1981, St Clair Drake Papers Box 8, Folder 34, Schomburg Center for Research in Black Culture, New York. Andrew Rosa has written that Cedric expressed regret for not including Drake in *Black Marxism*. His biographical essay reads Drake as part of – perhaps as heir to – the Black Radical tradition. See Andrew Rosa, "To Make a Better World Tomorrow: St Clair Drake and the Quakers of Pendle Hill," *Race and Class* 54 (July–September 2012): 67–90.

43 On the founding of NCOBPS, see Joseph P. McCormick, "Beyond Tactical Withdrawal: An Early History of the National Conference of Black Political Scientists," in Michael Mitchell and David Covin (eds), *Black Politics in a Time of Transition* (Transaction Publishers, 2012), 159–78; and The Task Force Historical Record on the Founders of the National Conference of Black Political Scientists, "Chronicling our Legacy of Leadership," *National Review of Black Politics* 1 (January 2020): 80–131. See also the oral histories of Mae King and Mack Jones in the APSA/Pi Sigma Alpha: African American Political Scientists Oral History Project, Louie B. Nunn Center for Oral History, University of Kentucky Library.

44 Elizabeth Robinson, personal communication, April 12, 2020.

45 Mack H. Jones, *Knowledge, Power, and Black Politics* (SUNY Press, 2014), 32.

46 Cedric J. Robinson, "Malcolm Little as Charismatic Leader," in H. L. T. Quan (ed.), *Cedric J. Robinson: On Racial Capitalism, Black Internationalism, and Cultures of Resistance* (Pluto Press, 2019), 279.

47 Ibid., 285.

48 Ibid., 287–8.

49 Ibid., 268, italics mine.

50 Ibid., 292. This particular reading of the transformative power of charisma would be extended in Cedric's dissertation. But perhaps here is a great place to mention that the charismatic situation and its connection to the wider Black masses were also grounded in his elaboration of the collectivity of the Black

Radical tradition. On these connections, see Erica Edwards' reading of Cedric and her distinction between charisma and charismata in her *Charisma and the Fictions of Black Leadership* (University of Minnesota Press, 2012), 118–19.

51 Advancing the study of Black politics within the dominant frame of American political science was the goal for many Black political scientists who participated in the founding of NCOBPS. Not all shared the position advanced by Mack Jones, that of ultimate autonomy and a break from the discipline both organizationally and epistemologically. On this debate, see McCormick, "Beyond Tactical Withdrawal," 163–9; and Jones, *Knowledge*, 33.

52 Seidelman and Harpham, *Disenchanted*, 149–86; Ricci, *Tragedy*, 133–75; and Albert Somit and Joseph Tanenhaus, *The Development of American Political Science* (Allyn and Bacon, 1967), 173–94.

53 Ricci, *Tragedy*, 159.

54 Ibid., 188–90; Seidelman and Harpham, *Disenchanted*, 187–200.

55 Charles Drekmeier, interview with Natalie Marine-Street, Stanford Faculty Senate Oral History Project, Stanford Historical Society Oral History Program Interviews (SC0932), Department of Special Collections & University Archives, Stanford University Libraries.

56 Robinson, interview.

57 Ibid.

58 Ibid.

59 Cedric J. Robinson, Outline of Dissertation, n.d., CRP.

60 Norman Cohn, *The Pursuit of the Millennium* (Oxford University Press, 1970).

61 See Zevedei Barbu, *Democracy and Dictatorship: Their Psychology and Patterns of Life* (Grove Press, 1956) and his *Problems of Historical Psychology* (Grove Press, 1960).

62 Cedric J. Robinson, *The Terms of Order: Political Science and the Myth of Leadership* (University of North Carolina Press, 2016), 6. This newer edition – the most readily available and accessible – is mostly identical to the dissertation version of the work so the following citations will correspond to it.

63 Ibid., xxx.

64 Ibid., 9.

65 Ricci, *Tragedy*, 275–88.

66 Robinson, *Terms*, xxx.

67 See Ricci, *Tragedy*, 114–205.

68 Robinson, *Terms*, 16–17.

69 Ibid., 21.

70 Ibid., 22. At the turn of the century, Arthur Fisher Bentley famously dismissed such "artifactual innovations" as "soul-stuff," perhaps indirectly influencing generations of political scientists to view "ideals" as inconsequential to the mainsprings of political activity. See his *The Process of Government: A Study of Social Pressures* (University of Chicago Press, 1908), 26–7.

71 Robinson, *Terms*, 29.

72 Ibid., 31.

73 Hannah Arendt traces the historical evolution of authority in her *Between Past and Future* (1961). In a footnote to *Terms*, Cedric argues that the choice to focus on the historical, rather than the psychological, was a "conceptual error," that "more properly" might be understood "not as an error but a myth consequent to the strategy" of the text. Perhaps it was Arendt's "submission to liberal political philosophy and theory" that prevented her from being able to recognize the psychic dimensions inherent in these issues. See *Terms*, 227n54.

74 Ibid., 35.

75 Ibid., 36.

76 Here is Cedric: "Conceptualizations of social order can range from the design of Aristotelian and Burkean 'constitutionalities' and anarchistic rationalism to the law-fulfilling dialectic of Hegel and the historicism of Marx – from station to process" (ibid., 38). This is to say that this desire for order is a product of the construct of a "political" genealogy, emanating from the Greco-Roman foundations to the Enlightenment. It is important to note that this predilection was not a function of any particular ideology but of a culture.

77 Robinson, *Terms*, 38.

78 Jessica Blatt writes that political scientists, such as the intrepid academic entrepreneur Charles Merriam, "put great stock in the idea that scientific methods could anchor political judgment and point to possibilities for 'social control' in the face of rapid social, economic, and political change." *Race and the Making*, 7.

79 Ibid., 45.

80 Robinson, *Terms*, 60.

81 "Yet groups are acknowledged as failing because of their particular leadership and/or in spite of their particular leadership *but never because they possessed leadership.*" Ibid., 49, italics mine.

82 "For Machiavelli, distinguishing his thought from the earlier traditions, political authority rested from its inception in the cradle of power, force, and violence." Ibid., 32.

83 Ibid., 54.

84 Ibid., 55. The questions raised in the work of Carl Schmitt, particularly the idea of a "friend-and-enemy distinction" and that of "the decision," are perennial ones for political theory. The context of the emergence of his thought – Germany in the interwar years – is particularly critical to understanding questions of liberal political theory and of authority. See his *The Concept of the Political* (University of Chicago Press, 1996) and Carl Schmitt, *Political Theology: Four Chapters on the Concept of Sovereignty*, trans. George Schwab (University of Chicago Press, 2005). As a legal and political scholar concerned with order, he shared the same concerns as Cedric. But as a former Nazi jurist, he of course felt that order should be preserved. The curious revival of his thought came after Cedric finished his dissertation, but that this embrace happened at all provides an indication of the interests of political theory in the West. See Jens Meierhenrich and Oliver Simons, "A Fanatic of Order in an Epoch of Confusing Turmoil," in Jens Meierhenrich and Oliver Simons (eds), *The Oxford Companion Handbook of Carl Schmitt* (Oxford University Press, 2016), 3–70.

85 Robinson, *Terms*, 106.

86 Ibid., 77.

87 Ricci, *Tragedy*, 73.

88 The third chapter, "The Question of Rationality," engages Rudolph Sohm, William James, Sigmund Freud, William Reich, Eric Fromm, as well as Cohn, whom he had studied with at Sussex. Together, they are read as intellectuals that attempted to explain or understand the (sub)consciousness of "followership" and the "social movements" that required followers. Of these attempts, Cedric writes: "the events of the first thirty-odd years of twentieth-century western social and political history provoked crises in the West's epistemologies, crises in its meanings,

explanations, and understandings. In the specific attempt to comprehend the social movements of that period, one reaction was to reach back to the theologians. A very different reaction was to resurrect the nonbehaviorist efforts in psychology" (Robinson, *Terms*, 78).

89 Ibid., 103.

90 Ibid., 108.

91 Ibid., 109.

92 Ibid., 110–14.

93 Ibid., 120.

94 Ibid., 123. Weber treats charisma in his *Wirtschaft und Gesellschaft* (1922), which has appeared in numerous English translations.

95 Cohn, *Pursuit*, 38.

96 Robinson, *Terms*, 148. See also Max Weber, *Ancient Judaism* (Free Press, 1967).

97 Robinson, *Terms*, 152.

98 Ibid., 153.

99 Ibid., 160.

100 Robinson covers some of the major contributors to anarchist theory, from those considered egoists – Max Stirner, Sergei Nechayev, and Friedrich Nietzsche – to those who were revolutionists – Pierre-Joseph Proudhon and Peter Kropotkin. See ibid., 175–85.

101 Ibid., 185.

102 Ibid.

103 Ibid.

104 This genealogy is traced to the typology of African societies first presented in Meyer Fortes and E. Evans Pritchard, *Introduction to African Political Systems* (Oxford University Press, 1940). The "epistemocentric" basis is found both in the title of the text and in the association of the quality of stateless societies as a "political phenomenon." See Robinson, *Terms*, 190, 199.

105 Cedric J. Robinson, "Museums of Knowledge and Streams of Consciousness," *Praxis Center*, February 17, 2020, www.kzoo.edu/praxis/museums-of-knowledge/

106 Robinson, *Terms*, 202. The Ila-Tonga were incomprehensible to the British because they were "without networks of social and political machineries which would have made their demarcation convenient to those primarily familiar with European political

history." Ibid., 191. Cedric relied on and critiqued the work of the anthropologist Max Gluckman to come to an understanding of the *mukowa*. It was both a system of face-to-face relationships and an expansive network of relationships that extended to include ancestors and the spirit world. It encompassed all of these seen and unseen community members as it also functioned as the ground for day-to-day life. But this view was enabled through Cedric's reading of Gluckman's anthropology against and alongside the work of African philosophers like John Mbiti. See Robinson, *Terms*, 192–6. On the Ila-Tonga, see Elizabeth Colson, *The Plateau Tonga of Northern Rhodesia* (Manchester University Press, 1962).

107 Robinson, *Terms*, 196.

108 Cedric asserts:

> As political science, sociology, and economics (and their progeny in schools of history) have evolved into scientism – the progression of empiricism, analyticism, and quantitativism from approach to ideology – their probings into the nature of human organization have become situation-specific to a particular case of that organization: western industrialized society, and have settled down into a tangential, self-indulging universe of queries and data indices. And as they have done so they have sought the measure and dimensions of reality by positing for every particle in their systems and existence exorcised from the presence of any other thing: reification. (Ibid., 198)

In coming to terms with the question of how societies in Africa made meaning, anthropology's colonial legacy on the continent must be brought to bear. Objective knowledge was the basis for domination. Much as sociology has been understood under the rubric of measuring and realizing "social control," so might anthropology. On this question, see inter alia Bernard Magubane and James C. Faris, "On the Political Relevance of Anthropology," *Dialectical Anthropology* 9 (June 1985): 91–104.

109 Robinson, *Terms*, 199.

110 Ibid., 200. This recalls the dozens. On its African connections, see Elijah Wald, *The Dozens: A History of Rap's Mama* (Oxford University Press, 2012), 135–51.

111 Robinson, *Terms*, 201.
112 Ibid., 202.
113 Ibid., 203.
114 Ibid., 212.
115 Ibid., 214–15.
116 Mary Agnes Lewis, review of *The Terms of Order* by Cedric Robinson, Raya Dunayevskaya Papers, Reel 15934, Volume 15, Section D, Item 7 Page 1, Archives of Labor and Urban Affairs, Wayne State University.
117 Ibid., 7.

Chapter 4 Beyond Racial Capitalism

1 On the strike, see Paul Foot, *The Postal Workers and the Tory Offensive* (SW Litho Printers, 1971).
2 Elizabeth Robinson, personal communication, August 7, 2020.
3 "The Black Action Movement, 1970," Box 107, President (University of Michigan) Records, Bentley Historical Library, University of Michigan; "Discussion with: Attorney Cynthia Stevens, Attorney Ron Harris, Attorney David Lewis, Professor Niara Sudarkasa. 'The Organizations and Significance of BAM' (part 1)," Department of Afroamerican and African Studies Records, 1966–2010, Bentley Historical Library, University of Michigan.
4 Matthew Johnson, *Undermining Racial Justice: How One University Embraced Inclusion and Inequality* (Cornell University Press, 2020).
5 Robin D. G. Kelley, *Freedom Dreams: The Black Radical Imagination* (Beacon Press, 2002), 73.
6 Cruse, a former member of the Communist Party, writes:

> White radical social theory (i.e. Marxism), as practiced in the United States, has only been truly applicable as it concerns the history of white people and white classes. When it comes to Negro history, Marxism invariably departs from truth. Marxism could not deal with the fact that just prior to the Civil War, two opposing trends were firmly established in Negro leadership thought, and have persisted to this very day. As pointed out earlier, this conflict was between the

integrationist (Douglass) and the nationality (Delany) strains. It can be shown that Marxist-Communism has been able to wield political influence in Negro life only during those periods when the integrationist trend was predominant. (*The Crisis of the Negro Intellectual*, Morrow, 1967, 226)

Cedric Johnson reads Cruse's adoption of these ideas through the lens of ethnic pluralism, arguing that Cruse's view of culture was static and that his view of Black politics sustained by cultural difference was more conservative than radical. See Cedric Johnson, *Revolutionaries to Race Leaders: Black Power and the Making of African American Politics* (University of Minnesota Press, 2007), 23–33. Yet among Black nationalists, his view of self-determination remained a point of departure for the development of a critical intellectual genealogy of Black thought. See Jacob H. Carruthers, "Black Talk and the White Question: Reflections on Afro-American Critiques of African-Centered Thought," in *Intellectual Warfare* (Third World Press, 1999), 154–71; and Josh Myers, "The Still Rejected Strain; or How Black Thought is Enough," *US Intellectual History Blog*, September 21, 2017, https://s-usih.org/2017/09/the-still-rejected-strain-or-how-black-thought-is-enough-the-crisis-of-the-negro-intellectual-roundtable/

7 See the contributions to Jerry Watts (ed.), *Crisis of the Negro Intellectual Revisited* (Routledge, 2004).

8 Jordan T. Camp and Christina Heatherton, "The World We Want: An Interview with Cedric and Elizabeth Robinson," in Gaye Theresa Johnson and Alex Lubin (eds), *Futures of Black Radicalism* (Verso, 2017), 95.

9 Cedric Robinson, review of *How Europe Underdeveloped Africa* by Walter Rodney, *Third World Coalition Newsletter* 1 (June 1975): 15–16.

10 Archie Singham and Sylvia Wynter, "Opening Comments," The Revolutionary Legacy of C. L. R. James Conference, University of Michigan, Ann Arbor, Michigan, March 31, 1972, audio tape, CRP.

11 Cedric Robinson, "Opening Comments," The Revolutionary Legacy of C. L. R. James Conference, University of Michigan, Ann Arbor, Michigan, March 31, 1972, audio tape, CRP.

12 Darryl C. Thomas, "Black Studies and the Scholarship of Cedric J. Robinson," *Race and Class* 47 (October–December 2005): 2.

13 Ibid.

14 Chuck Morse, "Capitalism, Marxism, and the Black Radical Tradition: An Interview with Cedric Robinson," *Perspectives on Anarchist Theory* (Spring 1999): 6.

15 Robinson, "Opening Comments."

16 Elizabeth Robinson, personal communication, August 21, 2019; James Garrett, email communication, October 28, 2019; Anthony Bogues, "C. L. R. James, Pan-Africanism, and the Black Radical Tradition," *Critical Arts* (2011): 491–2; E. Ethelbert Miller, Amanda Huron, James Early, Aldon Nielsen, Kojo Nnamdi, Sylvia Hill, and Sally Schwartz, "The Legacy of C. L. R. James and His Influence on DC Activists," panel discussion, University of the District of Columbia, October 22, 2019, https://www.youtube.com/watch?v=yiS223imbD0.

17 Walter Rodney, "C. L. R. James and the African Revolution," The Revolutionary Legacy of C. L. R. James Conference, University of Michigan, Ann Arbor, Michigan, March 31, 1972, audio tape, CRP.

18 Sylvia Wynter, "C. L. R. James and the Cultural Revolution," The Revolutionary Legacy of C. L. R. James Conference, University of Michigan, Ann Arbor, Michigan, April 2, 1972, audio tape, CRP.

19 "C. L. R. James Conference Papers," Box 11, Folder 24: 3, Fernand Braudel Center Papers, Binghamton Libraries Special Collections, Binghamton University.

20 Ibid., 22.

21 Ibid., 29–30. It was not James's first pass at such a conclusion. See his earlier and more influential 1948 essay, "The Revolutionary Answer to the Negro Problem in the United States," in Scott McLemee (ed.), *C. L. R. James on the "Negro Question"* (University Press of Mississippi, 1996), 138–47.

22 Black Matters Committee, "C. L. R. James: Revolution in His Time," *Michigan Daily*, April 15, 1972.

23 Robinson approached Immanuel Wallerstein about publishing the conference papers with the "imprimatur" of the Fernand Braudel Center. See Cedric J. Robinson to Immanuel Wallerstein, September 21, 1976, Box 11, Folder 285,

Fernand Braudel Center Papers, Binghamton Libraries Special Collections, Binghamton University.

24 Thomas, "Black Studies," 2–3.

25 Ernest Allen, email communication, December 12, 2019. See also Ernest Allen, "Dying from the Inside: The Decline of the League of Revolutionary Black Workers," in Dick Cluster (ed.), *They Should Have Served that Cup of Coffee* (South End Press, 1971), 71–109.

26 Peniel Joseph, *Waiting 'til the Midnight Hour: A Narrative History of Black Power in America* (Henry Holt, 2006), 53–63.

27 Muhammad Ahmad (Maxwell Stanford), *We Will Return in the Whirlwind: Black Radical Organizations, 1960–1975* (Charles Kerr, 2003), 281.

28 Joseph, *Waiting*, 58–9; Ahmad, *We Will Return in the Whirlwind*, 242. On the Boggses, see Stephen M. Ward, *In Love and Struggle: The Revolutionary Lives of James and Grace Lee Boggs* (University of North Carolina Press, 2016).

29 For a full account of the League and these implications, see Ahmad, *We Will*, 243–83; James Geschwender, *Class, Race, and Worker Insurgency* (Cambridge University Press, 1977); Dan Georgakas and Marvin Surkin, *Detroit: I Do Mind Dying: A Study in Urban Revolution* (St Martin's Press, 1975).

30 Cedric Robinson to Harold Jacobson, January 29, 1973, CRP; Cedric Robinson, Curriculum Vita, 2001, CRP.

31 "Rules Threaten Some PESC Classes," *Michigan Daily*, January 25, 1972; "'I'm Encouraged,' Teacher Sinclair Says of U Course," *Ann Arbor News*, February 7, 1972. On Sinclair, see John Sinclair, *It's All Good: A John Sinclair Reader* (Headpress, 2008), 12–22.

32 "Community Control of Prisons, Class Discussion," n.d., p. 2, CRP.

33 "Community Control of Prisons, Class Discussion", February 15, 1972," p. 1, CRP.

34 Cedric Robinson, "Response to Community Control of Prisons Controversy," n.d., CRP.

35 "Community Control of Prisons, Notes on Discussions," n.d., CRP.

36 Robinson, "Response."

37 "Cedric Robinson, AAS 409- Charisma and African Diaspora" and "AAS 501- Anarchism and Violence" (Orientation Tape) –

Winter 1973," Department of Afroamerican and African Studies Records, 1966–2010, Bentley Historical Library, University of Michigan.

38 Darryl C. Thomas, interview with the author, September 22, 2020.

39 For a useful summary of this context, see Ronald W. Walters, *Pan Africanism in Africa: An Analysis of Modern Afrocentric Political Movements* (Wayne State University Press, 1993), 59–88.

40 John Vassall, "BSU: Thank You," *Colonial News*, May 3, 1968.

41 "A Boy's Dream of Great Things Leads to a Publishing House," *New York Times*, September 25, 1994.

42 *Student Course Guide Fall 1974*, p. 155, University Archives, Binghamton Library Special Collections, Binghamton University.

43 "SUNY Students Enjoy African Study," *Press and Sun-Bulletin*, September 30, 1974; Elizabeth Robinson, personal communication, August 10, 2020.

44 Immanuel Wallerstein, "Pedagogy and Scholarship," in Immanuel Wallerstein and Mohammad H. Tamdgidi (eds), *Mentoring, Methods, and Movements: Colloquium in Honor of Terence K. Hopkins by His Former Students and the Fernand Braudel Center for the Study of Economics, Historical Systems and Civilizations* (Ahead Publishing, 2017), 35–40.

45 On the social sciences and the world-system, see Immanuel Wallerstein, "A World-System Perspective on the Social Sciences," *British Journal of Sociology* 27 (September 1976): 343–52 and his *Unthinking Social Science: The Limits of Nineteenth-Century Paradigms* (Polity Press, 1991).

46 Terence K. Hopkins and Immanuel Wallerstein, "Preface," in Terence K. Hopkins, Immanuel Wallerstein, and Associates (eds), *World-Systems Analysis: Theory and Methodology* (Sage, 1982), 7.

47 Terence K. Hopkins, "The Study of the Capitalist World-Economy: Some Introductory Considerations," in Hopkins et al. (eds), *World-Systems Analysis*, 9–38; Terence K. Hopkins, "Notes on Class Analysis and the World-System," *Review* 1 (Summer 1977): 67–72; and Terence K. Hopkins, Immanuel Wallerstein, and Associates, "Patterns of Development of the Modern World-System," *Review* 1 (Fall 1977): 111–45.

48 See Immanuel Wallerstein, "Oliver C. Cox as World-Systems Analyst," in *The Sociology of Oliver C. Cox: New Perspectives* (Emerald, 2000), 183–93.

49 Kelvin Santiago-Valles, "Racially Subordinate Labor within Global Contexts: Robinson and Hopkins Re-Examined," *Race and Class* 47 (October 2005): 54–70. In this article, Santiago-Valles lists Oliver Cox, C. L. R. James, Aime Cesaire, Frantz Fanon, Sylvia Wynter, Ifi Amadiume, Saidiya Hartman, Lindah Mhando, along with Cedric Robinson, as scholars that added these analyses.

50 "Of the five most prominent founders of world-systems analysis – Terence Hopkins, Andre Gunder Frank, Giovanni Arrighi, Immanuel Wallerstein, and Samir Amin – three began their careers as scholars of Africa, and two (Arrighi and Amin) spent significant time in Dar es Salaam during the heyday of the Dar school in the 1960s and 1970s." Yousuf Al-Bulushi, "Thinking Racial Capitalism and Black Radicalism from Africa: An Intellectual Geography of Cedric Robinson's World-System," *Geoforum*, https://doi.org/10.1016/j.geoforum.2020.01.018

51 Hopkins, "The Study of the Capitalist World-Economy," 22, italics in original.

52 Ibid., 37n4. See Santiago-Valles, "Racially Subordinate," 62–4, for an extended treatment of Robinson's work in relationship to both this Black radical genealogy and world-systems thought.

53 On the history and aims of the CHSS, see Juan Andres Bresciano, "La herencia bruadeliana y el paradigma de los sistemas-mundo" (PhD Diss., Universidad de Buenos Aires, 2012), 90–2.

54 Immanuel Wallerstein, *The Modern World-System: Capitalist Agriculture and the Origins of the European World-Economy in the Sixteenth Century* (Academic Press, 1974). This was the first of four volumes tracing the expansion of the world-system from the sixteenth century to the twentieth.

55 Bresciano, "La herencia," 94–5.

56 Elizabeth Robinson to Immanuel Wallerstein, May 23, 1975, Box 11, Folder 287, Fernand Braudel Center Papers, Binghamton Libraries Special Collections, Binghamton University.

57 Cedric Robinson, "A Paradigmatic Comment," May 23, 1975, Box 11, Folder 287, p. 1, Fernand Braudel Center Papers, Binghamton Libraries Special Collections, Binghamton University.

58 Ibid., 3.
59 Robin D. G. Kelley, *Hammer and Hoe: Alabama Communists during the Great Depression* (UNC Press, 1990). On Robinson's role, see Robin D. G. Kelley, "Foreword," in *Black Marxism: The Making of the Black Radical Tradition* (UNC Press, 2000), xv.
60 Cedric J. Robinson to Robin D. G. Kelley, June 21, 1985, Robin D. G. Kelley Personal Papers.
61 Robinson, "Paradigmatic," 4–5.
62 Al-Bulushi, "Thinking Racial Capitalism."
63 "Seminar I: Group Formation and Group Conflict in the Historical Development of the Modern World-System," p. 11, Working Papers, Fernand Braudel Center, CRP; Fernand Braudel Center, Research Groups, 1977–78, Box 9, Folder 210, p. 1, Fernand Braudel Center Papers, Binghamton Libraries Special Collections, Binghamton University; Participants in Working Seminar I, 1976, Box 9, Folder 210, Fernand Braudel Center Papers, Binghamton Libraries Special Collections, Binghamton University.
64 Cedric Robinson, "Social Movements and the African Diaspora," Box 16, Folder 750, Fernand Braudel Center Papers, Binghamton Libraries Special Collections, Binghamton University.
65 Ibid., 2.
66 Ibid., 3.
67 For a critique, see Joshua Myers, "The Order of Disciplinarity, the Terms of Silence," *Critical Ethnic Studies Journal* 4 (Spring 2018): 107–29.
68 Robinson, "Social Movements," 3–4.
69 Ibid., 5.
70 Cedric J. Robinson, "Historical Consciousness and the Development of Revolutionary Ideology," *Review of Afro-American Issues and Culture* 1 (1979): 219.
71 Ibid., 221.
72 Ibid., 229, emphasis added. This quote is from Cabral's *Return to the Source* (Monthly Review, 1973), 68 – a regular on Robinson's syllabi while teaching at Binghamton.
73 This phrase was the subtitle to this critical opening section of the article. See Cedric Robinson, "Notes Toward a 'Native' Theory of History," *Review* 4 (Summer 1980): 45–8. It was also the title of a talk given at Binghamton's Afro-Latin Cultural Festival in

the spring of 1975. See Cedric Robinson, "The First Attack is an Attack on Culture," in H. L. T. Quan (ed.), *Cedric Robinson: On Racial Capitalism, Black Internationalism, and Cultures of Resistance* (Pluto Press, 2018), 69–74.

74 Robinson, "Notes," 48.

75 Ibid., 49.

76 Ibid., 58.

77 Ibid., 69–70. The Mwase-Kampingo account is in George S. Mwase, *Strike a Blow and Die* (Cambridge University Press, 1967).

78 George Shepperson, "Ourselves as Others: Some Comments on Cedric Robinson on George Shepperson," *Review* 4 (Summer 1980): 84.

79 Robinson, "Notes," 72.

80 Ibid., 75.

81 Hopkins et al., "Patterns," 54.

82 Morse, "Capitalism," 7.

83 John Aubrey Douglass, *The California Idea and American Higher Education: 1850 to the 1960 Master Plan* (Stanford University Press, 2000), 162.

84 Gerard Pigeon, Murad Rahman, Cynthia George, and John Cotton, "The Black Student Takeover at UCSB in 1968," *Kalfou* 2 (Spring 2015): 27, 35.

85 Cedric Robinson, "Retracing Black Radicalism" (lecture delivered at Western Michigan University, Kalamazoo, Michigan, February 9, 2013).

86 "Black Athletes Charge 'Racist Policies' by Athletics Department," *El Gaucho*, October 2, 1968; "400 Hear BSU's Grievance Listing," *El Gaucho*, October 8, 1968; "Blacks Take North Hall," *El Gaucho*, October 15, 1968.

87 Karen Miller, "Black Studies in California Higher Education, 1965–1980" (PhD Diss., University of California, Santa Barbara, 1986), 91.

88 "Proposal for a Black Studies Program at UCSB," April 17, 1969, p. 12, UCSB Living History Project, livinghistory.as.ucsb.edu.

89 "News Release Regarding Agreements to Help Resolve Campus Issues," *Daily Nexus*, May 30, 1975; "Negotiating Teams Release Information on SCA Demands," *Daily Nexus*, May 30, 1975; Miller, "Black Studies," 92–9; Gerard Pigeon, "UCSB Black Studies: An

Evolutionary Study, 1968–1979," University of California, Santa Barbara, Department of Black Studies Records, c. 1968–2003, Box 3, Folder 5, Department of Special Collections, UC Santa Barbara Library, University of California, Santa Barbara.

90 Gerard Pigeon, comments at Radical Thought: Toward Critical Social Theories and Practice, University of California, Santa Barbara, November 6, 2004; "People," *Jet*, April 19, 1979.

91 Brenda Gayle Plummer, "On Cedric Robinson and *Black Marxism:* A View from the US Academy," *Race and Class* 47 (October–December 2005): 112–13.

92 Robinson, "Retracing."

93 Ibid., 112.

94 "Symposium Set Here on Black Movements in Western World," *Daily Nexus*, February 5, 1980.

95 Plummer, "On Cedric Robinson," 112.

96 Avery Gordon, "On Lived Theory: An Interview with A. Sivanandan," *Race and Class* 55 (April–June 1974): 3.

97 Cedric Robinson, *The Terms of Order: Political Science and the Myth of Leadership* (University of North Carolina Press, 2016), xxx.

98 Ibid., v.

99 Camp and Heatherton, "The World We Want," 96.

100 Robinson, *Black Marxism*, 1.

101 Cedric Robinson, "On the Liberal Theory of Knowledge and the Concept of Race," p. 3. Lecture Notes, A.A. 100x, n.d., CRP.

102 *Student Course Guide, Fall 1976*, University Archives, Binghamton Library Special Collections, Binghamton University.

103 Peter James Hudson, "Racial Capitalism and the Dark Proletariat," in Walter Johnson and Robin D. G. Kelley (eds), *Boston Review: Forum 1: Race Capitalism Justice* (2017): 59–65.

104 See, for instance, Michael Ralph and Maya Singhal, "Racial Capitalism," *Theory and Society* 48 (2019): 851–81 and the contributions to July–August 2020 issue of *Monthly Review*.

105 Walters, *Pan Africanism*, 178–86; Rob Waters, *Thinking Black: Britain, 1964–1985* (University of California Press, 2019), 15–50.

106 A. Sivanandan, "From Resistance to Rebellion: Asian and Afro-Caribbean Struggles in Britain," *Race and Class* 23 (1981–2): 111–52; Minkah Makalani, *In the Cause of Freedom: Radical Black Internationalism from Harlem to London, 1917–1939* (University

of North Carolina Press, 2011); and Marc Matera, *Black London: The Imperial Metropolis and Decolonization in the Twentieth Century* (University of California Press, 2015).

107 Waters, *Thinking Black*, 35–6; Stuart Hall, *The Hard Road to Renewal: Thatcherism and the Crisis of the Left* (Verso, 1998). See Gus John's tribute to Cedric, "Tributes to Cedric Robinson," *Institute of Race Relations Blog*, https://irr.org.uk/article/tributes-to-cedric-robinson/.a

108 Walters, *Pan Africanism*, 127–69.

109 Waters, *Thinking Black*, 55–62.

110 Ibid., 51–4.

111 A. Sivanandan, "Race and Resistance: The IRR Story," *Race and Class* 50 (October 2008): 1–30.

112 Gordon, "On 'Lived Theory,'" 3.

113 Sivanandan, "Race and Resistance," 27.

114 Robinson, *Black Marxism*, 9. This article appeared largely verbatim in *Black Marxism*, so the citations will follow from this text. For the original article, see Cedric Robinson, "The Emergence and Limitations of European Radicalism," *Race and Class* 21 (October 1979): 145–70.

115 Robinson, *Black Marxism*, 9–10.

116 Ibid., 26.

117 Ibid.

118 Ibid., 28.

119 Ibid., 2.

120 Ibid., 308.

121 Waters, *Thinking Black*, 165–207.

122 Cedric Robinson, "An Inventory of Contemporary Black Politics," *Emergency* 2 (1984): 22.

Chapter 5 The Making of the Black Radical Tradition

1 Doug Rossinow, *The Reagan Era: A History of the 1980s* (Columbia University Press, 2015), 101–17.

2 Cedric Robinson, *Black Marxism: The Making of the Black Radical Tradition* (University of North Carolina Press, 2000), 71.

3 Rossinow, *The Reagan Era*, 139–60. Robin D. G. Kelley describes the moment of *Black Marxism*'s appearance as a "political cross-roads," an era in which "corporate wealth and callous disregard

for the poor and people of color" led to an uncertain future for Black political organizing, stuck between an emergent cultural nationalism and the decline of the leftist organizing of the previous decade and the structural difficulties facing Black politicians in the cities. See his "Foreword," in *Black Marxism*, xvii.

4 "Summary of Recent Work by the Black Action Committee," n.d., CRP; Cedric Robinson, Curriculum Vita, 2001, CRP.

5 Teresa P. Hughes to Cedric J. Robinson, April 26, 1979, CRP.

6 "KCSB Radio Program Attempts to Present Third World Perspective," *Daily Nexus*, November 14, 1980.

7 Elizabeth Robinson, 'Twenty-Five Years of the Third World News Review," *Race and Class* 47 (October/December 2005): 78.

8 "KCSB Radio Program."

9 "Panthers Host Meeting Talking US Aggression," *Daily Nexus*, January 9, 1984.

10 Tom Najem, *Lebanon: The Politics of a Penetrated Society* (Routledge, 2012), 34–42; Rossinow, *The Reagan Era*, 114.

11 "Grenada: What the White House Hides," *Santa Barbara News and Review*, November 10, 1983; "Jesse Jackson's World," *Washington Post*, December 29, 1983.

12 Andaiye, "The Grenada Revolution, the Caribbean Left, and the Regional Women's Movement: Preliminary Notes on One Journey," in Alissa Trotz (ed.), *The Point is to Change the World: Selected Writings of Andaiye* (Pluto Press, 2019), 37–46.

13 "US Vetoes UN Resolution 'Deploring' Grenada Invasion," *New York Times*, October 29, 1983; Rossinow, *The Reagan Era*, 114–15.

14 Cedric Robinson, "Running Unchecked," *Daily Nexus*, October 28, 1983.

15 "Grenada: What the White House Hides." For more, see Audre Lorde, "Grenada Revisited: An Interim Report," *Black Scholar* 15 (January/February 1984): 21–9; and Tony Martin, *In Nobody's Backyard: The Grenada Revolution in its Own Words* (2 vols) (Majority Press, 1985).

16 Robinson, "Twenty-Five Years," 80.

17 G. Pascal Zachary, "Cedric Robinson: Karl Marx and Beyond," *Santa Barbara News and Review*, September 17, 1981.

18 Cedric Robinson, "Outline of *Black Marxism*," 1977, CRP.

19 Zachary, "Cedric Robinson."

20 Robinson, *Black Marxism*, 29–30.

21 Jordan T. Camp and Christina Heatherton, "The World We Want: An Interview with Cedric and Elizabeth Robinson," in Gaye Theresa Johnson and Alex Lubin (eds), *The Futures of Black Radicalism* (Verso Books, 2017), 97–8.

22 See, for instance, Cedric J. Robinson, "Ventriloquizing Blackness: Eugene O'Neill and Irish-American Racial Performance," in Peter D. O'Neill and David Lloyd (eds), *The Black and Green Atlantic: Crosscurrents of the African and Irish Diasporas* (Palgrave Macmillan, 2009), 49–63.

23 Robinson, *Black Marxism*, 36–41.

24 Ibid., 43.

25 Ibid., 66. Though Cedric attributed the idea of "partial consciousness" to Marx, it was actually rooted in Engels's idea of false consciousness. It became an important aspect of Marxist thinking in the first half of the twentieth century and is most consistently linked to the ideas of Franz Jakubowski. See Friedrich Engels to Franz Mehring in Robert Tucker (ed.), *The Marx–Engels Reader* (Norton, 1972), 766; and Franz Jakubowski, *Ideology and Superstructure in Historical Materialism* (Allison & Busby, 1976), 103.

26 Robinson, *Black Marxism*, 45–6.

27 Ibid., 52–64.

28 Quoted in Robinson, *Black Marxism*, 64. The original quote is from a letter to Joseph Bloch and may be found in Tucker (ed.), *The Marx–Engels Reader*, 760–5.

29 Robinson, *Black Marxism*, 45. Here again, Marx was more prescient on the question of the political than were later Marxist theorists. In *The Terms of Order*, Cedric cites excerpts of "On the Jewish Question" and "Critical Glosses," arguing that "Marx, for the time being, achieved a reconciliation of the political and the anti-political: though a useful instrument, the political itself would be transformed by a deeper, more profound process – social revolution." Despite Marx's ideas about the state, later generations of Marxists have "understood the political in terms much more shallow and much less ambiguous than Marx himself." The necessity and/or persistence of leadership and state power are assumed in social science and among scientific socialists. Cedric

J. Robinson, *The Terms of Order: Political Science and the Myth of Leadership* (University of North Carolina Press, 2016), 3.

30 Robinson, *Black Marxism*, 65–7. On western radicalism and Enlightenment, see Jonathan Israel, *Radical Enlightenment: Philosophy and the Making of Modernity, 1650–1750* (Oxford University Press, 2001) and *Revolution of the Mind: Radical Enlightenment and the Intellectual Origins of Modern Democracy* (Princeton University Press, 2010). That this "radicalism" did not extend to those subjected to the vicissitudes of colonialism is likely less a contradiction of its principles and more a confirmation of them. See the contributions to Emmanuel Eze (ed.), *Race and the Enlightenment: A Reader* (Blackwell, 1997). Histories of Enlightenment's most prominent examples of revolution – the American and the French – have necessarily been rethought. The latter, with respect to its origins in preserving slavery and the former in light of the Haitian revolution, are important examples of Enlightenment's racialist flaws. See Laurent DuBois, *Avengers of the New World: The Story of the Haitian Revolution* (Harvard University Press, 2005) and Gerald Horne, *The Counterrevolution of 1776: Slave Resistance and the Origins of the United States* (New York University Press, 2014). Cedric's work focused on these questions, for sure. But his thinking was always attuned to what this "scientism" or "rationality," whatever its intentions, obscured about human life – that which could *not* be controlled. In 1976, he told his students: "Scientific thought does not resolve mysteries so much as it defines them out of existence – beyond rational consideration . . . Reality is not scientific reality. Scientific reality is that aspect of reality which is *manageable*, that aspect of reality which can be controlled. This is modern science, western science." Cedric Robinson, "On the Liberal Theory of Knowledge and the Concept of Race," p. 1. Lecture Notes, A.A. 100x, n.d., CRP (emphasis in the original).

31 Robinson, *Black Marxism*, 65.

32 Vincent Harding, *There is a River: The Black Struggle for Freedom in America* (Harcourt Brace Jovanovich, 1981).

33 Robinson, *Black Marxism*, 72–3.

34 Ibid.

35 Ibid., 72. On the question of essentialism, see Kelley's "Foreword," in ibid., xx. A typical claim of essentialism can

be found in Jonathan Fenderson, "Black Studies Post-Janus," *Black Scholar* 48 (Winter 2018): 3; and Michael Ralph and Maya Singhal, "Racial Capitalism," *Theory and Society* 48 (2019): 864.

36 From G. W. F. Hegel's *Philosophy of History*, quoted in Robinson, *Black Marxism*, 73.

37 "The obliteration of the African past from European consciousness was the culmination of a process a thousand years long and one at the root of European historical identity." Ibid., 82.

38 Ibid., 101.

39 "Columbian exchange" is from Alfred Crosby, *The Columbian Exchange: Biological and Cultural Consequences of 1492* (Praeger, 1972). See also Vera Lawrence Hyatt and Rex Nettleford (eds), *Race, Discourse, and the Origins of the Americas: A New World View* (Smithsonian Institution Press, 1995).

40 Robinson, *Black Marxism*, 91–100.

41 From Cox's 1959 *Foundations of Capitalism*, quoted in Robinson, *Black Marxism*, 110.

42 Cedric J. Robinson, "Oliver Cromwell Cox and the Historiography of the West," *Cultural Critique* 17 (Winter 1990–91): 19.

43 Ibid., 8, 14–16.

44 Cedric J. Robinson, "Capitalism, Slavery, and Bourgeois Historiography," *History Workshop Journal* 23 (Spring 1987): 128.

45 Ibid., 135.

46 Robinson, *Black Marxism*, 116–20.

47 Ibid., 121.

48 Ibid., 121–2.

49 Ibid., 125.

50 Ngugi wa Thiong'o, *Something Torn and New: An African Renaissance* (BasicCivitas, 2009), 31–65.

51 Nahum Dimitri Chandler, *X: The Problem of the Negro as a Problem for Thought* (Fordham University Press, 2014), 43.

52 Robinson, *Black Marxism*, 81.

53 Elizabeth Robinson, "Roundtable on Cedric J. Robinson, *On Racial Capitalism, Black Internationalism, and Cultures of Resistance*," panel presentation at the African American Intellectual History Society Conference, Austin, Texas, March 7, 2020.

54 Chandler, *X*, 56.

55 Robinson, *Black Marxism*, 130–4.

56 Cedric J. Robinson and Elizabeth P. Robinson, "Preface," in Johnson and Lubin (eds), *Futures of Black Radicalism*, 3.

57 Cedric Robinson, "Coming to Terms: The Third World and the Dialectics of Imperialism," *Race and Class* 22 (April 1981): 365. In an undated lecture, Cedric spoke to the dynamics of the industrial era more directly:

> As heirs of the tradition that history is inevitable progress, it is not surprising that we seldom connect the Industrial Revolution to the wars, migrations, famines, chronic under-nourishment, poverty, infant death and epidemics which also were its social and historical accompaniments. Yet it was the Industrial Revolution which gave the infant economic organization of capitalism its vitality – the capacity for concentrating enormous wealth. Capitalism, in turn, meant the centralization of social and political power for the purposes of maintaining that wealth and ensuring its further growth. Banking houses, stock and commodity exchanges, bureaucratic administration, the bourgeoisie and State armies became the dominant features of this new social order. And in their wake, the human destruction and social dislocation were considerable and worldwide. (Undated lecture on the Nineteenth Century, p. 2, CRP)

58 Robinson, *Black Marxism*, 312.

59 Robinson and Robinson, "Preface," 3. On Haiti, Robinson stated that the historical "relationship of the maroons to the Haitian revolution is still a matter of debate." But it ends up agreeing with those, C. L. R. James included, who argued that they "were an integral part of the disparate elements that crystallized" into the revolution. On this question, see Carolyn E. Fick, *The Making of Haiti: The Saint Domingue Revolution from Below* (University of Tennessee Press, 1990). Fick, a scholar with Detroit roots, was one of the many thinkers invited to engage with C. L. R. James in the early 1970s. Her work on Haiti builds from James's.

60 Robinson, *Black Marxism*, 164.

61 Ibid., 311–12.

62 Ibid., 166.

63 Ibid., 168.

64 Ibid., 170.

65 Ibid., 171.

66 See Asad Haider, "The Shadow of the Plantation," *Viewpoint Magazine*, February 12, 2017; and Charisse Burden-Stelly, "Modern US Racial Capitalism: Some Theoretical Insights," *Monthly Review* 72 (July/August 2020): 8–20.

67 Cedric J. Robinson, "An Inventory of Contemporary Black Politics," *Emergency* 2 (1984): 27.

68 Robinson, "Outline of *Black Marxism*," 2–3. The focus on the title has elicited much commentary. Although early indications included the eventual title, some other mentions of the title of the book included *Black Marxists and the Black Radical Tradition* or *Black Marxists*. See Cedric Robinson, "C. L. R. James and the Black Radical Tradition," *Review* 6 (Winter 1983): 321.

69 Robin D. G. Kelley, "Luncheon Talk," lecture presentation at the African American Intellectual History Society Conference, Austin, Texas, March 7, 2020. In the foreword to *Black Marxism*, Kelley writes: "The way they came to the Black Radical Tradition was more of an act of recognition than invention; they did not create the theory of black radicalism as much as found it, through their work and study, in the mass movements of black people," xv.

70 Robinson, *Black Marxism*, 170. On the questioning of enshrining, see H. L. T. Quan, "Geniuses of Resistance: Feminist Consciousness and the Black Radical Tradition," *Race and Class* 47 (October/December 2005): 46.

71 Cedric J. Robinson to Nancy Lane, December 8, 1977, CRP; Cedric J. Robinson to John E. Moore, August 19, 1981, CRP.

72 Cedric Robinson, "The Concept of Charisma and the African Diaspora," p. 2. Lecture Notes, Political Science 409, 1973, CRP.

73 Carole Boyce Davies, "A Black Left Feminist View of Cedric Robinson's *Black Marxism*," *Black Perspectives*, November 10, 2016, https://www.aaihs.org/a-black-left-feminist-view-on-cedric-robinsons-black-marxism/.

74 Quan, "Geniuses of Resistance," 46–7.

75 Davies, "A Black Left Feminist View." See her *Left of Karl Marx: The Political Life of Black Communist Claudia Jones* (Durham University Press, 2007).

76 Ibid., 43.

77 Camp and Heatherton, "The World We Want," 99.

78 Robinson, "Coming to Terms," 364–5.

79 Robinson, *Black Marxism*, 183.

80 Ibid., 184.

81 Charles Euchner, *Nobody Turn Me Around: A People's History of the 1963 March on Washington* (Beacon Press, 2010), 181.

82 Martin Luther King, Jr, "Honoring Dr Du Bois," in John Henrik Clarke, Esther Jackson, Ernest Kaiser, and J. H. O'Dell (eds), *Black Titan: W. E. B. Du Bois* (Freedomways, 1970), 176–83. On Du Bois's repression, see Gerald Horne, *Black and Red: W. E. B. Du Bois and the Afro-American Response to the Cold War, 1944–1963* (State University of New York Press, 1985). On this question, Cedric writes: "The opposition to Du Bois was grounded on deeper reservations: the recognition that his work had origins independent of the impulses of western liberal and radical thought. Thus, when his contribution to the American historical tradition should have been celebrated by its historians and scholars, the reaction of the academy was often vilification and neglect," *Black Marxism*, 186. "Caution and trepidation" is from Anthony Monteiro, personal communication, August 30, 2020.

83 "Du Bois was writing in the middle of a period where it was clear to him and a number of others that world capitalism was in a critical, perhaps fatal crisis. But *Black Reconstruction* is seldom read," Cedric Robinson, "Richard Wright as Marxist Theorist," lecture presented at The University of Michigan-Ann Arbor, November 15, 1978, Department of Afroamerican and African Studies (University of Michigan) Records, 1966–2010, Box 28, Bentley Historical Library, University of Michigan, Ann Arbor, MI.

84 Cedric Robinson, "Marxist Theory and the Black Savage: Du Bois' Critique in *Black Reconstruction*," 1975, CRP; Cedric Robinson, "A Critique of W. E. B. Du Bois' *Black Reconstruction*," *Black Scholar* 8 (May 1977): 44–50; Cedric Robinson, Curriculum Vita, 1981, CRP.

85 Robinson, *Black Marxism*, 186–95.

86 Ibid., 195.

87 Ibid., 196.

88 Ibid., 238.

89 Ibid., 228.

90 W. E. B. Du Bois, *Black Reconstruction in America, 1860–1880* (Free Press, 2000), 182–3.

91 Ibid., 14. And quoted in Robinson, *Black Marxism*, 238.

92 Ibid.

93 Ibid., 240.

94 C. L. R. James to Cedric Robinson, April 7, 1972 and C. L. R. James to Cedric Robinson, April 11, 1972, CRP.

95 Robinson, *Black Marxism*, 241–51.

96 Ibid., 266–70. See C. L. R. James, *Beyond a Boundary* (Hutchinson, 1963).

97 Robinson, *Black Marxism*, 262–3.

98 Ibid., 270–4. See also Minkah Makalani, *In the Cause of Freedom: Radical Black Internationalism from Harlem to London, 1917–1939* (University of North Carolina Press, 2011), 189–224.

99 C. L. R. James, *The Black Jacobins: Toussaint L'Ouverture and the San Domingo Revolution* (Vintage, 1963), 375.

100 Ibid., 283.

101 Ibid., 86. And quoted in Robinson, *Black Marxism*, 275.

102 James, *The Black Jacobins*, 88–9.

103 Robinson, *Black Marxism*, 278. See also Robinson, "Coming to Terms," 363–4.

104 C. L. R. James, "Lectures on the Black Jacobins," *Small Axe* 8 (September 2000): 75–6.

105 Ibid., 104.

106 Ibid., 108. See also Neil Roberts, *Freedom as Marronage* (University of Chicago Press, 2015), 110–11.

107 On these years, see Grace Lee Boggs, "Thinking and Acting Dialectically: C. L. R. James, The American Years," *Monthly Review* 45 (October 1993): 38–46; Paul Buhle, *C. L. R. James: The Artist as Revolutionary* (Verso, 1988), 66–99.

108 Robinson, *Black Marxism*, 179.

109 C. L. R. James, *Notes on Dialectics* (Allison and Busby, 1980), 181. And quoted in Robinson, *Black Marxism*, 284.

110 Cedric Robinson, "A Case of Mistaken Identity: Richard Wright and Gold Coast Politics," paper presented at the African Studies Association, Los Angeles, California, November 1, 1979.

111 Cedric Robinson, "The Emergent Marxism of Richard Wright's Ideology," *Race and Class* 19 (January 1978): 223.

112 In an unpublished portion of his analysis of Wright, Cedric enlarged upon this theme:

> Social science is exclusionary. Its practitioners follow conventionally defined procedures as their ideology. They worship a jealous god through which they are dominated. Other ways of penetrating reality or giving it meaning are dismissed as lacking in scientific legitimacy. They are understood by social scientists to be lacking rigor, as lesser forms. That is they are less precise, less logical, and less rational ... We must be clear that scientific knowledge is not *the* form of knowledge but merely *one* form. Moreover, we must concede that this scientific tradition is by definition hostile to other forms of knowledge. Among those forms is literature. (Richard Wright's *The Outsider*: Marxism and the Petit-Bourgeoisie, p. 3, n.d., CRP, emphasis in the original)

Novels by Chester Himes and Ishmael Reed were constants on Cedric's syllabi in Afro-American Studies. In his later career, he began to closely study detective fiction, namely the work of Pauline Hopkins. See Cedric J. Robinson, "The Black Detective in American Memory," in H. L. T. Quan (ed.), *Cedric Robinson: On Racial Capitalism, Black Internationalism, and Cultures of Resistance* (Pluto Press, 2018), 54–65.

113 Ibid., 233.

114 Ibid., 236. For Du Bois's statement, see his "Sociology Hesitant," *boundary 2* 27 (Fall 2000): 40.

115 Cedric Robinson, "Richard Wright: Marxism and the Petit-Bourgeoisie," *Race and Class* 21 (April 1980): 353–68.

116 Cedric Robinson, "Richard Wright as Marxist Theorist," lecture presented at the University of Michigan-Ann Arbor, November 15, 1978, Department of Afroamerican and African Studies (University of Michigan) Records, 1966–2010, Box 28, Bentley Historical Library, University of Michigan, Ann Arbor, MI.

117 Ibid.

118 Richard Wright quoted in Robinson, *Black Marxism*, 293.

119 Ibid., 292.

120 Cedric Robinson, "Introduction," in Richard Wright, *White Man, Listen* (Harper, 1996), xx.

121 Cedric Robinson, "A Paradigmatic Comment," May 23, 1975, Box 11, Folder 287, p. 1, Fernand Braudel Center Papers, Binghamton Libraries Special Collections, Binghamton University.

122 Robinson, *Black Marxism*, 288.

123 Richard Wright, quoted in ibid., 299.

124 Ibid., 291.

125 Ibid., 299–300.

126 Ibid., 302.

127 Ibid., 305.

128 Robinson, "Richard Wright as Marxist Theorist."

129 Robinson, *Black Marxism*, 304.

130 Ibid., 300.

131 Richard Wright, quoted in ibid.

132 Quan, "Geniuses of Resistance," 43.

133 Robinson, *Black Marxism*, xxxii.

134 Ibid., 316.

135 Ibid., 317.

136 Ibid., 318.

137 Paul Gilroy, review of *Black Marxism*, by Cedric Robinson, *City Limits*, November 25–December 1, 1983; Karim Alwari, "The Scarlet and the Black," *Afkar* (August 1984): 68–9; F. D., "Where Radicalism Began," *West Africa*, March 12, 1984; Errol Lawrence, review of *Black Marxism*, by Cedric Robinson, *Race and Class* 26 (October 1984): 100–2.

138 V. P. Franklin, review of *Black Marxism*, by Cedric Robinson, *Phylon* 47 (1986): 250–1; Cornel West, "Black Radicalism and the Marxist Tradition," *Monthly Review* 40 (September 1988): 51–6.

139 John McClendon, "Reading *Black Marxism* from the Standpoint of Black Intellectual Culture: 'The Black Radical Tradition' and C. L. R. James as Marxist Philosopher," paper presented at the Eastern Division of the American Philosophical Association, Radical Philosophy Association, Philadelphia, PA, December 2002, CRP.

140 Fred Moten, "The Subprime and the Beautiful," *African Identities* 11 (2013): 239.

141 Robert Molteno to Cedric Robinson, January 15, 1991, CRP; Robert Molteno to Elizabeth Robinson, June 10, 1997, CRP.

142 Again, H. L. T. Quan is instructive here. See "Geniuses of Resistance," 44. Gaye Theresa Johnson and Alex Lubin's volume, *Futures of Black Radicalism* (Verso, 2017) is valuable in this sense as well. See also the roundtable on *Black Marxism* for *Black Perspectives* for a more recent example of academic reception, at https://www.aaihs.org/tag/black-marxism/; and Bedour Alagraa, "Cedric Robinson's *Black Marxism:* Thirty-Five Years Later," *The CLR James Journal* 24 (Fall 2018): 301–12. The 2021 edition is also published by University of North Carolina Press.

143 Cedric J. Robinson, "Amilcar Cabral and the Dialectic of Portuguese Colonialism," in Quan (ed.), *Cedric J. Robinson*, 323.

144 Ibid., 324. The article later appeared in *Radical America* 15 (May–June 1981): 39–57.

145 Cedric J. Robinson, "Fascism and the Intersections of Capitalism, Racialism, and Historical Consciousness," *Humanities in Society* 6 (Autumn 1983): 325–49. Also in Quan (ed.), *Cedric Robinson*, 87–109; Cedric J. Robinson, "The African Diaspora and the Italo-Ethiopian Crisis," *Race and Class* (October 1985): 51–65.

146 Cedric Robinson, "The Book of Fascism," in "The Black Response to Fascism," p. 24 (unpublished manuscript), n.d., CRP.

147 Ibid., 3.

148 Cedric J. Robinson, "Fascism and the Response of Black Radical Theorists," in Quan (ed.), *Cedric Robinson*, 157.

149 Agenda for Medical Dedication with Alice McGrath, Comite Evangelico Pro-Ayuda Al Desarrollo, November 26–December 3, 1988, CRP; Cedric Robinson to Paul Oquist, January 23, 1989, CRP.

Chapter 6 Culture and War

1 On this political moment, see Andrew Hartman, *A War for the Soul of America: A History of the Culture Wars* (University of Chicago Press, 2015). On Black student resistance, see Joshua Myers, *We Are Worth Fighting For: A History of the Howard University Student Protest of 1989* (New York University Press, 2019).

2 "Police Arrest 141 Protestors at UC Berkeley," *Los Angeles Times*, April 16, 1985.

3 "Daylong Divestment Rally Ends in Arrests," *Daily Nexus*, April 25, 1985.

4 "UC Approves South Africa Divestment," *Sacramento Bee*, July 19, 1986; Robert Edgar (ed.), *Sanctioning Apartheid* (Africa World Press, 1990).

5 "New Chair of Growing Political Science Appointed," *Daily Nexus*, October 15, 1987.

6 Ami Chen Mills, *CIA off Campus: Building the Movement Against Agency Recruitment and Research* (South End Press, 1991), 89–90; Jon Wiener, "The CIA Goes Back to College," in *Professors, Politics, and Pop* (Verso, 1991), 94–8; "Critics Unsure About CIA Agent Chritton's Recent Appointment," *Daily Nexus*, November 10, 1987; "Chancellor Hires Controversial CIA Officer as 'Visiting Fellow,'" *Daily Nexus*, November 9, 1987; "Anti-CIA Rally Ends in Cheadle Hall Protests," *Daily Nexus*, November 6, 1987; "CIA Man's Role at UC Santa Barbara Reduced; No Recruitment," *Los Angeles Times*, November 7, 1987.

7 Wiener, "The CIA"; "Academic Freedom for the CIA," *Daily Nexus*, October 27, 1987; "Anthropology, UCSB, and the CIA," *Daily Nexus*, November 3, 1987.

8 Gerard Pigeon, interview with the author, August 8, 2020.

9 "Critics Unsure About CIA Agent."

10 "CIA Man's Role at UC Santa Barbara Reduced"; Wiener, "The CIA," 95.

11 "Government and University Relations 'Teach-In' Topic," *Daily Nexus*, January 27, 1987; "Chritton Not Given Renewal of Position," *Daily Nexus*, May 6, 1988.

12 "Rally Asks Student Body Support for Ethnic and Gender Standards," *Daily Nexus*, February 19, 1987; "Protestors Rally at UC Regents Meeting for New Requirements," *Daily Nexus*, February 20, 1987; "Faculty Reviews Ethnicity Program," *Daily Nexus*, May 1, 1987.

13 "CSAR Invites Speakers to Address Racism at UCSB," *Daily Nexus*, October 28, 1987.

14 H. L. T. Quan, interview with the author, September 21, 2020.

15 "Students Disrupt Meeting, Demand Ethnic Guidelines," *Daily Nexus*, November 18, 1988.

16 People Involved in the Hunger Strike to All Student Groups at UCSB, n.d., Box 17, Folder 6, GHP.

17 "Ethnic Requirement Gets Negative Vote," *Daily Nexus*, January 20, 1989; "Hunger Strikers Fast to End UCSB Racism," *Daily Nexus*, February 22, 1989; "2 UCSB Professors Hold Three-Day Fast," *Daily Nexus*, March 1, 1989; "UC Santa Barbara Protest Gains Support," *Los Angeles Times*, March 4, 1989.

18 Pigeon, interview.

19 Barbara S. Uehling, "Ethnic Studies Gets Personal," *Los Angeles Times*, July 29, 1989; "Incoming Freshman Class to Face USCS Ethnic Studies Requirement," *Daily Nexus*, September 15, 1989.

20 The Black, Chicano, and Native American Faculty to UCSB Campus Community, March 1, 1989, Box 19, Folder 6, GHP.

21 Mario Garcia to Barbara Uehling, October 26, 1989, Box 44, Folder 15, GHP.

22 Charles McKinney and Elizabeth Robinson, "Early Outreach Summer Camp – Draft III," July 27, 1989, Box 38, Folder 13, GHP.

23 Memo of Understanding and Intent Between Jackson State University and The University of California, Santa Barbara and Minutes, University of California, Santa Barbara Visit, June 26–8, 1985, CRP; Jackson State/UCSB Agenda Notes, January 10, 1989, Box 54, Folder 6, GHP.

24 Cedric Robinson to Manning Marable, April 28, 1987, Box 14, Folder 8; Gerald Horne to Barbara Uehling, April 6, 1989, Box 20, Folder 4; and Cedric Robinson to Barbara Uehling, October 13, 1993, Box 26, Folder 9, GHP.

25 Pigeon, interview.

26 Cedric J. Robinson, "Mass Media and the US Presidency," in John Downing, Ali Mohammadi, and Annabelle Sreberny-Mohammadi (eds), *Questioning the Media: A Critical Introduction* (Sage, 1995), 107.

27 Ibid., 108.

28 Cedric Robinson, "The Business of News," *Critical Times*, October 1, 1991.

29 Robinson, "Mass Media," 100.

30 Cedric J. Robinson, "Race, Capitalism, and the Antidemocracy," in Robert Gooding-Williams (ed.), *Reading Rodney King/Reading Urban Uprising* (Routledge, 1993), 73.

31 Ibid., 74.

32 Ibid., 75. See also Steve Fraser and Gary Gerstle (eds), *The Rise*

and Decline of the New Deal Order (Princeton University Press, 1989).

33 Robinson, "Race, Capitalism," 77.

34 Ibid., 78.

35 Ibid., 79.

36 Cedric J. Robinson, "The Value of Multiculturalism," p. 3, panel presentation, The University's Role in Political Correctness, Associated Students, University of California, Santa Barbara, January 16, 1992, CRP.

37 Ibid., 6.

38 "Speaking for the Subject" Conference Program, May 26–28, 1989, CRP.

39 Cedric J. Robinson, "White Signs in Black Times: The Politics of Representation in Dominant Texts," in H. L. T. Quan (ed.), *Cedric J. Robinson: On Racial Capitalism, Black Internationalism, and Cultures of Resistance* (Pluto, 2020), 185–6.

40 On Jackson's campaign and this question, see Jack O'Dell, "The Rainbow is Moving the US Toward Greater Democracy," *Black Scholar* 19 (March/April 1988): 24–8.

41 Robinson, "White Signs," 191–3.

42 Ibid., 186–7.

43 Cedric J. Robinson, "Manichaeism and Multiculturalism," in Christopher Newfield and Avery Gordon (eds), *Mapping Multiculturalism* (University of Minnesota Press, 1996), 116.

44 Ibid., 120.

45 Ibid., 119.

46 Ibid., 122.

47 Cedric J. Robinson, "Ota Benga's Flight through Geronimo's Eyes: Tales of Science and Multiculturalism," in David Theo Goldberg (ed.), *Multiculturalism: A Critical Reader* (Basil Blackwell, 1994), 389.

48 Ibid., 396–400.

49 See Sylvia Wynter, "No Humans Involved: A Letter to My Colleagues," *Forum NHI: Knowledge for the 21st Century* 1 (Fall 1994): 42–71.

50 "Key Quotes and Major Themes/Questions for Discussion and Proposed Solutions," The Two Reservations: Western Thought, the Color Line, and *The Crisis of the Negro Intellectual Revisited* Symposium, March 3–5, 1994, CRP.

51 Cedric J. Robinson, "Toward Fascism? Race, the Two Reservations, and the Materiality of Theory," paper presented at Stanford University, The Two Reservations: Western Thought, the Color Line, and *The Crisis of the Negro Intellectual Revisited* Symposium, March 5, 1994, CRP.

52 Cedric J. Robinson, "Cruse Revisited," unpublished paper, p. 4, 1994, CRP.

53 Cedric J. Robinson, "The Real World of Political Correctness," *Race and Class* 35 (January 1994): 79.

54 Black Studies I Syllabus, n.d., CRP.

55 Joanne Madison, interview with the author, August 8, 2020; "Popular Black Studies Lecturer to Lose Post," *Daily Nexus*, April 7, 1993.

56 Cedric J. Robinson, "Social Conditions Among the Black Peoples of the Americas," in *World Encyclopedia of Black Peoples*, Vol. 1 (Scholarly Press, 1975), 126–42.

57 Cedric J. Robinson, "Class Antagonisms and Black Migration: A Review Article," *Race and Class* 24 (January 1982): 47–60.

58 "UCSB Students Produce Black History Calendar," *Los Angeles Times*, December 1, 1994.

59 In emphasizing the "contextual," the point was to resist developing a narrative of an "imaginary and monolithic Black ambition." See Cedric J. Robinson to Cecelia A. Cancellaro, December 31, 1993, CRP.

60 Cedric J. Robinson, *Black Movements in America* (Routledge, 1997), 20.

61 Cedric J. Robinson, "David Walker and the Precepts of Black Studies," in Quan (ed.), *Cedric J. Robinson*, 349. Cedric gave this talk at least twice, at Ohio State University and Duke University.

62 Ibid., 342, 347.

63 Ibid., 349.

64 Robinson, *Black Movements*, 97.

65 Rayford W. Logan, *The Negro in American Life and Thought: The Nadir, 1877–1901* (Dial Press, 1954). Cedric titles the fifth chapter of *Black Movements in America* "The Nadir and its Aftermath."

66 Robinson, *Black Movements*, 98.

67 Ibid., 144.

68 There were advance reviews in *Booklist* and *Library Journal* and within two years academic reviews appeared in the *Black Scholar*,

Race and Class, the *Journal of Southern History*, *The Americas*, and the *Journal of American History*. A major review essay appeared in the *Boston Book Review*, juxtaposing the text with Manning Marable's *Black Leadership* (South End Press, 1998). See James Goodman, "Where Do We Go From Here?" *Boston Book Review* 4 (July/August 1997): 8.

69 "Black Studies Dept. Pushes Grad Program," *Daily Nexus*, January 7, 1994; "A Preliminary Proposal for a Black Studies Graduate Program," n.d., CRP.

70 Cedric J. Robinson, "What is the Nature of Black Studies?," n.d., CRP.

71 Cedric J. Robinson, "Slavery and the Platonic Origins of Anti-Democracy," in Matthew Holden, Jr (ed.), *National Political Science Review, Volume 5: The Changing Racial Regime*, (Transaction, 1995), 19. Also in Quan (ed.), *Cedric J. Robinson*, 127–45.

72 Classical Political Theory, Political Science 240, Syllabus, Spring 1990, CRP.

73 Robinson, "Slavery and the Platonic," 31.

74 Cedric J. Robinson, "In Search of a Pan-African Commonwealth," *Social Identities* 2 (1996): 165.

75 Ibid., 164.

76 See Cedric J. Robinson, "Du Bois and Black Sovereignty: The Case of Liberia," *Race and Class* 32 (October 1990): 39–50.

77 In a 2000 interview, a journalist asked Cedric if he believed in socialism. His response was: "Oh, yes. I have no sympathy with private property. It makes no sense to me at all." "The Return of *Black Marxism*," *Santa Barbara Independent*, February 24, 2000.

78 Robinson, "In Search," 167.

79 Cedric J. Robinson, "The Utopian Break: South Africa as Other," unpublished manuscript, n.d., p. 10, CRP. On the proposed volume, see Ntongela Masilela to Cedric J. Robinson, October 12, 1994, CRP.

80 Robinson, "The Utopian Break," 1.

81 Cedric J. Robinson, "On the Truth and Reconciliation Commission," in Quan (ed.), *Cedric J. Robinson*, 356.

82 Ibid. See W. E. B. Du Bois, "My Evolving Program for Negro Freedom," in Rayford Logan (ed.), *What the Negro Wants*

(University of North Carolina Press, 1944), 31–70, for Du Bois's evolving relationship with Truth. Cedric often cited Du Bois's invocation of the "Truth," as a product of an authentic history, in the final chapter of his *Black Reconstruction in America* (Free Press, 2000), 711–29. He was critical of its positivistic aspects, but its "moral authority" was of importance. See Robinson, "White Signs," 185. And then there is Mari Evans, "Speak the Truth to the People," in *Continuum: New and Selected Poems* (Black Classic Press, 2007), 22–3.

83 Lecture notes, *Political Science* 112, Fall 1979, CRP.

84 Avery Gordon, "Preface," in Cedric J. Robinson, *An Anthropology of Marxism* (Ashgate, 2001), vii–viii.

85 Ibid., 2.

86 The three foundations were English political economy, German philosophy, and French socialism. See ibid., 4–11.

87 Ibid., 16.

88 Ibid., 52.

89 Ibid., 40–60.

90 Ibid., 134.

91 Ibid., 156.

92 Ibid., 157.

93 See H. L. T. Quan, "Foreword," in Cedric J. Robinson, *An Anthropology of Marxism* (University of North Carolina Press, 2019), viii.

94 August Carbonella, "Towards an Anthropology of Hope," *Focaal* 42 (2003): 173–85.

95 Elizabeth Robinson, personal communication, August 21, 2019.

96 Margot Dashiell, personal communication, December 13, 2019.

97 Black Film Society, April 28, 1972, CRP.

98 Black Film Society, Advertisement, *Michigan Daily*, March 26, 1972; Cedric J. Robinson and Travis Tatum, Black Arts Films Proposal, September 28, 1972, CRP.

99 Cedric J. Robinson and Tom Denyer, "Liberal Fantasies and the Politics of American Movies," unpublished manuscript, p. 13, 1976, CRP.

100 Ibid., 17, 21.

101 Ibid., 19–20.

102 Ibid., 22.

103 Ibid., 28.

104 Cedric J. Robinson, "Black Women in American Films," *Elimu* 8 (Fall 1993): 1.

105 Cedric J. Robinson, "Blaxploitation and the Misrepresentation of Liberation," *Race and Class* 40 (July 1998): 11.

106 Cedric J. Robinson, "The Black Middle Class's Bad Ass Song," *Buname* (Spring 1974): 36.

107 Cedric J. Robinson, "Domination and Imitation: Xala and the Emergence of the Black Bourgeoisie," *Race and Class* 22 (January 1980): 147–58.

108 Cedric J. Robinson, "Indiana Jones, The Third World, and American Foreign Policy," *Race and Class* 26 (October 1984): 91.

109 Cedric J. Robinson, *Forgeries of Memory and Meaning: Blacks and the Regimes of Race in American Theater and Film Before World War II* (University of North Carolina Press, 2007), xii–xiii.

110 Ibid., xiv–xv.

111 Ibid., xi–xii.

112 Ibid., 14.

113 Ibid., 45–81.

114 Cedric of course critically engaged the text by Donald Bogle, *Toms, Coons, Mulattoes, Mammies, and Bucks: An Interpretive History of Blacks in American Films* (Continuum, 1995).

115 Among the moments that Cedric highlights are the United States occupation of Haiti, the lynching of Leo Frank, the exploits of Jack Johnson, and the vagaries of World War I. See Robinson, *Forgeries*, 108–18.

116 Ibid., 179.

117 Ibid., 205.

118 Cedric J. Robinson and Luz Maria Cabral, "The Mulatta on Film: From Hollywood to the Mexican Revolution," *Race and Class* 45 (October 2003): 1–20.

119 Robinson, *Forgeries*, 227.

120 Ibid., 247.

121 Ibid., 257.

122 Ibid., 260.

123 Ibid., 262–4.

124 Tommy Lott, "A No-Theory Theory of Contemporary Black Cinema," *Black American Literature Forum* (Summer 1991): 221–36.

Conclusion: I Am You

1 Darryl C. Thomas, interview with the author, September 22, 2020.
2 Bruce Cosby, interview with the author, September 10, 2020.
3 Joanne Madison, interview with the author, August 8, 2020.
4 Madison, interview. "Winners Chosen by Mortar Board for Professor of the Year Award," *Daily Nexus*, May 12, 1987; "Professors of the Year to Be Honored at Annual Banquet," *Daily Nexus*, May 27, 1992.
5 Robin D. G. Kelley to Cedric J. Robinson, November 5, 1984 and Cedric J. Robinson to Robin D. G. Kelley, June 21, 1985, Robin D. G. Kelley Personal Papers.
6 Robin D. G. Kelley, interview with the author, December 28, 2020.
7 Quan, interview with the author, September 21, 2020; H. L. T. Quan, "Roundtable on Cedric J. Robinson, *On Racial Capitalism, Black Internationalism, and Cultures of Resistance*," panel presentation at the African American Intellectual History Society Conference, Austin, Texas, March 7, 2020.
8 Quan, interview.
9 Tiffany Willoughby-Herard, interview with the author, June 25, 2020.
10 Fred Moten, interview with the author, September 23, 2020.
11 Avery Gordon, interview with the author, September 28, 2020.
12 Quan, interview; Marquez, interview.
13 Erica Edwards, "Cedric People," in Gaye Theresa Johnson and Alex Lubin (eds), *Futures of Black Radicalism* (Verso, 2017), 251.
14 Tiffany Willoughby-Herard, interview with the author, September 16, 2020. Damien Sojoyner and Tiffany Willoughby-Herard, "Preface: Unhushable Wit: Pedagogy, Laughter, and Joy in the Classrooms of Cedric J. Robinson," in *Black Marxism* (University of North Carolina Press, 2021), xxxv–xlvi.
15 Jonathan D. Gomez, Jorge Ramirez, and Ismael F. Illescas, "Cedric J. Robinson, Modest Audacity, and the Black Radical Tradition," *Kalfou* 3 (Fall 2016): 288–97.
16 Cedric Robinson, comments at Radical Thought: Toward Critical Social Theories and Practice, University of California, Santa Barbara, November 6, 2004.

17 Barbara Ransby, *Making All Black Lives Matter* (University of California Press, 2018).

18 Ruth Wilson Gilmore, "Foreword," in H. L. T. Quan (ed.), *Cedric J. Robinson: On Racial Capitalism, Black Internationalism, and Cultures of Resistance* (Pluto Press, 2019), xiii.

19 See "The Killing in Ferguson," in ibid., 354–5.

20 Cedric J. Robinson and Elizabeth P. Robinson, "Preface," in Gaye Theresa Johnson and Alex Lubin (eds), *Futures of Black Radicalism* (Verso, 2017), 7.

21 Cedric J. Robinson, "The Appropriation of Frantz Fanon," *Race and Class* 35 (July 1993): 79. I am grateful to Alan Minor who first characterized this phenomenon in this way.

22 Cedric J. Robinson, *Black Marxism: The Making of the Black Radical Tradition* (University of North Carolina Press, 2000), xxxv. See Robin D. G. Kelley's "Foreword" to the 2021 edition for a review of recent scholarship that engages Cedric's work.

23 Avery Gordon, interview with the author, September 28, 2020.

24 Notes on Conference: Two Reservations, p. 4, March 4, 1994, CRP.

25 Robinson, *Black Marxism*, 184.

26 Cedric Robinson, "Rethinking Black Marxism," panel presentation at Politics and Languages of Contemporary Marxism, University of Massachusetts-Amherst, December 6, 1996. Available at https://www.youtube.com/watch?v=_FX8xlhKHtI&t=5371s

Index